The Moon & I Confer

monte ceceri

THE MOON AND I CONFER

Monte Ceceri Publishers, LLC

For more information, educational pricing, and other resources, please contact Monte Ceceri Publishers.

Publisher's Cataloguing-In-Publication Data:
Eckstrand, Ed, 1946– author
The moon and I confer: Savannah radio commentary from P. T. Bridgeport / Ed Eckstrand
ISBN: 978-1-949512-02-1 (paperback)
ISBN: 978-1-949512-03-8 (eBook)
1. Creative nonfiction. 2. Nonfiction radio programs. 3. Radio commentaries. 4. Humor—Anecdotes. 5. Savannah (Ga.)—Nonfiction. 6. Illustrated works—Photobooks. 7. United States—Nonfiction. I. Title

Monte Ceceri Publishers
P. O. Box 60623
Savannah, GA 31420
www.montececeri.com

The
Moon
& I Confer

Savannah Radio Commentary
From P. T. Bridgeport

Welcome to My World

My name is P. T. Bridgeport. At least it is on the radio.

I'm not from Savannah, but I've migrated south every time I've moved. I spent decades in the Washington, D. C., area, engaged in far more "serious" industries than radio or writing. Those corporations and our nation's capital matured rapidly while I was there; my own pace was far slower. On retirement, the elegant and accomplished Ms. Hamden Bridgeport and I agreed that we were too old for four seasons and rapidly concurred on which one to eliminate. We came to Savannah after touring the Southeast for a number of vacations. Savannah was our first choice. Having lived here for a while, it still is.

Since arriving, we have been joined by Stink Bridgeport, who is probably a Carolina dog, at least mostly. He is actually a short-haired, mixed-breed mutt, but then so am I. My personal provenance is somewhat Scandinavian, but...well, I'll talk about it later. Stink is much more local than I.

Savannah, Georgia, is a town of about 150,000 residents, the last major city before you reach Florida as you travel down I-95.

It's a nice place to visit, and it's a nice place to live—but that's a tricky balance. The tourists might be happier if we ran a roller coaster up Bull Street between Broughton and Forsyth Park, but Savannah is a real place, not Disney World or Busch Gardens. Continue on to the Sunshine State for that theme park vibe.

In the early 1700s, General James Oglethorpe thoughtfully laid out squares in Savannah. They're still here, and we enjoy them and Savannah's good walking weather. You'll have to discover the beauty of the town for yourself—we're not going to hit you in the face with it. Savannah has places to see, events to attend, terrific restaurants. Everything's to be enjoyed at your own pace. Poke around; you'll see something that enchants you.

Because it's a real place, Savannah has things for residents and stayers for extended visits, too. The Port of Savannah has served the Southeast for centuries, and we have some fine universities, a commitment to art, and a sense that the coming years will make our community an even better one to settle in. We have problems, too, of course, but we're working on them the best we know how.

A few years back, I got involved with WRUU-LP 107.5 FM, Savannah's community radio station and just one example of the Hostess City's spirit. After listening to the station's many great programs since it began, I decided to try being a host and see what it was like from the other side.

The program committee asked, "What do you want to do with this show?"

I didn't know. I knew what I didn't want to do with it—I didn't want it to be one of those old-time pop shows, with stacks of hot wax. A friend of mine actually offered up a stack of hot wax, but it was large and unwieldy and had been sitting in his garage for twenty years. I declined it. Maybe by eliminating what I didn't want, I thought, I could figure out what it was that I did.

WRUU accepted my proposal and put up with me while I learned the ropes (the ropes I have learned thus far, that is; I'm still a little fuzzy on phone interviews). I found an interesting and intelligent group of radio-heads, and I love being a part of them.

WRUU's Orlando Montoya, Leigh E. Rich, and Brian Renner

"We are Savannah Soundings, community radio with global soul." That's the WRUU slogan, and you'll hear it about once an hour (and maybe more). The station is affiliated with Savannah's Unitarian Universalist Church on Troup Square.

We subscribe to the Unitarian Universalist code of ethics, which is a pretty good set of rules for life, but that doesn't mean we're serious about everything. We play different kinds of music and produce thought-provoking talk shows, from community matters to global concerns. WRUU was started by a bunch of dedicated folks as interesting as they are intelligent. I'm not one of them, so I can say that. Most of them are still here, week in and week out. But we're like the city—we're not going to scream at you. You have to listen to understand what we are trying to do.

Right now, you can hear my voice on Fridays and Saturdays. First, Leigh E. Rich and I host *Beyond the Liner Notes*, Brian Renner's old program. We play music that addresses a single topic, like the letter *z* or road songs or songs about gems. (Or when we're feeling very meta, songs about radio.) Then I spend an hour with Leigh on *Listening to Literature* (now in "volume two") on the shotgun side of the stagecoach. My job on that program is to give listeners the impression I know something about books, and sometimes I do.

On Saturdays, I'm in the "hot seat" for a little adventure called *When the Moon Sings*. I play powerful music that can only be appreciated though quiet listening, just as the twinklings of twilight steal across our meadows of marshes and river canals. You might hear film scores, jazz, new age, classical, or folk music—anything from solos to symphony orchestras. And then I talk a bit, too.

Now and then on the program, I interview people from the art community or just those who I think are interesting. Before I put on headphones, I spent a few years in and around Savannah's art scene. It's large and diverse. The Savannah College of Art and Design lives here (that much, you likely know), as do active programs in our other universities. And then there is Savannah's huge community of independent artists, which the city always has had, going back to colonial days.

Nearly every week, I also spend seven or so minutes musing about the moon (and other things), contemplating moments in my own life and the world in which we live. This book is a compilation of those thoughts, from the inauguration of *When the Moon Sings* in 2017 on into 2020. The viewpoints expressed in this book do not necessarily reflect those of WRUU, its license holder, or its staff, but the proceeds will go to help support WRUU. While we are affiliated with the church, we are run by volunteers and completely self-supporting, and radio requires a certain amount of funding to translate our efforts into airwaves.

The book would not be possible without the efforts of several people who kindly shouldered responsibility for parts of the process. **Leigh E. Rich** is a canny critic of art and literature who handled the publication. The mysterious **Martha** did the editing, as a byproduct of several years in much more serious ventures. Martha lives west of here, but she pitched in anyway. So did **Carol Andrews**, whose careful eye and sharpened pencil caught things at the eleventh hour that I no longer could. **Stink Bridgeport** requires two walks every day, without which many of the ideas for this book's contents would never have come to fruition. Finally, Ms. **Hamden Bridgeport** provides the time and sense that make P. T. Bridgeport possible. As always, the content is my responsibility, rather than that of any of these fine people, four-footed or otherwise.

Autumn ~ Winter 2017

That's Brian Renner, not me. Brian is more photogenic, even from that angle.

St. Vincent's

Autumn comes to Savannah like the airplanes into Hunter Field—first audibly and then visually. Acorns and pinecones flattening under car wheels make a sound, unlike the pine needles and live oak leaves that fall later.

We are now deep into autumn. Our daily highs aren't even lows in August.

Amid the grounded foliage, I went to the WRUU studio during the day and passed the square through which the scholars of St. Vincent's Academy amble on their way to and from class. They walk briskly, with purpose now, perhaps because they are fully engaged in the love of learning... and maybe because of the persistent north wind. Each scholar responds to those two things in different proportions.

Autumn is when you must suffer the indignities of long pants and socks once again—the T-shirts and shorts go to the side of the closet, and the warmer things come front and center.

So we spend these days in reflection, and great amounts of reflection just leave me hungry. Fortunately, Thanksgiving comes at the end of the reflective period and then Christmas with all its joy and effort. It won't be until after the holidays that we face the cold reality of acting on those autumn reflections.

Stay calm and stop carrying on.

Marsh Life

If you've been listening to me on WRUU, you've probably concluded that I am not a native Savannahian. And you are quite right. Technically, I might not be a Savannahian even now (with or without a loosening of the not-so-tacit "three-generation" proviso), since I live east of the city on one of those islands in the mouth of the river. We are well outside the city limits.

Our island is just south of the ship channel. If you go to the edge of the island and look in the right direction, the superstructures of the tall container ships tower over the trees. When the Christmas decorations go up, I wonder if we don't look like a distant carnival to the seamen on the ships' bridges.

It is early in the holiday season on our island. Houses have started to sprout colorful lights, and they glow softly and attractively through the morning fogs. The houses that have the most elaborate embellishments are often those that once staged pretty intricate Halloween displays as well. These houses usually contain children (whether in spirit or in age). Perhaps the next great idea will involve lights that glow orange before October 31 and turn green and red (or blue and white . . .) after Thanksgiving. What a boon to parents—put up lights in the middle of October and you won't have to take them down until after the New Year. Once and done.

We will string some lights, too, but perhaps not just yet. The holiday is full of shopping and baking and the next great feast and festive gatherings that we must negotiate at the same time. Our decorations are not conspicuous anyway. We install lights and the odd lawn ornament, but we do that to please ourselves. Our heirs and assigns live elsewhere, complete with careers, mortgages, and their own trimmings.

Our island has some neighborhood traditions: There's a blowup Santa on a motorcycle that's been an annual visitor for years and another in a sturdy, well-lit helicopter, complete with lights imitating whirring blades. Last year, I noticed a number of Darth Vaders festooned in Christmas attire, illuminated or otherwise. I had a little trouble with the thinking there, so I consulted a number of experts at the sage age of single digits. They thought it was a dandy idea and, therefore, so do I. Wisdom consists of seeing the world through new eyes now and then.

We won't have a white Christmas this year—or likely in any other year. We will have a greenish-brownish one. Maybe we'll get as close as gray if the fogs continue to roll in.

Savannahians think of snow as humidity that has picked up some bad habits on the street. Having lived in snowy areas before, I agree. Snow is certainly pretty, but like many other pretty things, it is labor-intensive, expensive, and a nuisance to be around for very long. And it comes with a family: ice, freezing cold, howling winds. You might want to date snow, but you'd never want to marry it.

December is our month of gratitude. We end the prior month with a national thanksgiving, and then we proceed to the rituals that demonstrate our appreciation for friends, family, color and light, and maybe even life itself. The presents, decorations, and baking are part of those rituals and tokens of a greater gratefulness.

There are worse ways to spend December.

The Holidays

It is winter. I can tell because the Internet tells me so. Some days it feels like winter, and other days it doesn't, but the Internet is positive that we are in the fallow period.

I can tell it's winter because, via cyberspace, I saw a picture of a sign in the window of the Richard III Sporting Goods store. Like most merchants, they are having a pre-holiday sale. The sign said, "This is the Winter of Our Discount Tents." I don't know where, in reality, Richard III Sporting Goods exists, and like much else on the 'Net, I fear it may have been made up.

I can tell it's winter because I also see Christmas gifts for cats. I don't spend time seeking out feline exercise wheels or jewels that you slip over your furry friend's tail to brighten up its rear end, though I see them when I'm online. I know cats. Cats have lived with me, and I have an inkling what cats would think about these things. There isn't a cat that doesn't know what to do if its rear end needs attention. The resident dog, Stink, does the same thing. Jewelry isn't part of the fix.

I can tell it's winter because the college ice hockey season is half over. For some reason that escapes me, Savannah media doesn't cover college ice hockey very well. Just to keep you up to date, St. Cloud State is having a wonderful season, and they are the top-ranked team. They just edged out the University of Denver, Clarkson University in Potsdam, New York, Notre Dame, and Cornell, who are also top-ranked teams. That's the top five. I love any sport where the top-five teams include an Ivy League school and three others nobody ever heard of. The Frozen Four, the college championship tournament, is in Saint Paul this year, and the ice will probably be better than when they played the finals in Tampa ... or at least drier. (Tampa temperatures create puddles.) I'll try to let you know how things are going as the season progresses.

I can tell it's winter because several people I know have established a close personal relationship with their ovens. That includes me. We all have traditional holiday treats that we create for friends and neighbors. My favorite is *Pfeffernüsse*, the German ginger cookie, but I mainly bake bread. The Bridgeports have a strong Scandinavian element in their heritage, and that includes *vört limpa*, a sweet rye that involves brewer's wort, the grains left over after you use them to brew beer. It also has anise and some citrus flavors. You have to try some to understand how good it is.

No discussion of Scandinavian cuisine would be complete without mentioning *lutfisk* or, if you are Norwegian, *lutefisk*. This is the traditional Christmas Eve supper. Time won't permit me to give you the particulars, but if you happen to have five pounds of air-dried stock fish, a pound of slaked lime, and a pound of washing soda hanging around the house, have I got a recipe for you. If you ask, I'll put it on the *When the Moon Sings* Facebook page.

Lutfisk takes a few weeks to prepare, so it's too late for this year, but if you pull lots of cod out of Wassaw Sound next summer, go ahead and air-dry them. I can guarantee a Christmas Eve supper you'll never forget, no matter how hard you try.

I am almost ready for Christmas, and I will stay almost ready until around New Year's. That's okay—the refinements I didn't get to this year will guide me next year. One of the charms of the holiday season is that it gives you lots of chances for a do-over.

Tomorrow is Christmas Eve. For everyone's sake, if you must go out, drive slowly and carefully. And please bring grandma in for the night. If she's wandering around the streets and gets hit by Santa's reindeer, we'll never hear the end of it.

The Stars

It was dark as I traveled to the WRUU studio tonight. The stars were igniting as I got to that stretch of road by the Frank W. Spencer Park. There aren't many houses as you cross the Wilmington River, which winds past the park, and the stars show up brighter without the light from the ground. You might know the place: It's where the old, wrecked boat quietly falls apart alongside the marsh. I had a moment of wonder, or at least as much of one as you can have on the Islands Expressway.

The stars—all that unknown out there, light-years of it. The unknown is lit by huge balls of energy powered by forces we don't quite understand. If you could get near them, you wouldn't survive (which is okay, because you wouldn't last for the journey, even at the speed of light). They provide a sense of wonder all right, and some humility, too, about how fragile we really are. Of course, there are some big balls of energy powered by forces we don't quite understand right here on Earth that could use that same lesson.

But this thought, and my own motorings, intervened in this moment of wonder. I passed the Waffle House and the Parker's after that, and they landed me squarely in the present. Still, thinking of the stars put me in mind of a friend I'll call "Popeye the Sailor Man." Popeye is an aerospace enthusiast. That's an understatement, like saying that LeBron James shoots hoops now and then.

Popeye regularly attends aerospace events he can get to, like rocket launches—he lives a few hours from one of the lesser launch pads. He also attends most of the natural space events, like the total solar eclipse. He went to Saint Louis last year to see it, a journey that took several hours and much effort. I stayed in Savannah and was treated to several hours of rain. I did take a picture of the rain clouds, but it didn't have the same impact.

Popeye tells me that we (the planetary "we") have had a recent visitor, a mysterious oblong object as big as a football stadium that flew through the solar system. By the time astronomers found it, it had passed us and was headed back out somewhere near Jupiter. Because it's oblong, some folks in the unscientific community decided that it might be a rocket ship from outer space. So the scientific community looked at it and reported that the surface of the thing was composed of "carbon-rich gunk."

What a description! If you think about it, that covers a lot of ground. The broken appliances I took to the dump and the old wrecked boat by Spencer Park are composed of carbon-rich gunk, too. So is the driver of the truck who cut me off on the Islands Expressway.

Popeye is also interested in the air force's footage of the unidentified flying object. I saw the film. There was a blob of light that curved in a twenty-degree turn across the aircraft monitoring events and then, according to the pilot who saw it, maneuvered and sped off much faster than our jet could. We don't know what it is, but we know what it isn't—weather balloons or something of the sort.

Oh, I could mention other things as well, like the Geminid meteor shower, but that's not the point. Popeye and all his friends have never lost their sense of wonder about space. Neither did Walter Cronkite.

At a more grounded level, I get the same sort of feeling when I see houses blazing with Christmas lights and their reflections bounce against the waters of the marsh. When I was very small, people usually told their children to act like it was Christmas all year long. Nobody ever did. Maybe that's too much to ask. But maybe if we kept our sense of wonder, the rest might fall into place. Wonder fosters appreciation and sometimes even reverence. It's something that you see in the best of scientists. Maybe we can make it contagious.

Christmas With Nelson Algren

It's been a very Savannah Christmas.

The day before Christmas, I had to come to the WRUU station (for reasons not worth mentioning) and very early. It was sixty-five degrees, and I almost regretted the jacket I wore. On the way home, I followed a truck pulling a boat; somebody was going to spend Christmas Eve trying to find Moby sea trout. I, however, was fishing for other things. I stopped at the drug store, because like a lot of other people, I had discovered that I didn't have enough ribbons and tape and gift tags. We remember to buy gift wrap but not the accoutrements until it's almost too late. The only alternative is to find out too late.

The store door was one of those automatic folding jobs, and it had jammed, so employees had folded it open. By that time, the outside temperature had risen, so it didn't make any difference. Some of the guys who were frantically picking through the gifts section were in T-shirts, and I saw a few in shorts.

As I wandered around during the day, I witnessed Christmas Eve things transpiring—a boy and his dad walking through the woods; a girl and her parents bicycling past Saint Andrew's; kids playing in the front yard. We think of Christmas as a family holiday, but on the very day we have new stuff from under the tree to explore and a huge meal to try to digest. The time or will to interact with others is moderate at best. Christmas Eve while the sun still shines is when the real interaction is.

But as I said, it was a very Savannah Christmas. Weather in Savannah is like a poker game—you don't expect to get the same cards every hand. The late Nelson Algren said that his three rules of life were:

1. Don't eat at a place called Mom's.
2. Don't play cards with anyone called Doc.
3. Don't lie down with anyone who has more troubles than you.

Well, about two o'clock, Doc showed up. To that point, the day had been a full house, kings over jacks, or maybe a low diamond flush. Doc put an end to that. The skies opened with a steady soaking rain, not the one-hour marsh-flooders or all-day dribbles we normally get. The temperature, which had gotten close to seventy, started to nosedive.

Christmas morning, Doc was still dealing. The ritual dawn dog walk took place in forty-four-degree weather, with a wind that Texans call a blue norther. I think of Christmas Day as mainly an indoor time, even in the typical Savannah clime, but at the halfway point of our chilly stroll, we saw a boy and a girl shooting new basketballs at a new driveway hoop. They were in pajamas, the fuzzy kind that have feet. The kids were of an age when it's a moral victory for the ball to reach the bottom of the net. Their older sister showed us her new unicorn. It was large and floppy.

For us older folks, this year for the holiday season Microsoft brought us a Creator's Update for Windows 10. In addition to adding several wonderful features I either can't or won't use, it obliterated many things I rely on. I am still using Office 2007, and so one of my e-mail accounts froze. I can still get to Word and Excel, and maybe some other things, but only after a long-ish conversion routine that one doesn't need at any age. I spent part of the holiday giving myself work-arounds for all of that. Sometimes you get the perfect gift from yourself. I have other thoughts about the Creator's Update for Windows 10, but I will save them for a less thoughtful and contemplative forum.

That wasn't all there was to Christmas. It had moments that were immensely valuable to me and some that would just be puzzling to anyone else. They don't even bear description.

But that's the whole idea. As much as we make holidays and other events communal, the value lies in what it means to each one of us. I can tell you I had a good holiday; if I tried to tell you why, you might laugh. Some of it is the effort we put into an event in the first place, some is what comes out of it.

Which brings us to New Year's Eve. We do nothing for it. The old year can find its own way out, and this one especially. Many of our neighbors welcome the budding year with bursts of gunpowder that make our island sound like the Fourth of July and the Battle of Gettysburg all rolled up into one.

Despite that, let us all have a good 2018—every one of us. We've got one coming.

Winter ~ Spring 2018

Humidity with bad habits

It Snows

Not so long ago, I spent a few days in a small town in central Georgia.

The stay wasn't completely intentional: State and local officials had demanded that those of us who live near the coast go somewhere else until the circular weather passed north of us. In this town, I had found a room in an establishment that accepts dogs. It turned out that the room was much more suitable for the dog than it was for us, but we were refugees and couldn't be that picky.

Do-it-yourself food also was necessary, and that is one of the few do-it-yourself categories I can handle. Groceries were available only at a big-box store—a place that carries garden tractors and desktop computers as well as Asiago cheese.

Since many of the people in this town work outside, I checked the store's non-food aisles for outdoor stuff. I found a pair of felt-lined chinos at a really good price. My rational side asked, "What are you going to do with lined chinos in southern Georgia?" My other side responded, "Bargain! Bargain! Bargain!" I went for them.

Hooray for the irrational, totally impulsive voice that somehow helps us adapt to changing circumstances. Now back home, I've been wearing the lined chinos since Monday.

It is cold for Savannah. Last week, my holiday pal—an intermittent resident—returned to Saskatchewan, where it is much colder. But, here, it is cold for us. I put gas in the truck a few days ago, and it dribbled out of the pump at a rate of about a gallon per minute. The lady inside explained that the network controlling the pumps was slow because it didn't like the cold. I've never seen cold that could slow down a computer network.

Then, there was a front-page story in the newspaper: "Savannah Delights in Winter Fun," and possibly, if you had given up on doing anything useful, delight you did.

Possibly, though, the reporters didn't get out to the islands, because both bridges to the mainland were closed for good portions of a couple of days.

Possibly, they didn't try to use the Truman Parkway, which was shut down due to the storm.

Possibly, they weren't on Victory Drive, trying to turn left onto Abercorn in order to get to the Southside. Many, many of us were, because the Truman was closed.

Savannah wasn't set up for winter fun. That's just not us.

But this flirtation with freezing is an aberration. Soon enough the weather will readjust to Savannah sensibilities that rebel at any more than two layers of cloth. The lined britches will again fade into a remote corner of the closet. We grow gators and sand gnats, not polar bears and blackflies. We have some things in common with our northern neighbors, like mosquitoes and traffic, but we are unique in many respects. The warmth will return.

This is weather for a Brunswick stew or shrimp and grits. We are humans, and we can adapt.

Martin Luther King Jr. and Jean Shepherd

This week was the anniversary of Martin Luther King Jr.'s birth, and that always brings Jean Shepherd to my mind.

Shep was a radio hero for me. I discovered him at that stage of my life when I had figured out that I had a place in the universe and wasn't sure what to do with it, or even if I wanted it. Of course, I didn't think about it in those terms. I had just discovered the wonders of acne, and I was micro-focused on that as a challenge.

Shep grew up during the Depression in an industrial town outside Chicago, was drafted during World War II, and went to college on the G. I. Bill after the war. He had wonderful stories about each of those experiences. If you've ever seen the movie *A Christmas Story* about Ralphie and the BB gun, it was based on a Shepherd story, and Shep did the voice-over in the film.

At the time I listened, Shep had a very late-night show on WOR in New York, which I could get even though we lived halfway to Boston. He told his stories conversationally, complete with pregnant pauses; he aired his impatience with sponsors; and he invited the audience to play along with his passions. He periodically told his listeners to throw open the window and scream, "Excelsior, you fathead!" I did that once, but it didn't have the same impact in an agricultural community in central New England. The cows that grazed behind our property looked at me funny the next day, but you couldn't expect the cows to get the subtleties of the message. Maybe that was his point.

When he discovered that the best-seller list was compiled from books requested rather than those actually bought, Shepherd instructed his listeners to ask for a specific book with a title that he made up. They did in such numbers that the title shot near the top of the list. It created such a furor that he and two friends rented a hotel room for a weekend and wrote the book. I read it several years later; it was a terrible piece of work.

One night in 1963, Shep showed up strung out and road weary at the radio station. He'd gone to Washington, D.C., for Dr. King's march and speech. He'd gone as a marcher, not as a celebrity. The organizers had rented crosstown busses to make the trip, and he sat on one just like everyone else. Back in New York, for the next hour, Shep talked about the experience. It was a string of impressions, large and small, from someone who knew how to make great radio from impressions.

Now that we know what an important moment that was, we find it being turned into history, and history usually contains a certain amount of mythology. But that's for historians to sort out.

If you want to know what it was like to be there, to be in the crowd, you could do worse than to listen to Shep's broadcast. There are sites on the 'Net that devote themselves to Shep's radio work, and you can find it on one of those. Because he goofs around for the first few minutes or so, you might start listening around the seven-minute mark.

Shep had a full measure of human foibles, but he was a radio man, and he knew important when he saw it. If you pick out human foibles, do it right and start with yourself. There are mornings when I look in the mirror at that saggy, shaving-cream-encrusted face, and I say to myself: "Excelsior, you fathead."

The Flu

I went to the drugstore the other day, and some of the staff and a few of the customers were wearing masks as a flu preventive. That makes perfect sense. If somebody gets the flu, the last place they'll stop before they collapse in a heap is a drugstore. But it reminded me of some pictures I've seen that were taken during and after World War I, when an influenza pandemic circled the globe near the war's end. The masks haven't changed that much.

That flu pandemic is what medical authorities fear today. The so-called Spanish flu killed something just below a hundred million people worldwide and around 675,000 in the United States. Many of those who died were the youngest and strongest. The flu causes the body's systems to overreact, throwing it into toxic shock.

The virus is known as a "quick-change artist," and this year's version isn't the same kind and isn't likely to cause that much damage. But it's still the flu, and even if it doesn't kill you, it's no fun. I went online and looked for recommendations on how to avoid this season's strain. As usual with the 'Net, there were many sites with a wonderful variety of ideas. The more authoritative stuck to the basics, like getting a flu shot, degerming your house, and taking your meds if sick. The more colorful spoke about sacrificing animals in the light of the moon or chants and dances. I don't know about where you work, but the maintenance staff of the radio station got fairly upset at the idea of a martyring a goat in the studio. That seems to be a nonstarter here.

There are some really rudimentary things you can do to cope with the flu. And some of them are rather appealing.

First, avoid crowds. That's a great one right there. I can't remember the last time I said, "Oh whoopee! I'm in a crowd." If you are in a crowd, there will probably be one person who's saying something like, "Oh, it's just my allergies," as if a temperature of thirty-four degrees with a north wind around twenty miles an hour is going to make the ragweed in South Carolina bloom.

Second, if you get the flu, stay isolated as much as you can. That not only prevents you from inflicting your flu on others, it also prevents them from catching your attitude. I don't care how much of a paragon of humanity you are, you aren't that person when you have the flu. You won't be a lamp to anyone's feet or a light unto their path until you get well.

Whenever I don't feel good, I sit in bed and sulk until I feel better. I should mention that my wife, the former Hamden Willimantic, is a medical professional and has other ideas. "You are the worst patient ever," she tells me. Medical professionals have not yet understood the benefits of sulking, and they interrupt it with kind offers of medicines or more pillows. Sulking is like meditation: If it's interrupted, that spoils the benefits.

Third, and this is my idea, do not try to carry on with your life, even if you can do that from your sickbed. You will spend the next month apologizing to the people with whom you interacted while you were achy and stuffed up. Read a book, turn on the radio, listen to music. It's time for you to take things in, not put things out. Treat yourself to something sleep-inducing if you get bored. Lower your expectations of yourself.

The flu is like stupid: You can't fix it, but sometimes you can avoid it.

The Uses of February

February has arrived in Savannah. That means spring is almost here. Oh, it's true. Flocks of twittering birds are filtering through the trees, lawns are starting to show some growth, and the algae in the drainage ditches out our way is getting even greener than it was. I saw my first palmetto bug today, and a woodpecker (who was obviously new at the game) tried to bore a hole in the tin roof of my shed.

I asked a birder friend whether these new bird flocks would stay or whether they were headed to someplace north, someplace that probably needs birds more than we do. She peered at them, shrugged, and said "LBJs." In birder talk, that means "little brown jobs," birds that blend in with their environment so well that you can't tell one sort from another without checking their driver's license. It seemed a shame to ask such musical creatures for ID.

Daily temperatures are variable now—we had one day with a high close to room temperature—but even on the cooler days, the sun shines brightly and warmly. It's almost time to go out and do things. Almost.

The radio station had a table at the Forsyth Farmer's Market this morning, and I almost went down. I had already been out once for the dog's morning ramble and decided that it was a little chilly for me. It will get better, and then I will go. If you see someone napping under the table, wake me up and say "hi."

At the beginning of January, we said, "Out with the old, in with the new." Some of us said that with vehemence this year. Because nature laughs at our wishes, it promptly froze everything in place for a month. Maybe that's over with now, and it will be easier to "out" old things and "in" new things. If you made New Year's resolutions, now would be the time to start working on them, especially if they require being outdoors.

According to *The Old Farmer's Almanac*, we are to have another snowstorm at some point in February. A number of people have told me that. I looked it up, and sure enough, the *Almanac* predicts snow sometime before the sixth. But I also checked an online weather site that was more optimistic than the old farmers of Keene, New Hampshire, prognosticating sometime last September. They are about as accurate as, oh, Pennsylvania groundhogs, and I need more reliable data. Two snowstorms in one year would be some sort of record for us and not really a terrific achievement.

In Savannah, we almost always focus not on snow but on water.

Out on the islands, many of us have boats parked somewhere near our houses. Another sign of spring is that many of them are sprouting "For Sale" signs. The Bridgeport driveway is innocent of marine craft, being offered for sale or not. Ms. Hamden, in her pre-Bridgeport existence, piloted rather large sail craft in her sunnier West Coast days. I have some experience myself: I once crewed on a twenty-hour trip down the length of the Chesapeake Bay and up the Potomac River. It was an unforgettable experience. I have become a strong advocate for putting lights on barges if you are going to tow them along sea-lanes in the middle of the night. Some of the people we encountered were less rabid on the subject. I am also fond of making sure that your engine will run for twenty hours if you take a twenty-hour trip. Part of life on the water is that there are even fewer guarantees than there are on land. And so our driveway remains free from transport that must be "captained" and "crewed."

February is the edge of spring in Savannah, and that is an improvement on February in other places. The sun is warm, and the mosquitoes are mostly still larvae. We can attune our wishes to nature, rather than expecting nature to accommodate us. On the whole, it seems more sensible anyway. January reminded us of that rule.

The Melt

At the halfway point in the season, I promised to keep all you Savannah fans listening to WRUU informed on the college hockey season. Well, here we are closing on tournament time, and the top-ranked teams are now St. Cloud State, Cornell, the University of Denver, Minnesota State, and Notre Dame. If you follow only ice hockey, Notre Dame is a large school in Indiana that has done well of late, and I understand they are very adept in other sports, too. We are getting close to the playoffs and the Frozen Four, which will be held in Saint Paul this year at the beginning of April. If you like dark horses in the tournament, keep your eyes on Clarkson, Northeastern, and Bowling Green. And the true Cinderella team would be Mercyhurst, which is cleaning up in a less regarded league. Now would be the time to book your tickets if you would like to be in Saint Paul in April. I have no such plans.

The hockey season is well and truly over in Savannah. Even since last week, the jonquils have bloomed, the flowering trees have started to . . . well, flower, and my blue truck has turned green from the pine pollen in the air. So have my friends who have allergy issues. 'Tis the season to be wheezy.

It is difficult right now to sort out those with allergies and are not contagious from those with the flu and are. It's even difficult to sort out myself. I cough and occasionally suffer from drip, both nasal and postnasal, and I wonder which misery is responsible. Perhaps it matters little for me, as I am still afflicted, of course, but passing on miseries seems like the wrong thing to do. This is one of those times when a loose affiliation with society seems wiser than a tightly knit community. Those times occur frequently.

Out east of the city, it is migration season. All those boats that have been hibernating on trailers are making their annual journey to the waterside. They will spend the warmer months in the sea, possibly mate (scholars debate about what really occurs), then come back to land in the late fall. The forecasters expect that there will be a slight increase in their numbers, which is okay, with no risk of being placed on the endangered species list. And like the Canada geese, there are always some that choose not to wander far from home, and they are ever with us.

That's outgoing migration. Incoming, we have the annual flocks of Girl Scout cookies, a part of the season I especially enjoy. I keep my eyes peeled for plumages of forest green, which may mean Thin Mints or Samoas are nesting nearby. I have been fairly successful in finding them in past years and look forward to more this year.

I have made my first uncoated forays into the backyard. A grapefruit tree grows there, and previously, when I wore several more layers of clothing, I went and harvested the bounty. But the tree is perhaps thirty feet tall, and many of the fruits are too high for me to reach even with devices made just for that. I was left to picking up the ones that had fallen after the freeze, and if I had waited any longer, the newly arrived wasps and such would have disputed my right to move them. So, in a few less layers, I now watch from a distance, possessing neither stinger nor fruit.

But this is spring, which is not constant. There will be cold and warm, fog and bright sun, howling winds and delicate calms.

Spring has been sung about since we started singing. Most of those songs use rebirth as the theme, but one of my favorites is "Águas de Março," or "The Waters of March," an old tune by Antônio Carlos Jobim. The song declares that spring is the end of all strain and imparts joy to the heart. Jobim was Brazilian and fully familiar with the rigors of summer, as familiar as we are. Yes, summer has its problems this far south. Spring—and the promise that water will stay liquid and the landscape will again become life-giving—does bring joy to the heart, even with the prospect of summer ahead.

The Wearing of the Yellow

Next week, Savannah wears its green. We also put it in fountains, beer, bagels, eggs, and anything else that will hold the dye. I haven't seen intentionally green bacon or pizza yet, but that doesn't mean that somebody isn't out there whipping up a batch. If you visit Savannah just after the ides and you see unexpected things in what we fondly imagine is Kelly green, keep calm. It's a Savannah thing.

But that's next week. This week, we're wearing our yellow. The pines are churning out clouds of pollen—it sweeps into the air and down the streets and sticks to anything with which it collides, including us. When it storms, the rain washes it onto the curbs and into the gutters, and there it dries until the next shower. It might even interfere with finding a parking place. If you have tooled into town this week, you probably think that there are bus stops on every corner. Look closer. Chances are, that yellow section is dried pollen, not paint, and you can park there after all ... assuming you have a credit card or a boatload of quarters.

Pine pollen is how we know spring has arrived. That, and the temperature drops and climbs in forty-degree increments, the wind either squalls or disappears, and torrents of rain flood the streets, followed by crackling, humidity-less days that dry them again—leaving a yellow residue, of course. But spring is no more predictable here than anywhere else. We have had windy days lately, and we're due for more. East of the city, where asphalt blossoms and the verdant squares decline, the wind has tinted the roads with a dusting of pollen. It rolls around like flakes up north after a flurry of snowfall.

I wandered around a few forested areas this week; one expanse had a rich, sweet smell. It was like honeysuckle that has started to bloom, but more pungent. I looked around, and there was a clump of jasmine just about to flower. Imagine that—jasmine in February! This was Confederate jasmine, not Asian jasmine. Confederate jasmine grows somewhat more slowly; Asian jasmine eats lamp poles and small buildings.

Such is spring in the South. In the North, where they still can't be very clear on the concept this time of year, the college hockey season continues. The national standings changed very little this week, though the conference champions were crowned. They are Mercyhurst, Cornell, Boston College, St. Cloud State, Notre Dame, and Minnesota State. But we still have the conference playoffs to go, and there's no guarantee any of them will be in the Frozen Four. There are several potent teams not on that list—for example, Northeastern, which had the top-three scorers in its league and the top-rated goalie. Northeastern also just won the Beanpot, symbol of Boston hockey supremacy. So all you college ice hockey fans in Savannah, stay tuned. It will be an exhilarating Frozen Four in Saint Paul. With the winter they're having, just getting to the stadium may be pretty exciting.

Here in the South, it's pretty easy to tell tourists from residents. Those visiting from farther north are walking slowly, taking in the sights that make Savannah what it is. Locals are frantically busy. There are landscapes to be planted or portrayed in paint, music to be played, and porches and gardens to be explored. Northern visitors don't have to worry about finishing outdoor activities until November or so. Our indoor season starts about the middle of June and, in some years, the middle of May.

But if you are a visitor, we will stop and share our bounty with you. Come paint a landscape or listen to some music. Sample some of our signature cuisine—like shrimp and grits. And if you order grits next week, don't be surprised if they are dyed green. It's a Savannah thing.

The Wearing of the Green

It's Saint Patrick's Day. In Savannah, we turn the standard American celebration into an art form. We don't just hold a parade, we have a multiple-day fête, and if you happen to manufacture green food coloring, boy, do we have a market for you.

Well, let the good times roll. But truth be told, this has always been a holiday about which I've been a wee ambivalent. I have a bit of Irish blood in me, not on the Bridgeport side but on my mother's. Her mother's generation and the generation before had many Irish immigrants. Most of them were Catholic; some were Protestant. In those years, the difference between being Green and being Orange might be life and death. There's an old joke: A man gets stopped in an alley by a group of ruffians. One of them snarls, "Are ye Catholic or Protestant?" The man says, "I'm an atheist." The leader stops for a moment and then asks, "Are ye a Catholic atheist or a Protestant atheist?"

Against all expectations, the Orange and the Green got along fairly well in my mother's family. They weren't close, but they were polite and respectful. The Greens would have a Saint Patrick's Day celebration, and the Oranges would come. And one year, so did we.

The first part of the evening was sufficiently tame—dinner was good, beer was plentiful, and everyone was on best behavior. Early enough to get home and late enough to be polite, the Oranges dribbled away from the festivities. And then things got strange.

The old men put aside the beer and pulled out drinks that do not foam when poured. I was underage for anything stronger than Yoo-hoo, but I figured it out later. They sat in a tight circle around the kitchen table, the bottle in the middle, and tried to determine, yet again, who killed Cousin Michael. That's what I'll call him.

Cousin Michael had become energized with independence. He had strong ideas on the future of the homeland and became an organizer for Michael Collins in Galway. One night, the constables found him dead, battered almost beyond recognition, in a Galway alley.

This was not sectarian—this was political. The suspected murderers were, like Cousin Michael, Catholic, but they didn't like Michael Collins, and they weren't too crazy about Cousin Michael either. Many of the old men tippling at the table had known both Cousin Michael and his contemporaries, and his death was a matter of family honor. They spoke in passionate low tones, with the threat of violence in every word. Apparently, they did this every year on Saint Patrick's Day. They were not just talkers; if they had ever reached a conclusion, Galway would have seen more bloodshed.

I asked my mother's Uncle Willie about it. Uncle Willie was one of the Orange relatives, a gentle man who wanted nothing to do with any of that old country history. He advised me, in so many words, to forget about it. But I never have.

Some people make fun of the American Saint Patrick's Day—too many buckled hats, too much beer, too much pseudo-blarney. That isn't authentic enough for some. Well, anything authentic has a dark side, too. On the whole, the way we do Saint Patrick's Day, which can be loutish, is far better than plotting mayhem. If I do not celebrate the day in the same way as you, perhaps it is because in my formative years I witnessed an authentic observance. I cannot recommend it. Go drink something green.

The Good Old Days

In the year I was born, more than twenty-five thousand children in the United States contracted polio, which was then called infantile paralysis; 1,845 children died of it. While looking up this sad statistic, I found a grim picture of a hospital ward for those with the disease. It had thirty-four patients, thirty of whom were in iron lungs. But that was a good year. Just before the vaccine was developed, there were fifty-eight thousand cases and more than three thousand deaths. Mind you, this was before the whole idea of medical insurance, and iron lungs were expensive. Back in the good old days, gravely ill children not only broke the heart, they broke the bank.

My parents were children of the Depression. Before marriage, my mother worked at the headquarters of a large insurance firm. They paid her (and most of the other female employees) almost enough to live on. In those days, people smoked to take the edge off their hunger—and that wasn't just a few people either. Back then, lunch counters kept a sharp eye on their ketchup bottles lest some needy person try to make tomato soup from its contents and hot water. If you were in a friendly restaurant, the waitstaff would bring a few packages of crackers whenever a customer ordered hot water.

We lived on the edge of a city—still urban but with actual suburbs a short drive away. The suburbs were multiple acres of identical homes far enough from downtown to make each trip to the city a dawn exercise and each trip home a journey in darkness. We had milkmen who got up at two o'clock in the morning to deliver dairy products for a salary of a penny or so a bottle and scissors-grinders who often had to choose between feeding their horses and feeding themselves. The lunch counters automatically put out hot water and soda crackers when a scissors-grinder parked his horse in front of the shop.

In our area, most of the neighborhoods were ethnic. Ours was considered Irish, though fewer than half the residents were actually Irish. The surrounding neighborhoods were mostly Italian. That was a big deal in those days—cross into the wrong neighborhood at night, especially as a kid, and you were likely to suffer indignity, if not injury. And any neighborhood besides yours might be the wrong one.

Ethnic identity was strong in those days. Boston College, where most of the students were of Irish heritage, was described as being within "rioting distance" of Boston University, where most of the students claimed Italian ancestry.

It was pretty much the same in every city in the country. The ethnicities might change, but the narrow attitudes were identical.

I could go on about the politics and the social mores of that era, but that isn't the point. Nor am I trying to impress you with how difficult things were when I was young.

When I got on Facebook the other day (yes, I still use Facebook), I found yet another canned post reminding me how wonderful the old days were. This particular one was about raising kids—how kids were polite and always changed their clothes after school and always did their homework. Why yes, they often did, because if they didn't, their parents would beat them silly and exhibit other behaviors that would result in a police presence today (and rightfully so). Look up some of the battered children statistics. It was a thing back then. Facebook commentators often forget crucial facts.

Facebook is an electronic monument to the fact that many people can type faster than they can think. I accept that. Many of the thoughts posted thereon are wryly amusing; some small number are intentionally so.

People today have much more freedom than they had back in the good old days. In those days, having the wrong ethnicity or having poor parents or having ideas other than the norms would limit you, if not kill you. This new freedom includes the right to post dumb things on Facebook. I try to remember that when I see yet another post pining for the days of the Mafia, stagflation, and the Korean War.

This particular throwback (the commentary about raising kids) ended with a request for others to repost the commentator's words. He did so using grammar that defied any relation to the sentence diagramming that we were taught in the good old days, and the last sentence ended with three exclamation points.

That makes reading it my fault, for those are signs that the words aren't worth one's focus. Sometimes I skip to the end of a post to check for them. I should have done that this time.

The price of liberty is eternal vigilance.

Yellow Journalism

I am in the middle of a book called *The Murder of the Century.* The century in question was the nineteenth, and the murder happened in New York. As murders go, it was sensational but rather small potatoes. Some boys playing around the East River saw a package floating along and retrieved it. Inside was a headless, legless torso, skillfully separated from the missing pieces.

Bodies floating down the East River were not common but not unknown either. The police took due notice, but then the newspapers got wind of it. The newspapers of the time were heavily into sensationalism, and this case fit their needs. The two largest papers in New York, the *World*, headed by Joseph Pulitzer, and the *Journal*, headed by William Randolph Hearst, went head-to-head in covering the case. Both papers sent swarms of reporters to mine every aspect and every detail. In fact, the reporter swarms were able to cover much ground that the police couldn't, and they contributed to the eventual arrest and prosecution of the suspects. Did the suspects actually do it? I don't know—I haven't finished the book yet.

The problem was that for great stretches of time in between discovering actual facts, the papers made up stuff and reported things from other sources that couldn't possibly be true. In fact, the papers developed corporate opinions about the whole thing. The *Journal* was intent on disproving the *World*'s published theories and vice versa. Every sensational article sold more papers, and the greater the sensationalism, the more papers it sold.

Today we call that yellow journalism. My personal term for it is "jerk warfare." Unless you get your newspapers from the rack at the grocery store checkout line, you probably haven't run into it much. Most newspapers today follow standards of behavior that would paralyze either Pulitzer or Hearst.

So we're through with that nowadays, right? Not so fast. Did you turn on your computer this morning? Have you scrolled through any social media? There are people there who make Pulitzer and Hearst look like choir boys.

Some are homegrown—every garden produces weeds. Some are true believers in whatever, and some get themselves funded by true believers in whatever. Well-paid true believers and even false believers show up frequently in all media, but TV and commercial radio seem to have a large number. There are even larger swarms on the 'Net. Most of them don't seem to have the country's best interest in mind, and in fact, some of them don't—we are learning interesting things about the technical capabilities of countries both north and south of Mongolia.

Anybody who uses social media sees the output. If you Facebook (yes, now a verb), it takes only one of your polarized friends to like something, and there it is on your computer, invading your home, reaching through your eyes into your brain. Politics aside, you see flat-earthers, anti-vaxxers, and every other sort of opinion about everything. Most of them believe that blurting out their opinion will be enough to convert you. If they use Twitter, the blurting is mandatory.

These are the modern jerk warriors, and the impulse has lots of appeal. I have learned from multiple sources that high-ranking officials of our very own government indulge themselves in jerk warfare.

Since few pulling the strings of social media will check users' facts, you must. I mean from anybody. There are sites on the 'Net for fact-checking. There's a whole list of ways to combat this, but they are mostly common sense.

Jerk warfare hasn't done any of us any good, either individually or collectively. The only people it benefits are the ones who cash in on it, like Hearst and Pulitzer before them. So here's the thing about jerk warfare: It only works when jerks follow the warriors. Ignore them, and they disappear.

It's not that I think anyone out there is part of the problem, but I sure do think you are part of the solution.

Chowing Down—Way Down

I like ethnic foods, and Savannah has its fair share.

Before I came here, I lived near a large city that had a restaurant for almost any sort of cuisine you can name and maybe a few you can't. I remember one that devoted itself to the cuisine of a central Asian country—one of the ones that end in "-stan." They had pictures of yurts, tractors, and cement plants on the walls.

We ordered the buffet (it was lunchtime), and that was a mistake. I had no idea what I was looking at on the steam table; it was all brightly colored conglomerations of things. I wound up making decisions by whether the colors coordinated with the rest on my plate. A busboy saw my assortment and involuntarily tittered. I'd have gone back for a course of properly selected edibles, except the -stan food did not appeal to many other people and the restaurant disappeared.

Like my former home, Savannah does not have a Scandinavian restaurant that I can find. Very few places do, and that interests me because my ancestors came from Sweden.

Many Scandinavians hail from places where they grew Vikings. My particular ancestors sold low-mileage dragon ships and gently used oars to the pillager wannabes. Which, if you want to live a low-risk and sedentary life, makes great sense—I come by my lifestyle honestly. There are a few Scandinavian restaurants in the Upper Midwest, but they are either scarce or missing elsewhere in the country.

The lack of Scandinavian foods is not a tragedy in my life; I grew up with them and have had enough of many of them to last a lifetime. Some are delicious, but quite frankly, many are not. You only need a map to determine why. My people came from an area that's on the same latitude as northern Labrador in this hemisphere. The growing season is short for just about anything, and large, high-maintenance beasts such as cows are in short supply. Two things were readily available: fish and root vegetables. So that's what they used.

When you go to an ethnic restaurant, you are eating the food of the common people, cleaned up of course. Pizza came about because the peasants had cheese, dough, tomatoes, and spices. The folks up in the castle were eating stewed nightingales, or whatever the medieval equivalent of surf and turf was.

One of the key ingredients in these dishes is spices, and the Scandinavians fell short even there. The spice trade emanated from the Mediterranean, and Scandinavia was the last stop before traders headed home. What Scandinavians saw had been picked over and rejected by wholesalers up the length of the Atlantic coast.

Traditionally, Scandinavians use either flavorings with a long shelf life, like almonds, ginger, caraway, and orange peel zest, or things that nobody else in the West could find a use for, like cardamom.

Cardamom is more popular lately. According to the 'Net, the health benefits of cardamom include gastrointestinal protection, cholesterol control, prevention of cancer, relief from cardiovascular issues, and curing dental diseases and urinary tract infections. Cardamom possesses aphrodisiac properties and is also used as an antidote for impotence. However, it still tastes like cardamom, and the 'Net is not known for scientifically accurate statements.

The Scandinavians integrated all these spices with their fish and root vegetables. When they did use land beasts, they used every last part of them.

The Napoleonic era ramped up the cuisine considerably. The Swedish royal family ran out of even vaguely related candidates for the throne, and they asked Napoleon for help. Napoleon sent them Count Bernadotte, who had no real love for fish and roots. Many of the more delicious things now have strong resemblances to French foods. *Plättar*, Swedish pancakes, are doppelgängers for crêpes and are used in the same way.

The most notorious Scandinavian dish is *lutfisk* or, if you are Norwegian, *lutefisk*. Now it is a traditional Christmas dish. Before Napoleon, I suspect it was the beginning of "eating up what you have stored because you can't fish in the howling North Sea and when the Baltic is frozen over for the season."

Some weeks before you attempt to eat *lutfisk*, get yourself a wooden tub and into it place the stockfish that you air-dried over the summer. Add water and industrial lye. I want to know who came up with that, and I'm even more interested in what they used before industrial lye was a thing. Incidentally, if you are set on by thugs, air-dried stockfish make perfectly serviceable hand weapons, having the same characteristics as a cricket bat.

The lye eventually breaks down the fibers of the stockfish, and you spend the rest of the weeks changing the water and leaching the lye out of the fish. After the process is complete, the stockfish is no longer suitable as a hand weapon, but the smell will drive anyone away. (The Mongol hordes never reached Scandinavia; I think I know why.) With preparation complete, you boil the result (this removes some of the rich odor but by no means all of it), top it with a cream sauce, and serve with potatoes and peas. And pepper—lots of pepper.

The Vikings who toured Europe in the spring had a reputation for being a surly and rapacious lot, a reputation that is fully justified. If they ate this and similar things from the winter solstice to the vernal equinox, maybe we can understand their attitude.

Awaiting Response

When I staggered to my computer first thing this morning, it informed me that a brown bear can eat forty thousand moths per day.

This earth-shattering news was accompanied by a picture of a mother bear and three cubs, none of which looked like they had been on the moth diet lately. They were strolling by a stream, possibly looking for something with more protein and less fiber. The mother seemed somewhat agitated, and so did the third cub, the one bringing up the rear.

I imagine the cub had just said, "Ewww, not moths again." If it wasn't that, it was, "Are we there yet?"

All of this floated through my consciousness just after I turned the computer on, before I even put in the password. Fun facts are part of the screen saver supplied by the operating system, along with pleas to sign up for things and notifications that I have earned some sort of points for something. I paid attention to the bears because it was the last thing I was able to do without a struggle.

I wanted to read the newspaper. I do that online because the paper there covers things that happen outside the Coastal Empire, and I am one of those worrywarts who thinks that wider news might be important. The paper I read online puts out a print edition, too, though not where I can get at it—we're not talking about *The Real Truth Tribune* or *Smash the System Daily* here. I was looking for facts, not opinions.

I pulled up the newspaper site. After a semi-suitable pause, the headlines appeared on my screen. Now, from long habit I read the comics first. It's sort of a tune-up before I get to things that are more difficult to process. So I clicked the comics section. The screen went blank, and the little notification box said, "Awaiting Response From . . ." It didn't tell me who it was awaiting the response from, but it was the newspaper site. Now, from long experience I know what that means. It means that I am going to have to wait while my Internet provider and the Web site figure out a way to communicate with each other. I also know that my provider's communications skills are about as good as North Korea's.

So I opened another window and started to go through the social media. I do that because I am officially charged by an organization to do so, even though other things get in the way. A friend of mine reposted a three-year-old message from somebody whose son was a Marine who encountered somebody who was rude to him. Of course, the message wanted you to share if you think it is wrong to be rude to Marines. I switched back to the newspaper. It was still awaiting response, so I looked up the other incident instead. I do not favor being rude to Marines, but this looked fishy.

Well, maybe it happened and maybe it didn't, but the person who originally posted the Marine message opened up a site for people to send money if they think being rude to Marines is wrong. That apparently didn't do the trick, because two years later, the ex-Marine and an accomplice were arrested for sticking up convenience stores. This is all true—you can look it up yourself.

I switched back to the newspaper; the comic I asked for had appeared. I read it and went to the next. I got most of my other computer work done while "Awaiting Response From . . ." showed on the first window. Then, I went on to the sports section and the rest of the paper, interrupted frequently by the same message.

There are several lessons here, and maybe I'll talk more about them in the future. But I wonder if I go through 40,000 "Awaiting Response From..." messages during the day, and I wonder if I shouldn't be looking for something more nutritious.

Rain

It rained an authentic Georgia rain on Monday. At ten o'clock in the morning, it was as dark as just before sunup. Before that, the sky had turned gray—if you are an artist, it boiled with darker shades of Davy's gray, accented by swirls and pools of Payne's grey, that grim Prussian-blue-tinted kind. When a Georgia sky turns Payne's grey, it means business. By mid-morning, you couldn't see the clouds; the water coming out of them obscured your vision.

I happen to know that because I was supposed to sit at the art gallery that morning, and we open at ten. I parked half a block from the gallery and walked through the downpour. For these occasions, I have a hooded warden's jacket from northern New England, built for stumbling around in wet forests. If you haven't seen one, they are made of medium-weight polyester, come to just above the knee, and have a minimum of seventeen pockets. However, my particular jacket is well aged, and well-aged polyester does not hold together well. Sewn seams loosen, and taped seams unstick. My warden's jacket has become "unseamly" in several areas. Monday's rain showed me exactly where each seam has fallen away.

The other feature of this jacket is that it's like Las Vegas—what goes into the pockets stays in the pockets. Monday, that was mostly rain. I found that out Monday night when I accidentally emptied four or five ounces of rainwater from one of the side pockets onto the rug. If you buy a jacket like this, you should know it retains water extremely well, especially the hood if you don't use it.

Biblical scholars suspect that Noah's ark made landfall on or near Mount Ararat in Turkey. When it rains like the biblical

flood here, I start to wonder where Noah started his voyage. I can't say for sure, but I'm almost certain the first body of water he hit after he cast off was Wassaw Sound.

By two in the afternoon, the weather had improved to dreary. The clouds were visible then, and they dropped only a fine mist with occasional bursts of heavier rain for people who thought they could go out without getting too wet.

When I returned to the Islands, one of my neighbors mentioned that we had gotten more than two inches of rain for the day. When you are surrounded by water—and much of it is a river that collects everyone else's water—you watch things like that. Well, two inches isn't even close to a record, but it's a wet day, even for Georgia. We're actually pretty dry most of the time, but when rain comes, it comes hard and fast.

By Tuesday dawn, the showers had passed. The air still had lots of moisture and a slight chill when the dog and I took our morning walk. But there was no wind, and the plants had absorbed the moisture. The whole neighborhood had that sweet, oily scent of jasmine and honeysuckle. Some of the aromatic roses contributed scents as well.

Savannah is back to sandals weather now, and it's almost time to switch to short pants permanently. By May, it could be hot and sticky. Around here, April showers bring April flowers—May can take care of itself. I like that about this place.

Gardening and Reuniting

This was an agricultural week out at the Islands Home for the Slightly Bewildered where I currently reside. We have a few weeks left where it is neither too cool nor too warm to rearrange the backyard, and this was one of them. The winter was not kind to many of the plants, and the jury is still out on some of the late season tropicals. But the smilax and the false grape vines have survived well and are choking out the plants that I actually want. While I was dealing with them, I noticed that the sand gnats are back in full force, too.

Smilax—that's the thorny vine with heart-shaped leaves that sneaks in among your azaleas and throws long tendrils of thorns all over the place. Here, we also call it cat vine and bull vine. It comes from a tuber, and the only way you can get rid of it is finding and digging up the tuber. I understand that you can make a pretty fair pipe bowl from the tuber and that the young shoots taste like asparagus when boiled. I will test those theories in my next incarnation.

The dog Stink accompanies me on these occasions. He is much better at digging than I am, but we can't seem to agree on location. On the rare occasions when we do, he digs up what I've just put down, and that causes confusion and sometimes resentment. Much less of that happened this year, because there is a new dog in one of the yards that backs onto ours. The two dogs carry on an extended dialogue that sounds like the peace process is falling apart. That leaves little time for digging.

When we came inside, I found more information on my class reunion. I generally don't pay much attention to reunions, but this is one of those big anniversary years. If this were a wedding anniversary, you'd have to wear a cummerbund at some point or go somewhere that would require at least two changes of planes. Either that or all your relatives would descend on you and make snotty comments about how your diet seems to revolve around corn chips but they're only saying that because they love you. Then, they bring out a large cake. That kind of special anniversary. For the reunion, the university will gather us together and congratulate us for outliving our education, and we will present ourselves to the friends of our youth as a more or less finished product.

Part of the preparation for these festivities was a trivia quiz. I failed it miserably. Another was filling out a questionnaire: Now that you've grown up, who are you anyway, and how did you get there? And because some of your ex-classmates think they are Marcel Proust or maybe James Joyce, limit yourself to a five-hundred-word response.

At first, that looks too limiting. Describe decades of my life in five hundred words? But if they're looking for accomplishments, winning third place in the church photography contest fifteen years ago won't make much of an impression. Maybe five hundred words is too many, after all.

Did you win a MacArthur grant or increase the gross national product of Burkina Faso by 8 percent using first-world waste products to increase crop yields? Did you rescue helpless children from a raging river, provide critical programming that ensured the success of the space station, or hit the Powerball lottery? I didn't. Once I pulled a cat out of a storm drain, but that didn't impress anybody much, not even the cat.

I didn't double the price of lifesaving drugs or drive a van into a crowded sidewalk either. But the questionnaire didn't want details on what I didn't do.

For inspiration, I looked on the wall of my office, where I have a few plaques and awards from the days when I was still becoming somebody. In the business world, that's known as an "I Love Me" wall.

I helped some kids pass their GED exams. Not bad, but not exactly front-page news. I contributed to the success of an organization. That organization no longer exists; apparently it needed more success than I could contribute. I made some invaluable contributions to a computer system that actually succeeded and is helping control air traffic today. The contributions are unspecified, as they should be, and at best it was enlightened self-interest—I have to use airlines, too.

What else? I once made a film on what to do if your equipment catches fire. It turns out that what you do is pretty intuitive, but it was aimed at trainees, so a film might be necessary.

Well, okay, that needs work. Now that I am a semifinished product, what am I? I get much commentary on this and how to make it better. I do the usual things: Garbage goes to the street on Friday and recycling every other Wednesday. The dog tours parts of the island twice a day. As for the rest, I deliberately stay a beta version of me to which I add new features, like talking on the radio. I've been doing a radio program since Thanksgiving, and anybody who thinks I have it down hasn't watched me in action. If you don't add new features every once in a while, everybody gets bored with you. Including you.

I managed to get to somewhere around four hundred words before I ran out of steam. But here's the thing—had I won a Nobel Prize, provided comfort and security to untold thousands, and been recognized by Congress for my contributions to humanity, I could appear as some sort of miracle worker to the people who read the questionnaire results. But when I arrived back home, the garbage would still have to go out and so would the recycling and the dog.

That's life.

Sick

My first year in Savannah, my ears and sinuses clogged up starting around Saint Patrick's Day and ending after the glorious Fourth of July. My system was getting used to Savannah's palette of allergens. Oh, Virginia (from whence I came) has allergens, too, but they apparently lack the variety and persistence of those in the Coastal Empire. My ears and eyes clogged shut, and my nose earned itself one of those 26.2 stickers you see on the autos of marathon runners. I impressed everyone I met as an old fool who couldn't hear, couldn't see, and spoke in phlegmy phrases that trailed off into a sniffle. I probably am an old fool, but I usually hide it better than that.

Every year since, it's been something, but it hasn't been everything. This year, I had periods of mild discomfort, but nothing really to speak of. Until last week.

Coming into the studio, my sinuses announced that they were feeling humid. Leaving the studio, my personal National Weather Service announced that a tropical depression had formed just inside my eyebrows, and it was time to bring the pets inside and nail plywood across the bigger windows. By Sunday, I was dizzy. Most people call that being light-headed—I don't know why. My head felt heavy, very heavy. My forehead was overheated, even though the rest of me was chilled. This was no allergic reaction. I had a fever, and not just spring fever either. I was officially sick.

I don't get officially sick that often, but I have enough experi-ence to know what to do. First, put on enough layers of clothing for a trip to Siberia. Second, take some green pills. Third, go back to bed and pull the covers over my head until it all goes somewhere else. The green pills are important. They have all those physical medicines that the manufacturers say they do, though not enough—never really enough. But one of the mag-ical ingredients suspends my ability to care anymore. And if I care, that's bad. First I get bored, and then I get angry. Boredom and anger never heal an aching body.

With this particular spell, mostly I slept. I slept until that point in the afternoon when the dog usually has some exercise. The dog announced this by reaching up and dragging his paw, claws included, across my shoulder.

"I don't care," I mumbled and rolled over. There was further negotiation but to no conclusion. Negotiation only works when both sides care enough to go through the process. I didn't.

Around sundown, the chills and fever seemed to have left, and I woke up. The dog looked up at me. Dogs have a way of telling you what they want without moving a muscle. It's in the eyes, and I suppose it's because when a dog wants something, it is with passion and complete conviction. Cats do not have that quality, though daughters sometimes do—I've had experience with them, too.

So I got out of bed, took off the Siberian excursion outfit, and put on Savannah togs. We walked around the neighborhood, spreading tiny droplets of the illness among the Spanish moss and pine needles. We didn't meet anyone, thank heavens, but when we left the house, I sneezed on the thorny vines that have infiltrated the azaleas. For the record, smilax is resistant to chills and fever; it is still there today, growing as robustly as ever. Analog thinking has failures as well as successes, particularly that which is influenced by sinus pressure.

When we got home, I discovered that I was not as free of the illness as I thought. I took more green pills and went back to bed. There I stayed until I was able to get to the fridge and take some light refreshment. I don't know what it was; it was whatever was in the fridge. I didn't care.

My wife was a surgical nurse before retirement. Before she left the profession, she helped put people back together who could be put together. That included installing aftermarket carburetors and valve lifters in people whose original equipment had worn out. After she left the profession, she did the same thing for horses for a while. Her first impulse is to nurse. While all my sickness was happening, she sat in her chair and made no comment.

Clever woman.

Over the years she's learned that what I need when ill is to be left alone. Here are some phrases that only irritate me when I'm sick:

"Would you like me to ... "

"Here, take some (whatever). ... It's good for you."

"Should we go to the emergency room?"

And so on. I did not hear one of those phrases—not one—while I was sick.

I am well now. My sinuses have dialed back to "humid," and I have that dramatic cough that signals you are just about over whatever you had. The dog is being walked on his regular schedule. In a day or so, I will be well enough to apply more time-tested strategies for removing smilax.

But first, I think I owe my wife a dinner out.

Summer 2018

Righting

A friend of mine on Facebook just posted a quote. No big news there, but it's a little more complex than that. This is an actual friend, not just somebody I've swapped cute electrons with. We have broken bread together, hitched rides in the other's motor vehicle, jointly worked on interesting projects, and occasionally blessed each other's hearts in the heat of some discussion.

An actual friend—you remember those.

Anyway, the quote is from Victor Hugo, and it says, "A writer is a world trapped inside a person." It attracted her because she has published a number of things about her world—so some of it is no longer trapped. Moreover, she has done so in an utterly entertaining way. If you have read the story of the Hootchie Cootchie Pickler, you know who I mean.

The quote attracted me because I have about two-thirds of a novel finished. When I was younger, almost everyone who had manually mowed the grass and polished the DeSoto sat down in the evening and worked on either a novel or a screenplay.

None of those things happen that much anymore, but some of us are still writing. Books seem to be out of fashion now. They've been replaced by incoherent howls of fifty words or less transmitted electronically to people who are looking to have their blind prejudices validated. Nothing in their worlds is trapped inside them, though you often wish it were, unless you are looking to have your blind prejudices validated.

The business of creating worlds is a thorny one. You must know your world intimately. If you don't, one of your readers will surely know more about it than you do and will comment publicly with something along the lines of, "If you don't know the streets of Quebec better than that, go back to repairing bicycles!" This is disconcerting, and more so if the comment is accurate.

The second part is that if you are going to write ninety thousand words or more, you are going to dredge up things that you've thought and done because you can't make that much up from mere imagination. In other words, you are going to have to reveal yourself to people. Some of those people will look over your most treasured thoughts and scrawl "You stink" on some rating board. They will probably also misspell "stink." The computer industry has already given us electronic pencils, but these people are waiting for the development of the electronic crayon.

You wrestle with your demons, and they wrestle with theirs. If you are actually going to publish the book, you have to pay more attention to yours. Many of them aren't demons at all; they're just consequences of some plot detail you slid into an early chapter. If you decide that Sheila or Gertrude is pregnant in chapter one, she's probably not going to feel like single-handedly defeating the hordes of the devil king Fnerg while armed only with a rapier and a red magic marker in chapter eight. Readers notice things like that.

If you think about it, any form of creativity is a world trapped inside a person. Music is certainly that way, and so is art. Good artists can portray landscapes or people or ideas or nightmares well.

Great artists bring you into their world where such things exist.

Stumbling through the here and now with a world trapped inside you is unpleasant, to say the least. Creative people are frequently not the best-adjusted, content, and caring individuals. It's like a pregnant Sheila or Gertrude character—when you have to pay attention to the world inside you, the outer one suffers. Those who stalk creativity will excuse their social disabilities by pointing to the large crop of lunatics, addicts, and narcissistic megalomaniacs whose books we read, music we listen to, and art at which we gaze. They imply that, left to their own devices, they will produce something just as fine. Regrettably, fourth-rate poets and hack cartoonists can be as ugly and toxic as first-rate ones.

The best creatives I know nurture the world inside them as a job, something to be done well rather than sidelined whenever their outer worlds call. I try to do that. It doesn't always work, but I try. If I write about the streets of Quebec, I'm going to do research, maybe visit them, and really think about what they mean—I'm not just going to dribble down half-formed ideas, fueled by my estimate of my own brilliance. I'm terrible at repairing bicycles, so if I want to write, I have to know and maybe experience what I'm writing about.

I just wish that people who communicate electronically would take the same care, especially if their opinions have some impact on the real world.

Lhude Sing Cucu

This was a week of firsts at Casa Bridgeport. For the first time this year, the windows misted over because outside is hot and wet and inside is cool and dry. It'll happen several more times before the weather turns, but this week was the inaugural for 2018. Summer is a-comin' in.

This week, the corporation that manages our solid waste removal announced that our pickup day is changing. That shouldn't be a big deal, but we live intricate lives now—most people our age do. Basically, it means that I will have to empty the house on Tuesday nights instead of Thursdays. It also means I will spend part of Wednesday putting the container back together rather than reassembling it on Fridays. The folks who collect our solid waste use a mechanical device to lift the can to the truck and then return it empty. Fair enough, but the device is somewhat less than gentle, and the can frequently has to be reassembled before I can wheel it back up the driveway.

On Tuesday, I made my first sustained beach trip for the year. I'm out there a fair bit, but a sustained trip is where I load a chair, an umbrella, food, and a beach cart into the truck and bring along reading and listening material suitable for hours staring at the waves. The forecast called for light rain punctuated by the occasional monsoon, the same forecast we've had for the past two weeks. But the sky said otherwise, so I went.

When I got to the beach, the southeast wind was driving the waves against the shore, and I watched some other sustained beach tripper chase an upturned umbrella into the surf. No umbrella for P. T. today—that looked like more fun than I was up for. In place of the umbrella, I slathered myself in SPF 173.5. It does the job, but it smells like a coconut crab threw up on you. A seagull looked at me and gagged.

It was a good day mostly. Not many people go to the beach on "Monsoon Tuesdays," so I had plenty of beach to myself. Plus, we are getting some nice fruit now, and the sandwich still tasted good. I have a small cooler that keeps liquids cold, and it fits nicely in the beach wagon between the umbrella and the chair. Life seemed brighter.

I brought along a book that I was close to finishing. It's a history of Amsterdam. Amsterdam is an odd place: at once a pillar of conservative Dutch society and a refuge for people who have highly individual ideas of what constitutes appropriate behavior. The last part has drawn the attention of American political commentators. Bill O'Reilly used to sneer at the city and its ideas from time to time. For all I know, he still does; I don't track Bill O'Reilly's opinions that closely.

Amsterdam has been a major seaport for five hundred or so years. For all that time, the city has coped with a steady stream of visitors who do not look or act like Dutch locals, and the locals have developed ways of dealing with that. The word they use for coping with visitors is *gedogen*, which broadly means "tolerance." Essentially, you don't have to act like a proper Amsterdammer as long as you don't hurt anybody and you keep whatever you are doing to yourself.

The hippies of the twentieth century discovered *gedogen* and flocked to Amsterdam in large numbers. Much of their passion and ambition related to the ingestion of marijuana. That was okay with the Amsterdammers as long as the smokers kept it to themselves. Even today, there are coffee shops that welcome joint bearers. Oddly enough, if you light up something with tobacco in it, you will be shown the door. Tobacco isn't tolerated. In my dim past, I tried the tobacco-less stuff. It increases my appetite for chocolate, and I don't need that right now. I'm with the locals on that issue. But that's just me.

The next step up is regulation. If people want to do un-Dutch things openly, they can still do them, but their activities and suppliers are regulated. The Amsterdammer idea of *gedogen* is to manage what you must and ignore what you can. If what you are doing harms other people, heaven help you. You get the full weight of Dutch law.

Compare that with this side of the Atlantic. We involve ourselves in individual decisions, things that society really shouldn't deal with. I'm talking about things like gender, race, and religion. Nobody ignores anything or even manages it. We just pass laws against it. If a sufficient number of people are against something, there will be laws against it, whether it is society's business or not. We are terribly binary here, either legal or illegal; we go to the "heaven help you" option for many things that the Dutch ignore or manage. We don't ignore things—we become outraged at them and pass laws that forbid whatever offends some influential sector of society. That leaves the practice of ignoring to the people who are doing it. We have laws against pot, prostitution, and increasingly immigration, as well as numerous other things I could mention. We used to have laws against alcohol and divorce. They didn't work and were repealed.

Maybe we should try tolerance and management rather than legal options. Management always works better than adding more rules, even in the corporate world. Management means acting on individual cases rather than putting out a regulation that is supposed to apply to all situations and doesn't.

Personally, I use *gedogen* frequently in my life. I am *gedogen* about the new traffic light they put up on Johnny Mercer, anyone named Kardashian, and the current fad for kale. As I indicated, I'm rather *gedogen* about Bill O'Reilly. The gap between loving something and hating it is very wide. Wouldn't it be nice if we recognized that?

I wonder what would happen if we tried the Dutch *gedogen* in our hemisphere, maybe in a seaport that has many visitors in a year, with all sorts or philosophies and outlooks that the locals don't necessarily like or understand. If we do, I think I know just the place.

My Favorite Sin

As I came to the studio last week, it rained, a storm that any Georgian could proudly claim as truly native weather. I drove into it from the east; you could see the rain falling from a quarter mile away.

Once in it, the windshield wipers couldn't keep up, and everyone slowed down to the speed limit. I found parking fifteen feet from the station door and still arrived inside soaked. Where I live, the storm included hail—nothing serious, but I'm still picking up branches. One of my more meteorological neighbors said we'd gotten a half inch of rain in twenty minutes (and more than two inches total).

As the week wore on, the skies cleared and summer snuck in; temperatures penetrated the nineties in the middle of the day. Typically, the dog Stink surveys his surroundings twice a day, once in the morning and once in the afternoon. In the morning, we walk around the neighborhood pretty close to dawn. But afternoon walks are further afield, and I prefer doing them in midafternoon. No more, starting last week. Now our definition of afternoon extends pretty close to dinnertime.

Summer is the time when the living is easy, according to a gentleman whose residences on the East Coast never extended south of New York's Lincoln Tunnel. He further explained that fish were jumping and the cotton is high. Well, fish do not jump because the living is easy, and the cotton does not get high all by itself. Easy isn't the word I'd use. George Gershwin was a little distant from his expertise on that one.

Summer is the time when I can indulge in my favorite "deadly sin." A few years ago, I surveyed the seven deadly sins and selected my favorite. That selection has held up and will probably be around for the rest of my days.

It's not pride. Oh, I have my share of that, but experience teaches you that your ideas of your contributions and general wonderfulness are subject to other interpretations. The more experience you have, the less pride—unless you haven't been paying attention or if your sense of humor doesn't extend to you. If you think you've been a big deal, go out on a clear night and look at the stars.

Greed? Well, maybe, as long as it doesn't take a lot of effort. When the lotteries get large enough, I'll buy a ticket. I couldn't say if it's worth the effort. I've never been overcapitalized and have lived comfortably without that advantage.

Lust? Like five sets of tennis or spending a few hours trying to reel in a large game fish, I confess an earlier interest, but the truth is that I was never really that good at the skills required to pursue lust seriously. It's like quantum mechanics: I wish I were good at it, but oh well...

Envy? The grass is always greener, they say. Everybody sees the result of hard work, but nobody sees the actual work. I have pretty much what I need. Anything else would be a nuisance to maintain. If you want that million-dollar Mercedes, the one encrusted with Swarovski crystals, go for it. Some folks will envy you for it. Others will merely be amused.

Gluttony? Ooh, that's a contender for me. I perch on the knife-edge between gourmet and gourmand. But in the end, I can't really do a good job of that anymore. My digestive system has lots of miles on it, and a few pieces have fallen off. After a while, you get used to the fact that a lot of things I like don't like me back.

Wrath? Oh, that one is hot now. There are lots of people out there who are angry about stuff, and many of them think their anger will convince you that they're right. Pro tip: It's a chump move, even when done at the national level. I caught that fairly early in the game. Get angry and you lose the ability to think your way through things. When you see someone else who's angry, you know they aren't flying straight and level. Those people are really easy to manipulate. They say and do stupid things. Need proof? Turn on the news. Wrath never was my sin du jour.

The only one left is sloth, and that's my pick (or, well, perhaps it picked me). With just a little sloth, you can avoid the other deadly sins. You can be lusty and avaricious. You can be wrathful and envious. But you can't combine sloth with any other sin unless you curb your sloth.

Sloth is the sin for when it's too hot and sticky. Referring back to Mr. Gershwin, the living isn't easy; it takes too much effort to do things. When climates get extreme, people hunker down because they must. Farther north, they don't build igloos because they appreciate the modernist aesthetic for spare functionality. They need a warm place to survive and cocoon in frigid seasons, the opposite of what we need here.

Sloth also appeals to me personally. Experience tells me that once you've accomplished something, it just leads to other things that must be accomplished. Furthermore, people start to expect you to accomplish things, and that just makes further trouble. Take accomplishment too seriously and that leads you to the pride thing...and probably most of the other deadly sins, too.

Sloth is the sin for summer. Let us embrace it as a necessity. Maybe sometime I'll talk about which of the usual virtues I dislike most. But right now, it's too much work.

Marsh Life This Week

It was an eventful week out on the islands where I live.

First was the matter of drainage. The islands are not just clumps of land set carefully in the ocean so that Route 80 can run through them without too much difficulty. They are the Savannah River delta. Like most river deltas, water and land alternate pretty frequently out by us. Sometimes which you get depends on the weather.

We have creeks, marshes, and named rivers, but what we have mostly are drainage ditches too small to name that carry runoff water to the creeks, marshes, and named rivers. They run alongside the roads or, more properly, the roads run alongside them. Build a road over a drainage ditch and you'll be sorry one day, unless you do it very carefully.

Well, the county has decided to cover over one of the main ditches. As drainage ditches go, it does a fine job; however, it's neither fragrant nor picturesque, and some of the county's lesser lights dump shopping carts and well-aged tires and indefinable chunks of molded plastic into it. It is also the neonatal intensive care unit for a wide variety of insects with a taste for humans, and the survival rate is pretty high. It runs by a school, and parents fret about their kids winding up under a shopping cart or trapped in a tire. Covering it over seems like a pretty good idea.

However, actual wildlife lives among the shopping carts and larvae—mainly turtles. I am proud to say that we have had our second turtle rescue mission, where local residents muck around in the ditch and pick up fauna that would resent being covered over—mainly turtles. I don't have exact figures, but a fair number of turtles have been exported to other, friendlier surroundings so that work can go forward putting a lid on the ditch. May it continue to carry water seaward.

The second was a personal experience. Driving home from the grocery on Sunday, I was stopped by a traffic light in what a sign calls the Wilmington Island Commercial and Resort District. Someone had set up a smoker not far from the intersection. The most wonderful smells emanated from that smoker, with great chunks of meat being cured for later consumption. It reminded me of my childhood, which was spent in an area nothing like the Wilmington Island Commercial and Resort District.

In that memory of the place and time of my childhood, air conditioning consisted of opening the kitchen window. Many people cooked from the ground up; they thought premade food was suspicious at best. The apex of the local cuisine was the Sunday sauce, so called because it took most of Sunday to prepare. Directly after church, home chefs would start skinning tomatoes and chopping garlic. Spices in great quantities would be hauled out of cabinets, and those draped in aprons would consider whether this was a capellini Sunday or a rigatoni Sunday. Maybe orecchiette. Then would come the grating of the cheese, the chopping of peppers, and the rest of the process, the details of which were a family secret passed down from the time when the pot sat on an open flame in front of a cave. By three in the afternoon, you couldn't enter our neighborhood without drooling. The neighborhood had other characteristics that were less livable, so now I live here, not there. But those Sundays are a fond memory. Because they happened while I was still only partially grown, they may account in some way for the size of my nose.

The third event was on Tuesday, when we had the grand opening of a new traffic light on the main thoroughfare into the Wilmington Island Commercial and Resort District. It is precisely one-tenth of a mile from the preceding light and two-tenths from the following one. It will be educational to see how those lights are phased without turning the road into a game of Monopoly, where you keep on rolling bad numbers (and do not pass go).

I am a great believer in following national and international events. Those things count—they really do. The fourth thing that happened this week is the guy in the neighborhood here went to meet the guy in the neighborhood there. On the way, he met the guys we usually hang with and told them that we didn't want to hang with them anymore. He decided that the next-door neighbors up the street, with whom we've always gotten along, are as bad as the ones down the street, and he's never liked the ones down the street. At a certain level, they're making it neighborhood stuff, even though it's more complicated.

Well, if national and international events are going to turn into simple neighborhood spats—your kid made my kid cry and your dog pooped on my lawn and your trees are dropping leaves in my backyard and the rest of it—I'll wait it out. Oversimplification catches up to you eventually.

Maybe tomorrow I'll make a Sunday sauce.

Progress

A tinge of sadness passed through my life this week: Frank Harden died. He was somewhere in his mid-nineties, a Savannahian, and a radio man. After Frank left Savannah, he put together a wildly popular morning show with Jackson Weaver. Harden and Weaver dominated the Washington, D. C., radio market in the sixties and seventies, at one point getting a quarter of all radio listeners in the area.

Well, life goes on, I suppose. Back then, Harden and Weaver were an important part of Washington's culture, and Washington's culture has changed. So have I, even to the point of not living there anymore. The culture back then transformed into something else.

Cultures are born and die with some regularity. Nobody notices that unless the culture has persisted for a long time. Then its transformation seems sad unless you look closer.

I am in the midst of a book by an Englishman of Irish heritage, who went back to Ireland for an extended visit in the late 1990s. He was not pleased (in that particularly voluble English way) about what he found. He found tourists, lots of them, in the southwest, which is supposed to be unspoiled. He found new cottages everywhere; some were vacation homes for the more affluent, but some were actually homes for the Irish themselves. This seemed to offend him more. They apparently spoiled the view.

The old Irish culture was the product of poverty and an almost complete lack of contact with the outside world. The new Irish culture is based on more affluence and more communication. I suppose he would have been happier to find wizened peasants who still live in stone beehive huts and weave stout sweaters by hand and sell them at deep discounts. I must think he'd be happier if all the cottages turned into tumbledown farmhouses. He seemed to enjoy his visit with an old friend who had gone back to the land and lived the way the old Irish did.

Well, he might have enjoyed it, but the Irish would not have. Whatever their architectural defects, new cottages have reliable running water and electricity, insulation, and other comforts not known to stone beehive dwellers. If you've ever lived in a real stone house, you know that stone faithfully transmits the temperature of the outside, and that's unhappy in Ireland. The Irish voted for the new culture with down payments on cottages and the discovery that the tourist industry pays better than farming a small plot where the soil is an inch deep before you hit bedrock. They voted by being extremely clever with computers and computer-related businesses.

The same problem exists around the world. The Mayans in the backcountry of Latin America, the Yanomami of the Amazon rainforest, and every culture that has had its share of poverty and lack of communication are beginning to evolve. The problem for most of them is that they aren't evolving quickly enough.

Perhaps cultural change is essentially democratic. People hang on to their old culture when they see an advantage to it, and they change when that seems like a better deal.

When cultural change is imposed, it creates huge problems and sometimes huge losses. That includes when the authority decides to modernize everything, such as the millions of lives lost when the Soviet Union "modernized" Russian culture. It also includes when the authority decides that everyone should start over as peasants, such as in Cambodia and China. More millions of lives were lost, to say nothing of those that were blighted.

Democratic cultural change is evolutionary; people select what they want and what they can afford. In the United States, the culture changes constantly—cell phones, movie stars, music, what have you. This cultural agility is our primary characteristic, and it may save us from oblivion.

As it happened, I visited some of the same places in Ireland about the same time as that author. I saw happy, well-fed people. I stayed in some of those new cottages, and they were as comfortable as motels in America. I also had been to Ireland when Irish cooking was about as appetizing as English, only with bigger servings. On the trip in the nineties, the Irish were serving delicious meals, albeit the same six dishes wherever you went.

There are people now who swear that the culture they grew up in back in the fifties, sixties, or seventies was somehow better than what we have now. Sometimes that's faded memory; sometimes it's political conviction; sometimes it's just wanting to be young again. Whatever the reason, those people have beans in their ears, as we used to say. We live the way we do now because that's what a lot of people wanted. There are always problems with the way you live, and in solving them, you find new solutions and new problems. I haven't totally adapted either—there are some features of modern life that I can do without.

But I understand how it all works. I am patiently waiting for some of the more official personalities in the country to catch up.

Independence Day

This was the week of celebrating independence.

Happy birthday, United States! I am in the midst of enjoying your bounty.

Part of the bounty is peaches. This is the season of peaches. I don't mean the peaches you see in most grocery stores; I mean those grown within four hours or so of us. They are good—better than any peach that comes from anywhere else. We're also getting that good sweet corn now, which started in our southern neighbor state and is working its way north. From the other side of the country, we get the sweet dark cherries, and we get blueberries from just about everywhere. We're also getting fresh, ripe tomatoes, some of which are homegrown, and radishes that haven't been stored for years in some cold locker.

Is that America? It sure is. In other places, all these things might have been shipped overseas to pay for imports that the government decided it needed. Look up the curious history of

the Ukraine in the early 1930s. That what's grown here can be bought here is a perk of being here.

On our way to the afternoon ramble, the dog and I passed the Turner Creek ramp where boatmen launch their pleasure crafts. The parking lot was full of empty trucks and trailers waiting for their owners to return. Spending the day on the water is a terrific idea. One year, I watched the Independence Day fireworks from a boat anchored in the Potomac River. What an experience! And we could sleep on the boat until traffic dispersed—an even better experience (if you know a thing or two about D. C. traffic).

The dog and I strolled past an extended family assembled on a front lawn. At least I hope they were an extended family. There were more than twenty of them from three or maybe four generations. The grill was going, the fireworks were aligned, and in the humid heat, cans of various cooled things were being opened and emptied. You say that's kind of basic? Sure, but remember that there are places in the world where you couldn't assemble twenty people from a family because most of them were dead or had fled.

On Wednesday, which was actually Independence Day, the professional givers of narratives trotted out the normal opinions, but lately there are quite a few who don't have normal opinions. One of those decided that one of the political parties was going to start a civil war on that day. Many of them seemed to confuse Independence Day with Memorial Day, as if all we had to celebrate were dead heroes. We must certainly honor those heroes, but there's more to it than that. Things that we can celebrate about those who are living apparently make some people uncomfortable.

It seems that every other day we are besieged by alarmists, people who can see dark ends in every child's bright eyes or the romp of a joyful puppy. There are quite a few of them in positions of power right now. Independence Day is for celebrating what's good about us as well as what it took to get us here. Election Day is for making sure that we are governed by people who get that. Remember that in November.

Nobody should minimize the problems we have or the tasks we face, but we should also recognize that as a country we are doing pretty well. All of that starts with people having the basics—the good summer fruit, the friends and family, the occasional firecracker, or maybe a day on the water.

Patriotic songs usually operate on a much higher level than that. They are normally so intent on glory that they don't have room to acknowledge the problems or that much of the trick is meeting basic needs. But there are a few songs that touch on that thought. I'll end the show with one ... it's called "Little Pink Houses" by John Cougar Mellencamp (once named for the cat that also calls America home). Take a listen at its lyrics and see what you think.

Behavioral Crises

As a language, English fascinates me.

It's just as well; I have no facility in any other language whatsoever. Oh, I can usually sit down with a dictionary and puzzle a phrase out, but that doesn't work if you are sitting in a café in Turkey and decide you need the bathroom. I once nearly got into a yelling match with a ticket seller because we couldn't understand each other, and that was in London.

I took four years of Latin. It taught me that no great work of Latin literature used the grammatical rules that were drilled into us in the first two years. I took a year of Russian, and the only phrase I remember is the command to slice a cucumber—I'm not sure how often that would come up. I did pass a Tool of Research exam in Spanish, but it was technology-oriented Spanish, which uses a comforting number of words derived from English and is not much use if you want to know which road goes to Madrid. Especially if you are in Peru.

Did I mention that I am also directionally challenged?

So I am delighted when I learn a new English phrase, and that happened this week. The phrase was "behavioral crisis," which is apparently a term from psychology. In the article I was reading, this meant that the subject had done something stupid and probably criminal, but the writer couldn't use words like "stupid" and "criminal." When not in behavioral crisis, the subject of the piece did some valuable and attractive things and had influence that the writer did not feel comfortable discounting.

I looked the term up. According to my electronic friends at the Wiktionary site, a behavioral crisis is an "episode of mental disorder in a person that is considered unacceptable by the community, friends, family, or the person themself." Being contrary, I wondered which episodes of mental disorders are considered acceptable to community, friends, family, or the person himself or herself, but that's all right—I know what they mean. Sort of.

And that's the problem. As a term, it covers everything—from sneezing in the produce aisle to that which may be much more serious. And we all know people who consider sneezing in the produce aisle as big a sin as some felonies. Almost anything that somebody does is liable to be unacceptable to some of their community, friends, or family in some way or other. We jostle each other with beliefs and actions. That's a part of life.

Maybe the trick is to keep your unacceptable episodes to yourself. When I am sitting at the computer and something itches, I scratch it even if it's someplace where the scratching might be an "episode of mental disorder" were it done in public. Because when not in public, it's just an itch and fails to rise to mental disorder status. Most people are that way.

Most people. Occasionally, you run into somebody who basks in the attention that being unacceptable brings. Oddly enough, some other people admire that. If the basker is transparently greedy or commits some error of manners or performs some other antisocial act, the admirers will tell you that he's just being real. I never really understood that. We are all real. I am real and you are real, as real as Joseph Stalin or Pol Pot. Reality isn't bound up in acting like a stinker.

Maybe that's what the definition is getting at. If people have flagrant or chronic behavioral crises where they publicly and habitually do unacceptable things, then maybe the question of mental disorder comes into play.

Like most psychological terms, "behavioral crisis" has to be free of value judgments and apply to many different behaviors, from sneezing in the produce aisle to far more serious matters. It's a range of behavior, not just one.

I'm not sure why I became so fascinated with the term, but it occurred to me again and again as I read the news this week. It seems that there are an awful lot of behavioral crises being played out in public, and it looks like some people are trying to make a career from them.

It won't be very pleasant for the rest of us if they succeed.

Shirley and Sheldon

As everyone within earshot of the Chamber of Commerce knows, Savannah is called the Hostess City. That is absolutely appropriate: Our tourist industry is bolstered by our hospitality industry. For locals, it means that we employ untold numbers of hostesses, waitpersons, bartenders, and chefs. They are a significant part of our economy.

Therefore, I'd like to introduce you to Shirley and Sheldon. Shirley and Sheldon work in a seafood restaurant somewhere just south of Wilmington, Delaware. Shirley is a hostess; she brings you a menu. Sheldon is a food runner; he brings the food to the table once it's cooked. So here's the thing about Shirley and Sheldon . . . they're robots.

Shirley and Sheldon hail from China, and they cost about $20,000 a copy. Of course, they are going to be very low maintenance after that, and they don't call in sick. You guarantee a full shift every night with your purchase money, and they don't bother customers about tips. Shirley looks vaguely like Casper the Friendly Ghost in a purple bellboy uniform. She doesn't have a nose, her eyes are shaped like vitamin supplements, and whoever decided that Shirley is female didn't do it on the basis of phenotypic characteristics. But you can do marvels with plastic now—that'll be an upgrade for the next version. Shirley's about three feet tall and has two posts that hold the menu above her head. Sheldon is also three feet tall but resembles one of the piers of the Savannah River Bridge, with shelves to hold the plates. Both are mounted on what look like Roombas.

Shirley and Sheldon have their limits. Shirley works well for restaurants where customers can't see chalkboard menus. Sheldon is okay if customers don't mind transferring plates from his shelves to the table and if nobody is in a hurry—right now robots lack hustle. More complex situations will require better technology, if not human intervention. If you need extra napkins or the cocktail sauce isn't cold enough or the music is too loud, there's no point in looking for Shirley or Sheldon.

Before you write them off, however, consider your automobile. Is it a Model T Ford in basic black? No? My point is that technology advances. Corporations with funding and vision can produce a product that replaces living organisms. Your automobile might not be a Model T, but it's not a horse either.

Remember all those people in what we now call the Rust Belt, the ones who thought their assembly line jobs were safe? Many were left high and dry when their industries went away, but some were replaced with machines that could perform the same functions and do it cheaper and better. The auto industry in Japan retooled like that while American carmakers worried about fins and sound systems. The Japanese cars aren't stylish, but they last, they're easy to maintain, and they can be inexpensive. Some months back, Ford announced they were giving up producing sedans for a while. It's what you call a trend.

So the trend is away from human labor and toward the mechanical sort. It isn't even a new trend, and the organics don't win very often. The textile mills in Great Britain threw many weavers and other clothworkers out of a job in the early nineteenth century. Worse, the mills employed many children because they work more cheaply than adults and because the skill set of one uneducated child is pretty much the same as the next, so finding suitable replacements wasn't a problem.

The unemployed clothworkers resorted to sabotage. They called themselves Luddites, after Ned Ludd, a fictional apprentice who supposedly smashed some stocking frames. After a series of incidents, the British government sent in troops to maintain order. They did so with gunpowder and ferocity, and the clothworkers remained unemployed. They either found other employment, usually less well paid than weaving, or were forced to send their children to work in the mills.

The movement may have disappeared, but the term didn't. There are people today who oppose technology and call themselves Luddites or Neo-Luddites. Some of the thinkers of the last century, like Martin Heidegger and Jacques Ellul, to name two, flirted with the idea. Of the current crop, the only recognizable name is Ted Kaczynski. You may remember him as the Unabomber, who killed three and wounded several others with mailed explosives.

But Luddism or Neo-Luddism doesn't produce a product, and it doesn't make a profit. If you put out an initial public offering that details no profitable potential, that stock is going to tank. There is no money to be made in not doing things. So the outlook is still not promising for anti-technologists.

I don't think that Shirley and Sheldon will necessarily destroy the hospitality industry. They may not make any impact at all. But technology is edging its way into the field. There's a restaurant in Boston with a robot that cooks what are called "complex meals." Even checkout at stores is changing: How many self-serve lanes have you seen?

High-end and low-end restaurants will probably not even consider a Shirley or a Sheldon, not even advanced models. But the in-betweens might. In the midst of composing these thoughts, I went to lunch. I've been going to this restaurant for a while . . . most of the current waitstaff were still in grade school when I started. The hostess in this Hostess City café was also my server, and since I go there now and then, we've run into each other before.

She doesn't like me. Maybe she doesn't like anybody. I can't remember having done anything to make her life harder, and yes, I tip well. Anyway, she composes her face when I walk in, sometimes visibly, and we go through the ritual with great efficiency and little warmth. Today, I tried to imagine her with two posts where her arms are supposed to be and a menu dangling over her head. I couldn't quite get there, but it was close. She is still an improvement on Shirley. Rather, she is an improvement on this version of Shirley. Whether she is an improvement on the next version of Shirley remains to be seen. Whether there will be a new version of her also remains to be seen...people do learn.

Trade Wars

When I walked the dog today, the weather was beautiful.

The temperature was seventy-seven degrees; there was a light breeze from the north-northeast; the streets were still. The sun was bright but not hot, and there were fluffy clouds that filtered the light, giving it a golden glow. We extended the walk just a little because it was so nice being outside. I glanced at the clock when we returned—it was 6:42 a.m. In another hour, it would be hot.

I sat down to read a magazine, and the first thing that struck me was an ad. The centerpiece of the ad was a young woman in a flowing white dress, lounging on a padded chair in front of a huge live oak. She looked confused or thoughtful or maybe sleepy. Maybe she was wondering why anyone would put a chair like that outside under a tree. I don't know, so I looked for further clues.

In addition to the dress, she wore a leather headband and sandals equipped with leather greaves that reached almost to her knees. Perhaps she had just returned from a party in San Francisco in 1971. The chair must be a time machine. The ad was quite striking and attractive on the printed page. But where were the bugs—the mosquitoes and gnats and the chiggers hopping gaily from one frond of Spanish moss to another? How come her carefully arranged hair had not wilted with the humidity? There's no sense in asking; that question was outside of the context. The context of the picture was the magazine, just as the context of the weather was dawn. It left a nice impression, even though I'm not clear on what they were selling.

Context is pretty important but can be confusing. That's because we use our media for both information and entertainment. When you pick up some printed paper or turn on the TV or thumb through your smartphone or poke a computer's keys, you are going to be either informed or entertained. We've gotten sophisticated enough to understand that we ought to make the choice before we push the button. It's all too easy to get sidetracked with cute cat pictures or reruns of sitcoms from forty years ago.

Even though we know we need to make a choice before we push the button, avoiding getting sidetracked is still not easy. Information has taken on the trappings of entertainment, so it seems exciting whenever the news portrays people doing something entertaining, even if that something is wrong.

As a seaport, Savannah is always entertaining. I love to watch the ships edge up and down the river, because most of the seaports I've observed directly abut the salt water. It's fascinating to see a ship twice as tall as an island's tallest tree pass behind that island. The container ships, the Ro-Ros, the bulk carriers all carry the sight and smell of the exotic to land-lubbers like me. The entertainment of watching them has a practical side, too, by reminding us that those ships are essential to our economy.

My information sources tell me that we are now in a trade war. It was declared in a most entertaining way, complete with hard feelings, angry words, and melodrama. So far, so good. But the context of a trade war is fewer ships chugging up and down the river because fewer things enter and leave our port. And the context of fewer ships is a drop in numbers: the people we employ, the revenue flowing through the city, and the amount of goods and revenue that stays.

Many years ago, a gentleman with the unlikely name of John Horne Tooke said that the law is like London Tavern: You will get a poor welcome if you can't pay for your entertainment. It would seem that national policy is the same way. We have had our entertainment. I'm not sure we can foot the bill.

Wars of any sort are a tricky business. They involve a risk of losing, and in any war, there are Pyrrhic victories, or losses even when you ultimately win. Today when we experience such loss, it often is followed by various people offering "thoughts and prayers" (people whose track records suggest neither thinking nor faith). Some have decided that "thoughts and prayers" are but code words for doing nothing in a tragedy's wake. Thoughts and prayers are neither information nor entertainment.

In a real war, losses are recognized with "thoughts and prayers" because there is little to be done. Now, even when we experience domestic tragedies, thoughts and prayers too often are offered by those who can do something but won't. It's all very puzzling.

As a port city, Savannah would seem to be on the front line of any trade war. I'm going to beat the rush: I'm not just issuing thoughts and prayers for Savannah right now, I'm even thinking about what I can do. Let us see how we react to this trade war entertainment in the upcoming months.

Snartemo

The book on my desk has a picture of a sword hilt on the cover. The sword is worn and obviously aged, but it is a beautiful piece of work. The handle is elaborately decorated with designs that must have meant something when the sword was forged, and the boss has the same sort of intricacy. The boss and the hilt both gleam a pale metallic yellow, which can only be gold. The gold is only plating; underneath is a mixture of silver and tin. Gold is too soft for the sort of work a sword is expected to perform.

This is the ancient Snartemo sword. Even though it resembles a typical Viking weapon in design, it comes from an earlier day, sometime in the sixth century. And it comes from Snartemo, Norway, the place where it was found. When the sword was discovered, other goods were unearthed with it: a glass beaker with silver chasing, a bronze bowl, rare fabrics, and bear claws (and not the tasty kind). All of this was deposited in a tomb.

If you have an imagination, artifacts like these put it to work almost immediately. Picture yourself living in southern

Norway, with a life that involved a sword with a silver foundation, your very own silvered glass beaker, and rare fabrics. Oh and a gold ring—I forgot about that. It's enough to make you grow a beard and snarl a Norse curse, if that is within your capability.

Maybe you should tell your imagination to take the day off. Like many other grave goods, these belonged to somebody with excess capital and probably excess power. Not everybody in southern Norway had a silvered glass beaker—almost nobody, in fact.

That's what makes this discovery so remarkable.

The sixth century was the time of great migrations. People in the more habitable parts of Europe, feeling crowded, moved elsewhere. They were the European version of pioneers, but they didn't have Oregon or California as a destination. Like American pioneers, they were mostly farmers. The sword owner and his people wound up in southern Norway, which doesn't exactly have the same growing season as the Imperial Valley. (You don't run into Norwegian navel oranges that often.) Who knows. The goods found at Snartemo may have been made elsewhere and were part of the life of the pioneer prince before he left . . . wherever he came from.

So if you can imagine yourself living the good life in Snartemo fifteen hundred years ago, you can probably imagine the spirits of the people who actually lived then—turnip hoers and cod netters for the most part, circling around your head and whispering, "Good luck with that, Slick." They may include the actual owner of the sword.

We all have an irresistible urge to poke around in the past. There's nothing wrong with that, but we tend to give it modern values and then romanticize it.

I once met a woman, a friend of my wife, who was absolutely beautiful in many respects. She knew I had read some medieval history. She was going to some sort of costume party and wanted just the right finery, so she approached me for advice.

Her: What did they wear in the Middle Ages?

Me: Dirt.

Her: (being aware of my sense of humor) What else?

Me: Lots of things, but they mostly had a layer of dirt, too.

We established that the infrequency of bathing in the Middle Ages was not her primary interest and talked about costuming instead. I pulled out a copy of a medieval manuscript that showed people at work and play, both the peasants and the class she wished to emulate. She surprised me when she stopped short at one illustration, a winter scene with peasants huddled around the fire. One of them had pulled up his robe to catch more of the heat in the wintry chill. Peasants in the Middle Ages used underwear even less often than they used soap, and everything under his robe was visible. That didn't fit with her mindset. But all people had was wool, and wool does not make terrific undergarments, even if you can afford it. If you have ever wondered why cotton became so popular so fast, you might try wearing wool skivvies.

My wife's friend is scarcely alone in romanticizing the past. Before you attend any Civil War reenactment, consider that one man in five never got to the battle because of assorted camp illnesses like typhus, dysentery, and so forth. Many of them never made any other activity either. Camp illness deaths were quite common (and the battlefield itself was even far less fun).

The problem is that many of our ideas about the past come from novels with plotlines and stories that excite the imagination through heroics, romance, and nobility, rather than pestilence, famine, and flood. That's all very well for the narrative, but many people take that as indication of how things actually were. You can't call that real and leave out hunger, plagues, and failed crops, which were strong factors in what people did and how they lived—or didn't.

We might be better at realizing the downsides of more recent history. Nobody has proposed to recreate the Battle of the Somme or the Tet Offensive. But the further history is from the present, the stronger the pull to relive some part of it—without all the things that made it what it really was.

I have friends, good people generally, who immerse themselves in Renaissance festivals and alternate universes created by movies, board games, and comic books. There is an enduring passion for doing that, in part because those worlds work on a few basic principles that almost everyone can understand. But as nuanced and absorbing as they are, they are still partials—chunks of reality without the icky stuff. It's good fun, but that's all it is. Had the characters from such cosmoses actually lived, Ivanhoe would have had intestinal problems and the aged Han Solo would creak with arthritis like you wouldn't believe.

I don't know how my wife's friend dressed for the costume gala. It doesn't really matter. As I mentioned, she is a very attractive woman to begin with, so everyone else probably melted. But I will bet anything that there wasn't a single speck of dirt on the costume or on her.

We cling to our illusions.

P. T. Gets Lucky

If you have discount tickets to Burkina Faso, please let me know.

For those of you who are a little fuzzy on where that is, don't worry. I was, too. It's in West Africa, just north of the Ivory Coast, Benin, and Togo. It's a landlocked country with a transitional landscape between the rainier coastal regions and the drier Sahel. North of the Sahel, you run into the Sahara. If you learned your African geography way back, Burkina Faso used to be called Upper Volta.

Burkina Faso is not a wealthy country. I can only find figures for 2016, but at that time, its gross domestic product was around $12 billion. Spread that among the population of sixteen million and you get an annual income of about $750.

So here's the thing. Since the beginning of this year, people in Burkina Faso have sent me e-mails offering money to a total of about six percent of the GDP. This week alone, the offerings stand at approximately $40 million.

You'd be surprised at the variety of people who live in Burkina Faso. The digital dialogue wending its way into my inbox tells me a lot of them are sick, dying in fact, and they just want to find a good Christian home for the money they inherited from their parents or their husband. After praying a lot, they decided to e-mail me. But they aren't the only inhabitants. Mu'ammar Gaddhafi's daughter lives there, too, somewhat bitterly and convinced that the international community is looking to steal the money her daddy gave her before he left his career in international politics. She keeps on writing, though I haven't heard from her in a few weeks. She has one of the bigger stashes of cash, by the way. So if your name comes up in her prayers, count yourself lucky.

There are others as well, or so it seems. Most are officials of the African Development Bank, which apparently has an office in Ouagadougou, Burkina Faso's capital. At that branch a tremendous amount of unclaimed cash is lying around, and I'm told I can collect about 40 percent of it if I show up and flash my driver's license—actually, they can do it for me if I just fax them a copy.

By the way, most of those sick people bank there, too, so it's one stop to big bucks. I can't remember where Gaddhafi's daughter banks, but despite published reports, her law degree, and her status as an ex-colonel in the Libyan Army, she tells me she's living in a refugee camp near Ouagadougou, so maybe her finances reside there as well.

I don't know how the bank officials got my name. I doubt prayer had anything to do with it. Maybe they found my fingerprints on a candy wrapper.

So I can be pretty well off if I either give them all my banking information or show up myself. By the way, all of them think I'm just a terrific person; some of the bank officials even address me as "dear" or "darling" and trumpet my virtues before they get down to business. Apparently, I shine more brightly in prayers than I do at home.

Now, to get from here to Ouagadougou, you have to do some industrial-strength traveling. There's a discount package you can find for only $2,263; the next cheapest is $7,140. You leave Savannah at o-dark-thirty and go to JFK. There's usually a thirty-minute delay on that flight, but it's okay, you'll be at JFK until o-dark-thirty the next morning. That could be a problem—a one-night stay at any hotel near JFK is really going to eat into that discount. From there, you head to Casablanca and change again for the express flight to Ouagadougou. That's all kind of tough, but at least you don't have to go through Atlanta. Atlanta and JFK on the same trip is sensory overload as far as I'm concerned.

Which is what's wrong with the $7,000 trips. One goes through Atlanta and JFK and the other through JFK and Charles de Gaulle, which is the French equivalent of Atlanta. There's a $12,000 trip that makes its way through Charlotte and Madrid, but I dislike Charlotte almost as much as I do Atlanta.

I wouldn't even consider it, but on the days I get those e-mails, I also receive notices that my accounts in various banks are being suspended and I need to give them all sorts of personal information. They are mostly banks I didn't know I had any dealings with, but hey, maybe there's more cash there, too. And I need to do it quickly, because somebody's going to suspend my accounts unless I send them the needed information.

Oh, it's all too complicated. If you are writing me one of these letters because you are a listener, break down the stash into fives and pass one out to everybody in Burkina Faso. If the annual income is $750, an extra five is going to be a big deal. Do that, and maybe I'll be as good a person as you said I am.

Escapism

Escapism ain't what it used to be. I recently watched a program—and a fine escapist one it was, too—that ended with the hero pelting down an airport runway on a motorcycle. He was chasing the plane that held the woman he decided he loved, albeit rather late in the game: he, roaring along with desperate determination; she, teary-eyed that she was leaving him, unaware of his proximity. The motorcycle approaches the aircraft; she fusses with her bag, looking for tissues, I suppose. As the motorcycle pulls level, he waves wildly, but she stares at the emergency lighting along the center aisle. The aircraft speeds up and takes off. She never sees his grand gesture.

I was caught up in the program. So that was irritating. I do not sit inside on mellow Georgia evenings and watch television, only to have the tales turn out badly. I can venture out into the world at any point if I prefer that. But then my perspective returned. We had a thundershower, making inside the place to be, and I reflected that this program is part of a series. No doubt there will be future encounters.

I have had a busy August. I didn't plan it that way. Technically, there are no months that should require my complete attention, but if there were, August would not be one of them. Savannah Augusts are no time for accomplishment. I am told that the entire country of France goes on vacation in August—we don't do that, but we slow our pace to suit the weather. In my neighborhood, many people (comforted by the odd can of cool refreshment) put lawn chairs in their garages and watch the heat melt the asphalt. But this year I ignored that.

So this week, I decided to remedy that busyness. I traveled downtown and ate lunch at a restaurant I enjoy. It serves food with a tingly shrimp sauce with a dash of sriracha. But on this particular day, the sriracha was more of a marathon than a dash. That didn't offend my taste buds, but there were repercussions and consequences thereafter. When lunch was done, I visited a splendid secondhand bookshop to pick up reading for the remainder of the hot weather. I did find a few tomes, but the repercussions and consequences from the sriracha began while I was there and the visit was a little hurried.

The next day, I decided to go to the beach. This would be a modified rather than a full-scale trip, with the wagon to carry the umbrella and the chaise and all the things I might need for an extended stay. I would sit on one of the swinging benches, take a few photos, and reflect on the state of nature.

That's the sort of activity that August is made for. The schoolchildren of Savannah have reentered the classrooms, so there are fewer people beachside. The people who are there tend to be refugees from real life and not interested in accomplishment either.

I stayed on the sand for slightly less than an hour and did get some interesting photos. However, the tops of my already well-tanned feet got the full benefit of the ultraviolet rays and became ultrasensitive to the sandals I wore. The weather site I use recommends staying indoors between the hours of 10:00 a.m. and 4:00 p.m. This is fine advice for vampires and bats but not terribly practical for the rest of us.

So I had two days of escapism with less than Hollywood-quality results, just like that program. It's as if the hero had stopped the plane, won his love, and then discovered she snores and thinks his toenails are impossibly ugly and considers him a dolt for not listening to the Bay City Rollers rather than Miles Davis. Life as lived has its consequences.

Then there's the discomfort of living in a society that has a limited tolerance for grand gestures. Try to drive a motorcycle down an airport runway in real life and see what happens. The controllers in the tower will be something less than thrilled, since motorcycles are not part of their training. They will send people in uniforms to adjust the situation, and your careful explanation that you are the hero may not totally erase their concern. At least one of the controllers will have to make an emergency appointment with his shrink. And that's assuming you do not run your motorcycle into the path of some Gulfstream product that can blow you away with its exhaust, even if it doesn't actually hit you.

No, escapism isn't what it used to be. We have become more sophisticated, nuanced people, and the plots need to be more complex to engage us. That's even gotten down to the comic book level. There isn't a comic book hero or heroine out there who isn't neurotic, if not downright loony. They are all fond of grand gestures, and many of them wind up in movies, because even adults can relate to their weirdness.

So escapism is moving closer to what actually happens. That's okay—it somehow flatters us as complex and advanced beings. But when I watch the news at night, I wonder if reality isn't moving closer to escapism. There are grand gestures, harsh words, comic book script speeches. That's not okay. In real life, the repercussions and consequences become serious fairly quickly. Our ability to distinguish between the real and the fictional lessens, and that's not flattering.

One of my childhood heroes, Walt Kelly, said this: "The Now is alive with a curious life which defies the descriptive powers of such divers as swim ahead of the swine in search of pearls."

As a cartoonist, Kelly counted himself among those divers, and he was well aware of the difference between the "Now," which is what he called reality, and the people who cobble together tales—he and his fellow divers. The comic book approach to life almost always claims victims. Usually, they include the people who take that approach.

I'll go back to the beach soon, but the beach cart with the umbrella will accompany me.

Reunion

My moonflower vines started to bloom this week. I've noticed the leaves sneaking up the ivy that grows on one side of my mailbox, but today there were a few white flowers when I walked the dog at dawn. When the moonflowers bloom, it's time to get ready for the fall—in this case, hurricane season.

After the blow two years ago, I bought a generator, and last year we used it twice, once for a little more than two days. I decided to check the thing out. Motored equipment that sits idle for a while may not cooperate unless you pay some attention to it in between needs.

Good thing. When I rolled it out to the driveway and attempted to start it, the battery was dead. The manual was not where I thought I had left it, so I had to improvise. What do you do with a dead battery? Well, you take it somewhere and have it charged.

So I removed the battery. That took more than an hour. You see, the battery is held to the generator by a lock plate that requires a socket wrench to undo the screws. I use socket wrenches about as often as I use tuxedos, so the first trick was to find the thing. It turns out we have two sets. I found the wrench for one and the fittings for the other, and of course they didn't match. I eventually found the other wrench and freed both the battery and the terminals. Then I looked at the battery for a while.

Apparently, the manufacturers of batteries haven't gotten around to charging via a USB port or anything of the sort. The terminals were incompatible with any chargers I happened to have lying around. So I looked it up. I couldn't find anything that looked right. The people who made the generator have a help line, so I called that. I spoke with a very nice, cheerful lady from the Upper Midwest.

"My battery is dead, and I need to charge it."

"Yes sir . . . "

"How do I do that?"

"You plug it in, sir."

It turns out there's a port on the control panel, and you don't have to remove the battery at all. They even supply the charging wire—it's a cell phone-type setup, not a computer setup. Of course, that meant I'd have to put the battery back on the generator and find the wire. I looked in the box where wires for equipment we threw out ten years ago might live, and there it was. The next trick, of course, was to find the manual.

Probably in the drawer where we keep manuals for equipment we threw out ten years ago.

Another sign of fall is that I have been invited to spend a weekend at the school that prepared me for the wider world. This particular year is a special event: I will get some sort of recognition that I have outlived my education. For a number of reasons, I decided to attend this one, even though it means a bit of travel.

There are two big happenings—not counting having doughnuts with the school mascot at eight in the morning—and there's a dress code for both. For the first, it's business casual; for the second, cocktail attire.

I know what business casual means. It means you wear one or more badges with really awful pictures of you on a lanyard. You match that with some shirt, usually a polo, with which you would wash the car if you weren't wearing it to work, because it was given to you by a distant relative who thinks she's still dressing dolls. The pants will have to be long to cover the fact that you don't wear socks unless absolutely necessary. The shoes should mask how you have put some miles on your feet and that mileage is starting to show. But this festival is somewhat north of here and late in the fall, so I might even bring socks.

But cocktail attire has me stumped. Cocktail parties went out of fashion while that school still housed me. As far as I know, they haven't returned. They've been replaced over the years by sit-ins, be-ins, encounter groups, group therapy, comic book conventions, and a host of other groupie events. Attire for these range from clothing optional to cosplay, dressing up as Parsnip Man.

From what I remember, the cocktail party was an occasion to dress pretty and talk small. You fluff your feathers, chatter about your significant but underrated position in life, and see who responds—something like the mating ritual of the lyrebird. Sometimes there was the romantic angle, sometimes not.

I never really got the hang of talking small, and I am not constructed for looking pretty. In truth, I never was. The cocktail parties I've attended have been dreary affairs, and there haven't been that many. I suppose I will wear a dark suit and loud shirt and try to find a tie that matches neither.

The cocktail party is the triumph of manners over ideas. Having actual ideas is tantamount to having too much gin. But maybe there's a place for that now. We live in an age where people blurt out their thoughts, especially the ones they haven't considered very well. Our online capabilities are a monument to the ability to communicate over the ability to think. Twitter demands incomplete grammar and thought and attracts many who believe that their talent for sound bites will beget acolytes who will bask in that talent. But the search for acolytes is usually a difficult and a sad business, even if you generate some. Acolytes tend to be accommodating, not critical. They might even believe that truth isn't truth, if the leader says so.

I do remember one thing from cocktail parties: If you put ginger ale in a champagne flute and hang a slice of lime on the lip, you will look exotic and remain polite. I hope they have diet ginger ale.

Autumn 2018

The south side of the cathedral

Obvious

Last week, a *Columbia Journalism Review* editor with the intriguing name of Nausicaa Renner wrote an article in *The New York Times Magazine* on the word "obvious." How, if people look confident and tell you something is obvious, you tend to believe them. How, if you sense that they disagree with you, you retreat into obvious generalizations so that they can't voice their disagreement. And some things are so obvious, they don't need to be stated, but they usually are anyway. I thought it was a very good article but also very mid-Atlantic, something with which we here wrapped in the gentle curve of the Coastal Empire need not be too concerned. Then I drove by a sign: "Road Closed When Flooded."

The word "obvious" is a fuzzy thing with many shades of meaning, and when you state the obvious, you are sometimes hinting at things that are not obvious at all. To wit: For those of you allergic to either sunshine or beer, the road to Tybee passes through the middle of nearly ten miles of marsh. About half-way there, somebody has erected a sign that proclaims "Turtle Crossing."

In the middle of ten miles of marsh, that's fairly obvious. What you are supposed to do about it is less so. It's a two-lane road at that point, with about eight inches of roadbed on either side of the pavement before you drop off into said marsh. The road is high speed and well traveled, and with no room to maneuver, there aren't many options. I suppose the sign posters want you to slow down, although I'm not sure that hitting a turtle at a slower speed will make any difference to either the turtle or your car. Perhaps you're supposed to know that, if you wind up in the marsh because you ran over something, it was probably a turtle as opposed to a buffalo or a yeti. I don't know. The motivation is not obvious.

We, as a species, are a clever lot. In evolutionary terms, that means we can successfully adapt to a wide variety of environments. As the younger me was learning the art of getting a car out of a snowbank in New England, my wife was learning the ways of the sea on Guam. She is an experienced helmsperson on rather large sailing craft. Two different experiences entirely. But if you ever need to get your large sailing craft out of a snowbank, we might be just the people to have around. Not only are humans adaptable, we can pool our different communal and individual cleverness.

So things that are obvious to her remain opaque to me and vice versa. Our third resident, the noble dog Stink, has his own ideas of obvious, but this conversation is about humans; his ideas don't count. And that's just within the Bridgeport household. Widen it out to the neighborhood or metropolitan Savannah or greater Chatham County and the whole idea of obvious gets very fuzzy indeed.

Okay, so what are the minimum daily requirements for "obvious"? Well, to start, the obvious should be true. The roads will indeed be closed when they are flooded. I will concede that point.

But even "true" has become more sophisticated than I remember.

Back when I sculpted snowdrifts, there was true and there was false, and that was pretty much it. I suffered through many a classroom quiz based on that assumption. Now, according to what I read in the papers, there's "truth" and there's "alternative truth," and there's truth that really isn't true. I get that from high-ranking officials. I actually noticed it many years back when Britney Spears asked the general public if they could handle her truth. At the time, my answer was a resounding "no," and examining what happened after that, I think maybe she couldn't either. I'm guessing she's switched truths, though I haven't followed her closely enough to be sure. I bet she couldn't handle my truth either.

Truth is malleable now, I guess, though I have my doubts about that. Apparently, those high-ranking officials and their lawyers have embraced the linguistic philosophy of Britney Spears. I can't say that I'm surprised, but I don't think they can handle my truth either, not from what they are saying and doing. Unlike Britney Spears, they are supposed to represent me and my truths. Maybe we need to fix that disconnect.

This isn't new. Actually, I remember a U.S. Army major once telling AP journalist Peter Arnett that "[i]t became necessary to destroy the town to save it," a rather peculiar form of truth and certainly not obvious and maybe even not all his. That was the town of Bến Tre, back in the Vietnam days. As it turns out, we neither destroyed the town nor saved it, but the quote will live on.

We certainly live our own lives with our own outlooks—calling them "truths" is a little presumptuous. We seem to live in an age where people want to buy outlooks prepackaged off the shelf. They don't want to go to the trouble of constructing their own. But outlooks are like underwear: One size does not fit all. Maybe that's the great lesson of the twentieth century. Any number of thinkers—Lenin, David Koresh, Chairman Mao, Abbie Hoffman—insist that their way is the only one. Their ways all get threadbare and all start to smell, sooner or later.

Beautyberries

I sat in my home office contemplating a load of freshly washed laundry. It rested comfortably on the guest chair with room left for, oh, about a dozen ears of corn. And that was the point. I'll put it away promptly; that's five minutes of work. But we are beginning the transition to autumn.

In autumn, the ears of corn disappear, and the piles of laundry grow larger, since T-shirts and shorts are no longer comfortable outside dress. By the middle of winter, the laundry pile will barely fit on the chair, even with socks along the edges dropping to the floor. I've often wondered if the piles of laundry eat the corn, thus growing bigger and eliminating the corn at the same time. But that does not meet the requirements for logic, so I discard the idea. I'm old-fashioned that way; if things don't make sense, I discard them. I don't tweet them to my followers.

Autumn in Savannah is a stealthy season. The temperatures drop but not that much. You must look for other signs.

I walked around the Whitemarsh Preserve the other day, and there were a few bright orange butterflies flitting around. I believe those are the early arrivals of the monarch butterfly migration. If you have been growing milkweed on the periphery of your house, this is your season. By the end of the month, monarchs will cluster thickly around your house like cars around a Cracker Barrel on a major highway. Milkweed is the monarch butterfly's equivalent of decently spiced sausage and well-done home fries. Monarchs sit on the milkweed stalks and grumble about the traffic. One of the smaller ones asks if we're there yet. No . . . not yet.

I also saw that the beautyberries had turned violet; up to this point, they had been green. Beautyberries are a mint that grows vigorously in areas that no other plant wants to deal with. In the fall, the green berries morph into violet and then deep purple. This year, the ones in the preserve have very thick clusters of berries, since there have been daily deluges for much of the summer and they've responded. By the way, if you fancy beautyberries, you can probably find some at your local flower market, but those are cultivars and will be neither as vigorous nor as long-lived as the wild ones. When you find purple-tinged bird droppings on your truck, you know that one of your neighbors has successfully planted beautyberries.

On weekdays, tartan-clad students swarm thickly around the radio station. They are traveling from class to class, I suppose, and display a range of boisterousness, sadness, and distraction. You look at them and doubt the wisdom of growing old and leaving the world in their care. They look at you and wonder why the world isn't more messed up than it is, with the likes of you having participated. There's nothing like a little distance to create misunderstanding. And then you go your separate ways.

For people who plan, this is a busy season. Things have to get done before the holidays, and being outdoors is possible again. In the evenings, you can throw events that are dressier than T-shirts and shorts and don't involve kegs. If anyone has a gala-something or an annual-something and doesn't do it in the spring, it'll be done in the autumn. Of course, it has been too hot to do any real planning before this, so it has to be done now. You can hear the motors whine and the fan belts screech as the planners gear up for the event that has to be held on the most perfect weekend before the frozen turkeys arrive at the supermarket.

For businesses, September is the end of the third fiscal quarter. Are they happy? They are happy about as often as farmers. The fourth quarter is when you have to fix all the things that were wrong with the first three and simultaneously plan to meet impossible goals for next year. Oh, what fun.

And since this is an even-numbered year, elected officials must face the constituents in whose name they have been making decisions—or not making them, that's been the rage lately. Some time back, elected officials held town hall meetings where they faced constituents. They found that constituents asked questions that were just plain icky: sometimes challenging, sometimes abusive, sometimes disclosing that your performance wasn't everything your PR people said it was.

Many of those officials have gone to call-in town halls, where a communications line can drop at the first sign of ickiness. Technical problems, you see, because ickiness creates static in the line.

That's not a town hall; that's a call-in show, except not as entertaining. And I must ponder something quite a bit before I declare it less entertaining than some call-in shows.

I am informed by authorities who range from Billie Holiday to Frank Sinatra that autumn in New York pretty much consists of crowds that glitter and clouds that shimmer in our steel-reinforced skyscraper canyons one might find in a precisionist painting. That would include world-weary roués and cheery divorcées who lunch at the Ritz, the delight of first-nighting, and various other attractions. Actually, the words to that song were written by Vernon Duke. Vernon was a gifted and very interesting man, but he spent a lot of time in Paris and Santa Monica. I am told he discovered Sid Caesar. I am guessing that, while he was in New York, he didn't get out to Queens much, where I spent part of my life. My idea of autumn in New York is very different.

Anyway, we don't do autumn that way here in Savannah. I like it our way.

Hurricane Tracking

We had a radio station meeting this week, and I asked our other hosts about some of the topics I will address on air. Their reactions pretty much fluctuated from stunned silence to wry smiles. We have a wide range of ages among the station staff. Some are veteran human beings like me, with scars and medals and endless war stories, and others are just starting out and have many more campaigns left in them. I do not envy them—they are living in a world that I find too complex to deal with in many ways.

Here's an example. As I've mentioned before, I read a nationally recognized newspaper online because I can't get paper copies, at least not of today's news. Recently, as I was poking through the digital pages, my eyes flashed at the advertisements, just as they would in hard copy. One of them stopped me cold. It offered to instruct me on eight ways to tell if I am constipated. How technical and convoluted the world has become! Back in my day, we only had one way to tell, and it required no instruction. I have used that lesson my whole life, and it has served me well. Just for a second, I thought about clicking the link to find out what the other seven are, and then I decided that I knew enough about the subject and didn't care for any elaboration. Perhaps we don't need such sophisticated indicators.

This week, there's a topic that is on our minds here, whether we read nationally recognized newspapers or not. Weather. I am in the studio today, however, and the worst has not happened. The worst scenario (at least from our perspective) would have been Hurricane Florence coming ashore around Ocean Isle Beach on the Carolinas border, staying for a drink, and then bouncing southward toward us. If that had happened, I would not be in the studio. I would instead be experiencing the wonders of hunkering down in central Georgia, and you would too, probably. We are here in Savannah, so we were relatively unscathed. I have heard of people booking reservations in Dothan, Alabama, and Chattanooga, Tennessee. I was interested that somebody would drive to Chattanooga, because guess where the storm is going after it leaves the coast. I'll give you a hint: The winds on the edge of the storm are singing about boarding a train and being choo chooed home.

After many years without serious peril, we in Savannah have had two evacuations in two years. Here are some notes from my experience: First, after Matthew's initial blow in 2016, I spent a month cutting and hauling limb-fall to the street. I live on a circle, and all the residents on the circle piled their downed chunks of trees on the grassy median in the middle. That's where the county trucks pick them up. Three times we filled the circle to a height of more than six feet, and that's from seven houses. So these things are serious, and they stay with you. Out on Tybee, they piled debris in the parking lot for North Beach, a heap that made our circle look very small indeed. Our stack of tree parts stayed with us for months, until the last twisted piece of palm could be carted off.

Second, people are willing to pitch in and help. Your neighbors are, overall, a pretty decent bunch, no matter what you think of their politics or lawn-cutting habits or the color of the trim on any given house. In a genuine emergency, they'll help. Some of them will go way beyond expectations, and it probably won't be the ones whom you'd predict. That helpfulness includes people who are there because it's their job. Out our way, we had our power restored by linemen and linewomen from Alabama Power, who trucked in for the purpose. They were an incredible bunch of people, and some lasting friendships burgeoned. Our neighborhood claims dibs on Alabama Power if the situation here gets serious again.

Third, the farther you are from where the destruction is, the less pressing the problems seem. Hurricane Maria hit Puerto Rico in 2017; nearly three thousand people died. Parts of the island are still unhealed. Some federal officials swear that their recovery effort was a great success.

Let us hope that we (and any of our hurricane-vulnerable neighbors) require minimal assistance from those federal officials.

It's always easy to overreact to challenges like hurricanes. Some people see the end of the world in such things. If you are one of these, well, a cubit is between eighteen and twenty-one inches, and you should have started building your ark way before now. When you load up two of each species, forget about mosquitoes this time, okay?

It's also easy to underreact. It's not business as usual. With Florence, I am guessing we will have powerless hours, if not days, so I made sure the power generator works and I bought basics early.

Wholly aside from its potential as a refuge site, Chattanooga is said to be a pretty place with lots of outdoor activities and beautiful scenery. It even has its own typeface (did you know that?). But the drive time from here to Chattanooga is around six hours in the best of circumstances, and since it's on the same road as Atlanta, I don't see optimal traveling conditions. I'd like to go there someday.

But not this week.

Reasoning With Old People

I ran across a dandy word this week: abductive. It's a way to reason.

You've got deductive reasoning like Sherlock Holmes' forte; you've got inductive reasoning like most analogies; and now you've got abductive reasoning.

Here's the way abductive reasoning works: You start by making a set of observations, admitting that you haven't figured out the whole story. Then you make your best guess as to what's happening and what to do about it.

Think about that for a second. Isn't that the way things usually work? Unless you walk around in a deerstalker hat, it probably is.

The problem with inductive and deductive reasoning is that you need to know all the facts before they apply, and most of the time we don't. Even old Sherlock had to gather data before he came up with his reliably deductive conclusions, and finding clues took up most of the pages in the books.

I found another example of that this week. I went to have my annual wellness exam. The way my medicos do it is a two-visit process. First, you go in and have your blood drawn. Data gathering, right? I'm okay with that as long as I don't have to watch them stick that thing in my arm.

During the next part of the visit, they ask you standard-ized questions. Here's where it gets tricky. The questions are essentially inductive: The inquisitors look at a few things and decide that it might indicate some broader problem. But first, they nag you. Did I keep my appointment with my GI guy? Yes, the report's in your chart. How about the ophthalmologist? Yes, going next week. Then comes the good stuff. Do you snore?

I do, in fact. I've sat in waiting rooms and snored myself awake. When I do, the receptionists look pained. The others waiting are clustered around the television, supposedly watch-ing the family-friendly couple choose between a three-bedroom ranch that backs on to the steel mill or the four-bedroom that gets buried by snowslides every blizzard season. The patients (perhaps lacking patience) cast backward glances in my direc-tion. Yes, I snore.

Well, if I snore, I might have sleep apnea—that's where you stop breathing when you sleep. Do I want an apnea test? No, thank you. Neither the test nor the supposed cure is going to help my sleep. Aha, but that might be a clue. Do I have trouble sleeping?

The person asking me these questions was a professionally trained woman of just enough years to have some experience yet not enough to know the answer. I looked at her long, taffy-colored hair streaked with blondness and her carefully and attractively made-up face, and I almost laughed. Almost.

Look lady, I'm an old person.

I carry around a card from the government that certifies it. I'm doing this wellness visit in part because, in exchange for the card, they want me to get annual checkups, and I'm okay with that. People see me driving in my truck and they go twenty miles an hour over the speed limit to get around me, even though I'm doing ten over myself. In fast-food restaurants, counter people call me "sir."

I'm an old person. Old people have trouble sleeping. I don't sleep as deeply or as long as I used to. So sometimes I sleep more frequently, like in waiting rooms. Ask the receptionist who put on her earphones when I walked in—she's been through this before.

Of course I have trouble sleeping. I also have trouble doing lots of other things, and you don't want to know the details. I'll discuss them with the actual doctor, whenever I get to see her and if I decide they're worth discussing.

If the problem with the questions is that they are inductive, the problem with the philosophy is that it's deductive. A wellness exam starts with the presumption that I should be well. I disagree. I'm too old to be well. I remember what being well feels like, and this ain't it. Deductive reasoning only works when your hypothesis is valid in the first place.

Similarly, the inductive reasoning of the standard questions doesn't work either. I have gray hair; that doesn't make me feebleminded. I might be, but I'm not. Many of my marbles are left, though sometimes they rattle around. Maybe that's what causes the snoring. I see many people on the television and in the news whose hair is not gray, and I think you should be looking critically at them, not me.

Next week, I get to see the actual doctor. I've seen her before, and she uses abductive reasoning. I like that. I dislike the assumptions that go with the other sorts of reasoning—that whoever the observer is knows all there is to know.

I'd like to see more of the medical profession adopt the abductive attitude. Maybe, after that, we can persuade the politicians.

Eggplant

My thoughts this week ran to eggplant.

Well, maybe "ran" is overkill; they ambled or perchance stumbled.

Anyway, about eggplant. It's a member of the nightshade family, not the deadly version, but they're related. Eggplants were domesticated from thorn apples in two places, East Asia and the Indian subcontinent. According to botanists, eggplant is a berry, not a vegetable. If you are at a dinner party, that could be a fun fact to share (depending on whether you wish to be invited back). And if you are dying for a smoke, you're in luck if they serve eggplant. The seeds contain nicotinic alkaloids. Eggplant is also related to tobacco, you see. Some diners don't like the seeds, so maybe you can collect the seeds from other folks. Moreover, the eggplant skin contains vitamins and minerals, so be sure to swallow the stuff that sticks between your teeth—maybe wait until after the party is over.

I'm kind of neutral about eggplant myself. I've had some pretty good ratatouille, and there are some other things that work, too. The noble canine Stink turns his nose up at it, but I'm not that anti. Eggplant absorbs the tastes of the things you cook with it. It's like tofu in that regard, except it isn't made of bean curd. I can't eat tofu for two reasons: The first is that I can't digest it, and the second is that I don't want to.

So when I recently encountered the food page headline, "Think You Don't Like Eggplant? You Just Need a Better Recipe," I was surprised. I read on. Then the bulb lit. Eggplant is the new brussels sprouts.

The food writers of America, you see, go through these cycles where they all recommend something as a miracle food. They did it with spinach, they did it with brown rice, they did it with brussels sprouts. After that it was kale. Next up, eggplant.

The writers start with the supposition that all these foods are good for you. They forget that cooking has a lot to do with it. My favorite recommendations came during the brussels sprouts craze. You fry them, being sure to sprinkle blackening spices on them while they absorb all that great oil. Blackened brussels sprouts. That's got to be better for you than french fries, right? Well, maybe not. At best, they are better for you because you will eat fewer of them.

Eggplant is well beloved by people who resent the carnivorous aspect of human existence. I was first made aware of the existence of eggplant when I was served eggplant parmigiana. Eggplant parmigiana is an offshoot of veal parmigiana; you make it the same way as veal parmigiana, except without the veal. That is to say, you dip it in an eggy-bready mixture, fry it, drown the result in mozzarella and marinara, and dust it with Parmesan cheese to justify the name. You can bake it, of course, but only after adding enough oil that the difference between that and frying is negligible.

According to the top nutritionists at the P. T. Bridgeport Institute of Chowing Down, if you fry anything—anything at all—and then drown it in cheese, you aren't doing yourself any favors. And if you do anything else with eggplant, it's liable to taste like eggplant. Therein lies the dilemma.

I looked for a wider cultural context for eggplant and didn't find much. I wondered at the name: Why would you call that great purple thing an eggplant? Well, in days past, eggplants were much smaller, and they were white. They looked vaguely like hen eggs, if you can see a hen laying an egg with a spiny green stalk.

There is, of course, the Internet, where almost anything is anointed with a sexual connotation. That happened with the eggplant, too. Some say that eggplants resemble genitalia, and some use the eggplant as a placeholder. I do not see that resemblance at all. If you resemble an eggplant in that regard, run—do not walk—to the nearest emergency room . . . assuming you can.

The problem here is not eggplant but the human expectations for eggplant or, rather, the human expectations of other humans. The food writers suppose that eggplant, properly spiced and prepared like meat, might become a substitute for meat. One of the recipes in that article was a pretty standard treatment for shrimp tacos, except you use browned eggplant instead of shrimp. And browned, like sautéed, is a food writer's code word for "frying."

My personal problem is that, when I'm hungry, I want to eat food, not somebody else's sense of transcendental ethics. Eggplant is perfectly wonderful for people who like it and not for anyone else. There are those who avoid meat and feel better for it in some sense. I am not one of them.

We all have the unspoken conviction that if humanity would just follow our lead in some ways, humanity would be better off. That is not a misdemeanor unless it is spoken. When published, however stealthily, it becomes just another scrap in the information overload heap we all carry around with us.

I don't hate eggplant, but I don't particularly like it either. And I have much better recipes than the ones I found in that article. They just don't include eggplant.

Junk Mail

For dawn dog walks this week, I had to put on a jacket a few times. You remember jackets? The thing with the long sleeves you wear over your T-shirt? Think back to March or so. Maybe that's why the playlist this week has a few winter tunes—the seasons are changing.

One particular morning conversely felt pretty warm, and I decided to go out to the beach. I hadn't finished everything

around the house, so I took some paperwork with me in a brown plastic grocery sack. It's okay to go to the beach if I can get some things done while I'm there. That's according to me; the concept is less attractive to a dog that thinks we should go everywhere together. The city doesn't allow dogs on the beach, and there have been a few times when I wondered if they were all that thrilled with having me there either. I tend to bathe and shave after being-on-the-beach days, not before.

Some of the paperwork was actual work, but a lot of it was unopened mail. In the Château de Bridgeport, we have strategically located the recycle bin between the door and the mailbox. Advertisements and similar enticements never make it into the house. At this time of year, we start receiving catalogs reminding us that the holiday season is sort of imminent. There are people out there who believe that my gift list should include five-pound Lebanon bolognas, toothbrushes with LED lights, and so forth. The catalogs provide much of the heft when I roll the bin to the street. So the mail I took to the beach was the remainder, the stuff that might actually be meaningful.

The first one I opened was from the national committee of a political party. I was surprised by that. I am not affiliated in any way with that party or any other, for that matter. It was a four pager. I was to give them advice on the first three pages and write checks to attach to the last.

Now, I have lots of advice for that particular party, and I give it face-to-face to party representatives who visit me personally. They usually flee in terror before I finish, but that's their decision. So it's not like I don't have the words to inform them. But in the letter version, they ask the wrong questions—questions that don't have a right answer. You know the kind: "Would you prefer a toothache or a broken toe?"

There is a fashion for asking the wrong questions nowadays, and it's spread far wider than the political sphere. If you try to order something over the phone or you have a problem with something you ordered over the phone, you will more than likely be asked to take a survey. If you take that survey, they will ask you several questions about the agent and none about the reason you called. Was the agent polite? Yes, but the socks were purple. The problem here is that the company has outsourced trouble calls to an agency, and the agency cares about the call, not the reason for it.

I have taken surveys for most of my life. As I stumbled through various school systems, surveys (mostly thrown together in Minnesota, for some reason) were a regular feature. They tended toward the tedious. They specialized in asking the same questions three or four different ways, and the results were usually grotesque. I took one in high school that recommended "agricultural agent" as my best career choice. Some of the people I knew during my career in high tech would probably agree with that, but I don't. I know which end of the cow is for input and which is for output, but that's all. Not caring about what may come in between is a big part of my ignorance.

But surveys even infected my workplace. One year, we were all instructed to take the Myers–Briggs Type Indicator. If I remember correctly, I was an ISTJ. Okay, now what? Nothing, as it turned out. I note that Myers–Briggs was based on the work of Carl Jung. I wonder if he came up with that before or after the orgone box.

If meaningless surveys are your thing, you need only connect to the Internet. Several of my friends have sorted themselves into the houses of Hogwarts, matching their personalities to categories much the same way psychological magic determined that I belong to ISTJ. I do not Potter around, so I have resisted. Potterizing is the modern version of astrological signs. Whenever anyone asks me which house is mine, I always say the "Rising Sun." Those who are older get the joke, but many of them read things into it. Surveyors aren't interested in your particular answers, you see, they just want to aggregate numbers. The numbers will then be used to engineer statistics that prove their narrative is correct. The only question is how much engineering they'll have to do. Pigeonholing other people is usually wrong. Pigeonholing yourself smacks of delusion. But I am an ISTJ—you know how they are.

Anyway, the letter from that national committee wanted me to prioritize the planks in its platform. I couldn't do it—it really was a matter of comparing broken toes with toothaches. When I got home, I deposited the letter in the recycle bin. If I need that much bologna, I know a catalog I can get it from.

Winter 2018 ~ 2019

Virginia woods in the autumn

Other Woods

The woods were "lovely, dark and deep"... yes, Mr. Frost, yes indeed.

These were mid-Atlantic woods, and they swayed in a stiff and chilly breeze. My home woods, tucked far into the South, are mostly longleaf pine and live oak, and they are lovely, too, but in a different way. In the mid-Atlantic, there are more varieties of hardwoods, and they have a deeper, more textured feel. I lived most of my life in this sort of woods, and I have missed them.

The Northern trees were about to turn into their autumn colors but hadn't started yet. The stream gleamed in the sunlight as it chattered softly near my feet. Along this particular path, the watercourse averages a depth of about four inches. It is little more than a Savannah drainage ditch, but we have history, this stream and I. In times past, the dog of that era and I walked this path almost every day. This time, the woods were scruffier and more overgrown. The path apparently missed me, too, for it was narrower and less defined.

The woods surrounding the hotel had the same feel, though they had acquired large, multistory buildings at frequent intervals. The hotel was in an office park, a well-done office park, with the trees still defining the character of the land. But the buildings were prominent, and the sounds of the bordering interstate seeped through the leaves.

I was staying at this hotel in a small remnant of the mid-Atlantic woods to attend a college reunion. As I may have mentioned before, this was one of those years with a significant number. So significant, in fact, that the university presented us with medals for having survived our education, but that happened later. My classmates and I had been plotting other specifics of the reunion electronically for months—now it was actually happening.

The first event was informal, a small gathering at another hotel some distance away but reachable by subway. My rental car would convey me to the station and the subway car to my final destination. A friend with far more reunion experience told me to be prepared to meet classmates who look much older than I do. Before leaving my room, I stared at the mirror for a few seconds. Older, huh? Okay, classmates, beat that.

The subway ran well and on time and left me in a part of the city where the trees were memories and not even recent ones. I walked two blocks before I discovered I was going in the wrong direction—my urban pathfinder skills were rusty. I reversed course and arrived at the appointed place. As I entered, two of my classmates were exiting the elevator. We brayed at each other, then moved on to our appointed rounds. My part was to provide music, and I had programmed three hours of songs from our distant youth. We'd had a rather raucous distant youth, and as the reunion began, I turned the volume down.

The people were here for talking, not singing along to tunes we'd heard hundreds of times before. Eventually, the room contained something more than a dozen of us.

I looked carefully around the room. Yes, we had aged, and some had gone at it with more determination than I, but not many. There were a few, inevitably, who dressed elegantly and were coiffed beautifully, and they did not look much different from the days of yore. That group didn't include me.

Then I was swept up in conversations. Three hours of muted songs later, an old and trusted friend offered me a ride to the subway station closest to my hotel. When we reached it, I wandered around the parking garage for some minutes before I found my rental.

I need to brush up on those urban skills.

I won't describe the rest of the reunion here because it had mostly the same feel, just with larger groups of people. There were some twenty-five of us who had planned the student-led parts of the overall event, and each brought a new shine to the proceedings.

The university did its part, too. Over the years, like Ireland, it has prospered and learned to cook—at various times, we were served a variety of foods that actually tasted good. I flashed back to the old days, when an order of veal Parmesan resulted in a fried, breaded patty of some mammal, possibly a ruminant, topped with a square of Swiss cheese and no sauce.

You might imagine that all of this had a tremendous impact on me, and you'd be right. At first, I immersed myself in the familiar faces and voices and mannerisms of the others, and just that was pretty neat. But I had long discussions with a handful of the folks whom I hadn't seen for decades.

It was different, and it was better.

These people are an upgrade of their former selves. They've traded youth for experience and insight. They've become wiser and more interesting and far more capable. It was both fun and instructive to be around them. Some have done exciting things with their lives and some didn't mention any, but it was worth listening to and learning from all of them.

Like our youth, the reunion was over before we knew it. A few days later, I returned to Savannah/Hilton Head International early in the afternoon. Before I even rescued my luggage from the airport carousel, I had a double scoop of something nice from Leopold's, the first food I'd had that day. I drove home with no regard for traffic, for the first time since I had left.

Once home, I replaced the cold weather clothes I'd been wearing and got back into my Savannah attire—T-shirt, shorts, and sandals. The socks and closed shoes and thick jackets will come out again, but not just yet. The reunion gave me memories that I will cherish, from visiting with remarkable people to little details like a walk in the woods. I loved being there, back in the woods of my youth, but this is home and the place I want to be. I came to that conclusion while picking long pine needles out of the windshield wipers of the truck.

Like Mr. Frost and my classmates, I have promises to keep and miles to go—this was not a life-ending experience. I will keep those promises and travel the miles among the longleaf pines and live oaks.

Professionals

I'm not sure I understand the things that are happening today. But it's okay. Unlike most people who have reached my age, I never thought I understood what was happening when I was younger either. But sometimes there are clues in the past.

John Steinbeck wrote wondrous short stories about California during the Depression. I like short stories; they suit my tendency to fall asleep when in a comfortable chair. I can usually stay awake for the duration of a short story.

Some of Steinbeck's stories take place in Monterey on the California coast. If you go to Monterey today, there is little left of the town about which Steinbeck wrote—it has been overrun with golf courses, hedge fund managers, and trendy ideas.

Steinbeck's first set of stories is called *Cannery Row*. In it, you can easily tell the Monterey of the 1930s from the Monterey of today.

Two of *Cannery Row*'s major characters are Doc, who runs a marine biology supply house, and Dora Flood, who owns a whorehouse close by. Solitary, thoughtful, and somewhat sad, Doc lives by himself, but he is friendly and even genial with Dora and her employees.

Now, as much as Doc likes Dora and her crowd, he never patronizes her establishment. One of the other characters asks him why. He thinks for a minute and then says that he supposes that professionals have different ideas about the whole business.

Fast-forward to today. Our world has changed even more than Monterey. We have wealth and comfort that would be utterly alien to Depression life. This has allowed many of us to make livings as specialists in something or another. Some of us make very good livings, and many of Monterey's current inhabitants specialize in fields unknown in Steinbeck's time.

It is the way of things that, after somebody becomes a specialist and being a specialist proves viable, specialization becomes a way of life. In other words, people become pros. They read learned publications about the minutiae of their field; they seek others in the same field, maybe even forming associations for their personal betterment. Professionals or pros develop their own norms and their own language, unintelligible to generalists.

We assume that all these people are capable and experienced, and they usually are. We then assume that they will do what we want them to in a straightforward and economical manner. And right there is where things start to fall apart.

Professionals, you see, maintain themselves by doing their thing. Doing their thing is important, no doubt, but maintaining themselves is more important. Maintaining yourself means billable hours; it doesn't mean craftsmanship or love. It doesn't necessarily mean doing a thing in the most efficient manner either.

So the whole idea that a professional might be the best person to do a job may be in doubt. Frequently, artists or writers who do not depend on art or literature for a living—and, thus, don't have to spend their time marketing the product to live—might do a better job than those who do. Sure, the nine-to-five can be draining (and many of us dream of the patronage days), but amateurs sometimes have more ardor and energy to craft and consider...hence, the root of the word. The poet Wallace Stevens was vice president of a bank, linguist Benjamin Lee Whorf was a chemical engineer, and many artists and authors commonly teach their craft to maintain themselves.

There's nothing new about any of this: We've all seen and been professionals, and we know how it works, at least in an abstract way.

Every professional has overhead. Even Dora Flood, who was a kindly soul, noted rather grumpily that "some of [her employees] don't turn three tricks a month but they go right on eating three meals a day." With the whole idea of professionalism comes the idea of competition among professionals. And when there is competition, standards and usual practices start being bent in strange and convoluted ways. Sometimes the competition introduces practices that have nothing to do with functionality or the satisfaction of the customer. In fact, they usually interfere with both. Try shopping for a used car. The clientele of those professionals get the idea that they aren't getting what they paid for.

A bit more recently than Steinbeck, we had another observation: "When the going gets weird, the weird turn pro." That is true as well (thank you, Mr. Thompson), and if weirdness turns out to be sustaining, people will try to outdo one another. Next, clients (who may be otherwise kind and rational) will go along: "He may be a weirdo, but he's our weirdo." Or perhaps: "At least he's honest about it."

So Doc might be right—professionals really do have a different attitude about the whole thing. Maybe it's naïve to expect anything else. Sometimes the professional competition is so intense that the lack of ethics gives the entire profession a bad name. Sometimes that happens even in professions that are not known for ethical purity.

The Body Biologic

I will not "sing the body electric." Walt Whitman did that pretty thoroughly, and Ray Bradbury followed fantastically with another whole slant on the matter. Semi-creative people have been riffing off both of them for years. No, I will sing the body biologic instead. The body biologic is filled with wonders that only clog the circuits of the body electric with envy. One of these is lactase. Lactase is a curious substance. If you have it, you might not be aware of it; if you don't, you probably know all about it.

Lactase is an enzyme, and almost all babies have it. But what happens after the baby phase is very much up in the air. Some people, mainly of European and selected African, Southeast Asian, and even Middle Eastern heritage, go right on producing the stuff. Some people don't.

Lactase allows you to digest lactose, which is milk sugar. The enzyme sneaks up on those milk molecules and slices them, creating glucose and galactose. The body is okay with both of these, but whole lactose is a problem. When unsliced lactose passes through the stomach and cannot be dismantled in the small intestine, it creates bloating, nausea, diarrhea, and other conspicuously uncomfortable symptoms. If whole lactose reaches the colon, where bacteria live and work, the bacteria ferment it. That produces methane gas, which the body likes even less than lactose. The body will eject the methane by whatever means necessary, and it will do so whether you are in church or out on a hot date or wherever else. Sometimes noisily. A number of sociological complexities arise when that happens.

Even in people who had the right ancestors, lactase productions can be a problem. Well-aged bodies do not necessarily produce lactase as swiftly or efficiently as younger ones. The ice cream that perfectly delighted you at twenty might cause socially distressing symptoms at sixty.

So here's the interesting part: Humans didn't produce lactase until about seven thousand to twelve thousand years ago. We know this because geneticists have been extracting DNA from ancient bones, and the DNA string that creates lactase only shows up about then. Even so, only certain populations produced it. Why? Because it wasn't needed until then. If you bellied up to a Neanderthal bar and said, "Got Milk?," the bartender would laugh at you because he didn't stock it. You'd have to settle for something else—a flagon of river water or three fingers of blood or something like that. Only modern humans have used milk, and they only began to use it after they stopped hunting and gathering and started herding.

Humans didn't produce lactase until they started to use milk as a food. After some generations of bloating and diarrhea, somebody's DNA adjusted to this new digestion, and that person was an evolutionary success. Little wonder: Somebody who can get through courses of warmed Brie, sauerbraten, and scalloped potatoes and throw a few White Russians on top of it is going to breed more children than somebody who can't. That might still be true today.

Humans have flourished, while ancient people such as Neanderthals and Denisovans became extinct. Several reasons may have caused that, but maybe we can add the absence of lactase as one of them.

We are only beginning to understand the hard-and-fast rules for the body biologic. Some people can digest lactose late into life, some cannot. The ability to do so probably came from repeated exposure to life-giving milk foods, and so the body developed the power to break it down. If your ancestors came from places where milk was not a primary source of nutrition, you probably lack lactase persistence and have a higher risk of lactose intolerance.

The robot—the body electric in the Bradbury sense—has no way of making such adaptations. Circuits will be circuits; they cannot adapt to changes in the environment. They can be somewhat adaptive in the sense that they can react differently based on new data, but they can't change into other sorts of circuits.

All this lactase expertise comes from a book called *A Brief History of Everyone Who Ever Lived* by geneticist Adam Rutherford. He gets into the details, but he also makes them entertaining. One of my favorite parts is where he takes a long sneer at the Paleo diet and the supposition that it's better for modern people. No, it isn't. You aren't built for that anymore.

Modern genetic studies are now providing all sorts of interesting details about us, our ancestors, and our evolution. Before this, biologists looked at generations of finches, peas, fruit flies, and bumblebees for models of evolution, with the hope that the same mechanisms applied, and paleo-anthropologists poked at bones randomly preserved in a patchy fossil record.

Now we can query complete genomes from those scanty human remains.

Rutherford also takes to task the tree of life and says that it isn't a tree at all. It's more like a bucket of paint drizzled down an incline. The dribbles separate and merge many times before they reach the bottom (which is why you and I are genetically part Neanderthal and Denisovan). All those ideas about racial characteristics and purity are hooey, though Rutherford is far too British to use the word "hooey."

That poem of Whitman's ends with the following words:

> The thin red jellies within you or within me,
> the bones and the marrow in the bones,
>
> The exquisite realization of health;

O I say these are not the parts and poems of
the body only, but of the soul,

O I say now these are the soul!

If Whitman is right, then the soul is subject to evolution,
too, and that might cause some unease in those who try to
characterize the soul as somewhat static and beyond the realm
of physical laws. But that is probably beyond Rutherford's pay
grade, and it's certainly beyond mine. The "thin red jellies"
speak of change, and that in itself is a fascinating display.

Eternity

Recently, I have been haunted by the specter of eternal life.
As a concept, I mean, not personally. My readings as of late
have included things by medical mavens who think that living
far longer than a century is both possible and desirable; bioger-
ontologists who claim we can make the extra time pleasant and
fulfilling; and medico-mechanics who wish to replace random
body parts with aftermarket upgrades.

All this progress should make me happy, I suppose. When I
look at myself as not man but machine, I can spot some problems. The propulsion remains strong, and the engine runs well,
if at a reduced rate. But the audio and video sensors are going,
navigation fails occasionally, and avionics do, too. I am reduced
in the types of fuel I can use, and the exhaust system—well, we
won't go into that.

We, the excessively mature, like to think we are Warthogs.
For those of you not aeronautically inclined, the Warthog, or
A-10, is an aircraft first flown in 1972. It is neither fast nor
beautiful, but it does what it's supposed to do better than any
of its kind. Newer, faster, more gorgeous-looking planes can't
do the same thing. The comparison to older folks is appealing.
But even Warthogs need serviceable electronics and exhaust
systems.

Impending longevity should perk me up, but instead it gives me pause. There are ethicists and philosophers who worry about the ability to spew out formidable, long-lived fanatics through gene-splicing, like the Balrog factory in *The Lord of the Rings*, but we aren't that good at gene-splicing yet. These ethicists and philosophers are sometimes the very same who worry whether sentient robots might decide they don't like us anymore. Recently, the Boston Dynamics corporation released a video of one of its robots dancing to "Uptown Funk." On one hand, the robot did a better job than I could or, really, better than I ever could. On the other, I'm not convinced that dancing to "Uptown Funk" demonstrates enough sentience to raise the alarm—at least not yet.

What bothers me is having eternal life and still being here. In the past, when you developed a severe case of eternal life, you grew wings, learned to play the harp pretty decently, and wandered around the clouds free of vexations. Okay, that particular eternal life is a Western idea, but all religions and philosophies have a similar story.

In the oldest version from ancient Egypt, when you died your spirit flew off into the night to work the fields and make the pottery, just like you did when you were alive. Keeping your mummified body around was important because, when daylight arrived, your spirit flew back there to rest.

But the slightly less ancient Egyptians decided that this concept was flawed. They developed *ushabti*, little figurines with spirits that did your night job for you. Presumably, *ushabti* didn't require as much management as people, and you could relax rather than worry about whether the *ushabti* were taking a smoke break when they should be producing papyrus for the scribal trade. So even the ancient Egyptians bailed on an eternal life just like the one you lived on earth.

Excessive maturity has its compensations. One of the main ones is reduced expectations. And a lot of this is my reduced expectations of myself. It's not that I can't improve; I just have to be a little careful about where I put my efforts. I probably would be a better person if I were a better dancer, but that's a lot of effort at my stage of life. Besides, they have robots that do that now. Nor do I expect myself to be a captain of industry, a fireman, or an astronaut.

And those are just my expectations. With a longer life span, the expectations of others would skyrocket, too. When our life spans run to decades past a century, do you imagine the retirement age to stay at sixty-five? It can't, because we'll be expected to put our great-grandchildren through college and we'll lack sufficient grandchildren to fund Social Security. The idea of another forty or fifty years in the workplace does not exactly fill me with joy, even though my employers were pretty good people.

Many years back, a doctor who didn't know me well told me that I had to accept my own mortality. I've come to the point where I not only accept it, I depend on it. My time at the mortal table is limited, so I don't have that much personal investment beyond a certain point. That is wonderfully liberating. I can make mistakes without jeopardizing my career because I don't have one. I can reduce my interests to things that are actually interesting. I will leave snotty robots and colonization of other planets to somebody else down the road. I will happily miss the delay between extending people's lives and making them happy about it. Good luck with that—it sounds complicated and full of nasty surprises. I ask only to leave the table with as little fuss and inconvenience as possible.

So how do I want to be remembered? I'm not sure I want to be. It isn't like I won a war, cured a disease, or materially improved the lives of my countrymen. I am told that Richard Nixon conducted his time in the White House with his eye firmly on how history would judge him. He will be remembered, but perhaps not the way he anticipated. I doubt history will spend much time making any judgment about me. It might be better to avoid the whole process. I doubt I'll even qualify for a lovely parting gift.

A few days ago, I read a very nice poem by Ted Kooser, who won a Pulitzer and was the U. S. Poet Laureate for a while. Rita Dove, who has the same credentials, wrote an introduction to the work, and here's what she said: "Perhaps the best way to keep the spirits of loved ones alive is to allow them to continue living within us."

That sounds more like the right idea than hanging around with ill temper and faulty exhaust systems.

Oglethorpe

I sat on the cement bench in Chippewa Square while I enjoyed a warm libation with a cinnamon chip scone. Right there are two things I shouldn't be doing: I was supposed to be somewhere else and not indulging in sweets. But it's my call, right? Sainthood was never really a career option.

Anyway, the cement bench gives you a fine full-frontal view of General Oglethorpe in bronze up on his cement plinth. He looks rather grimly over your right shoulder. At present, Oglethorpe's cold eye seems affixed on the backhoe sitting idle behind a maze of temporary fencing and yellow tape. Part of the road around the square is currently under construction and is closed to traffic. I've seen the same look on modern-day merchants in the square as they contemplate such traffic impediments while the Christmas season wanes.

A curious fellow, James Oglethorpe. He founded Georgia, of course, but there was more to this Englishman than that. At the age of eighteen, he decided to soldier and did so in the company of Prince Eugene of Savoy, who led the Austrians against the Turks in the Balkans. Oglethorpe then served in Parliament and developed an interest in prison reform, which directed his interests to the New World. After founding Georgia, he returned to the old country to raise troops to defend the colony against the Spanish and got himself in the middle of

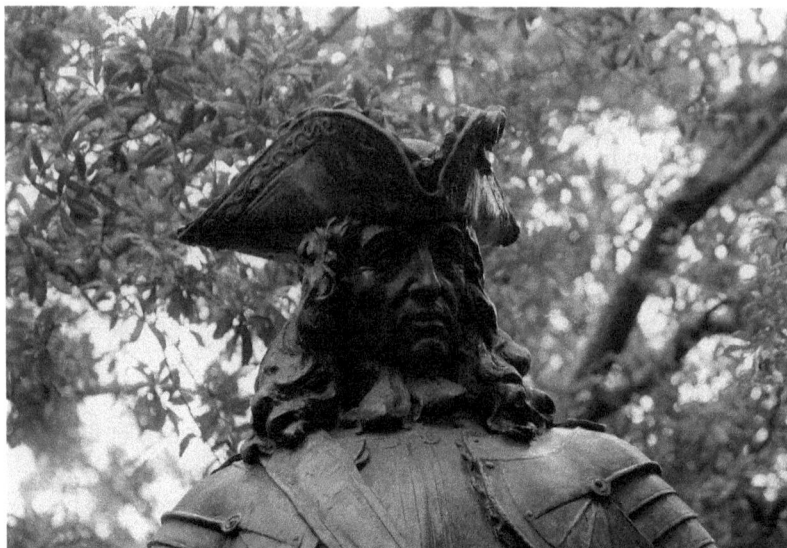

the Scottish rebellion of 1745. He turned his troops against the Scots and fought at Preston. And he never found his way back to Georgia again.

The statue itself is somewhat curious. Oglethorpe wears a knee-length coat with one of those long vests underneath and at least two pairs of britches. He has what appears to be another coat stuffed in his belt. The coat he wears flaunts armor on the shoulders. His sword points to the ground, and a cut palm branch lies disconsolately behind him. So this is a sculpture of him in Georgia, since there are remarkably few palms around Preston or the northern Balkans. Perhaps the grim look stems from wearing two sets of clothes in the Savannah climate, which frequently is uncomfortable with just one. Maybe the palm branch was the victim of a heat-rash-maddened Oglethorpe suffering in that outfit. I suppose he predated tank tops, but still ... The statue was created in a later age, of course, by people whose idea of bronzes did not extend to summer clothing.

A curious fellow. He founded Georgia as a refuge for the worthy poor, those in debtor's prison. In his time, you could be thrown in jail for owing money. Given the earning potential of those in prison, repayment of debts didn't happen that often, and being shipped to Georgia was a way out of debt—assuming you survived the transatlantic voyage, which one out of four or five did not.

He got his debtors, but they were soon overwhelmed by the Scots-Irish coming down the Great Valley this side of the Appalachians, who had their own notions of worthy and poor. He banned slavery in Georgia because he thought that would draw escapees from the Spanish colonies in Florida. It did, but it drew far more escapees from South Carolina, which became a sore point between Georgia and her northern neighbor. After he left Georgia in 1743, several of the more "pragmatic" Georgians purged the colony's laws of his odd slavery ideas.

After the Battle of Preston in Scotland, he followed and fought against one of the remnants of the shattered Scottish Army. Following one sharp action, he rested his own troops in the middle of a howling storm while the remaining Scots scampered away. Somebody, probably someone unfamiliar with Scottish storms, took umbrage at that, and Oglethorpe was court-martialed. The court exonerated him and promoted him to general, but he never commanded again.

Oglethorpe's life may be called a textbook example of good intentions gone wrong: Britain's prisons remained full of the poor, both worthy and unworthy. After he left the New World, Georgians not only embraced slavery, they gave it a big wet kiss—a love affair that lasted one hundred and twenty years. And he couldn't have been that happy about American independence; that wasn't at all what he had in mind when George II granted him the charter in 1732.

But good did come from Oglethorpe's efforts. The following generations of reformers instituted a saner prison system, banned slavery, and accomplished many of the things

Oglethorpe wanted in the first place. Oglethorpe is remembered. Contrast that with South Carolina, where many of the people and most of the philosophy came from the Caribbean—a region where slave-powered large crops were king and vast quantities of rice were produced along with a pernicious set of attitudes. Those "pragmatic" planters remain unknown.

Anyone who starts with a vision and good intentions is often plagued by critics, both during and after one's time, who point out the differences between plans and reality.

But the same thing is true for people who do things with no high intentions; in these situations, critics are equally adept at pointing. Unintended consequences result from low goals as well as high goals. And not all, but many unintended consequences can be as deplorable, if not worse, than the plans that gave rise to them.

And then there are those of us who are oblivious to the whole philosophical issue. As I swept scone crumbs from my shirt, a man ambled up to me, having determined that I was local. He pointed to the statue and asked, "Is that Chippewa?" The concept of having a statue and a square with different names had eluded him. I gave him a brief explanation and suggested that he go up to the statue and read the inscription. I noted that he was wearing one of those red baseball caps with the meaningless political slogan—you know the one.

Visitors often need orienting. But I couldn't shake the feeling that he was actually a local in need of a background briefing. After all, he was wearing one of those red caps—you know the one.

I Don't Know

I don't understand.

That's okay. I don't expect to understand everything. There are days when it's hard to understand anything. It's hereditary. I come from a long line of people who didn't understand everything, all the way back to the knuckle-draggers who figured out that whacking things with a club made them part of the food chain.

Not understanding everything became more complex when the knuckle-draggers began to form groups, whether they were families or hunting parties or yoga classes. Other people in the group understood things you didn't and vice versa. Some anthropologists think that we outlasted the Neanderthals and the Denisovans because we were able to socialize problems and find solutions from other minds. (That, of course, didn't stop us from interbreeding with them . . .)

But then, "I don't understand everything" became "we don't understand everything" because socializing doesn't provide solutions all the time. If the guy two caves down gets struck by lightning, you can socialize it all you want, but he is no less fried.

Not understanding everything may work well for one person, but groups don't like that answer. So they reach beyond their knowledge for answers. The first answer was "It's magic." But even the knuckle-draggers understood the use of logic when you don't have data; thus, that was offensive. That morphed into "It's God's will." Hierarchy was well understood even way back then, and their hierarchy had the unknowable at the top.

Here's how we go about things.

First, we are presented with an idea (or some magic or a pantheon of deities) that might help. If early indications are good, we attempt to apply the idea to everything. When it doesn't work for everything, we decide that it is totally fraudulent, like a false god. We then ignore it. Meanwhile, people ignore the benefits of the first idea, which may be substantial, if not universal. The search for a magical solution to all problems goes on.

We've become more sophisticated since the time of dwelling in caves, but curiously our approach has not. First, we decided that computers were magic and would solve every problem. In many cases, they merely replaced a problem with a more complex set of problems. Now the answer is genetics. Every physical problem you have can either be forecast or fixed using genetics. This is common knowledge among almost everyone but geneticists. They just smile wanly, just as the computer folks did, because they know better.

And no, I'm not talking solely about how the man in the street thinks and judges. Some fairly bright people with fairly good information think the same way and do the same thing. After the Sandy Hook Elementary School massacre, the commission investigating the murders asked for a genetic profile of the shooter. Some newspapers even speculated on what the commission might find. The commission didn't find anything significant that we know of because genetics is as much about the interactions of genes as it is the genes themselves. Even genetics researchers know very little about what genes do and next to nothing about those interactions. And genes aren't destiny. Social factors play a role—and likely a much greater role—than any one gene or host of genes. Maybe after fifty years or so, we'll know enough for a DNA profile to be useful, but not now.

When computers didn't save the world, we downgraded them as frauds, like pet rocks or lava lamps. We will do the same when genetics proves to have limits (which, with epi-genetics, may be occurring even now). We all have a notion that there is one simple answer to everything and the next big discovery may cure the economy, the balky washing machine, and occasional arthritis.

Maybe it has to do with how we educate ourselves. From elementary school through high school, almost every question has a right answer and a wrong answer. Right answers are complete and correct and wipe away all difficulties magically. One plus one equals two. After that, we learn that nature doesn't offer tidy, definitive answers for real problems. For every problem, there are a few pretty good answers and lots and lots of bad ones. One plus one might equal something else in binary.

We also find out that today's pretty good answer may not work tomorrow. Most of the things we define as problems aren't really problems; they're situations. And you don't solve situations—you manage them. Magical answers usually don't hold up.

Management is icky, of course. You can't just deliver an answer and then move on. Management means that you have to keep an eye on the situation and think about it and observe it, because things change and yesterday's answer may not be right today. You may have to find another answer that fits the situation today because there are added factors or new information to be considered. And because you are managing rather than solving, somebody might decide you are wrong. They might also decide that if you are not a genius, you are probably a dolt, and if you are not all powerful you must be a fraud. Magical thinking means that if you aren't all powerful and can't solve something, you must be a fraud. It's a matter of expectations—a magic bullet for everything or rejection of everything.

Magical answers, those bold epiphanies that ignore facts, are the enemy of real solutions. They usually result from oversimplifying a problem. When faced with data that contradict an oversimplified answer, magical answers reject that data. Can you think of an example? I can. And so the magical answer and the oversimplified problem remain in place—for now.

I don't deny the existence of magic. The universe worked long and hard to come up with you. Your eyes alone took countless years of development. Your ideas took thousands. Those ideas started with those knuckle-draggers and kept on developing until they came up with your particular perspective. Magic is when you don't see the time and effort that went into producing the effect.

I do deny that I understand everything, and I deny it categorically. I understand enough to manage myself through a day. Well, most days I do. The sum of human knowledge is beyond my comprehension. The way we all live is rich in variety and extends way beyond my experience. I'm just glad my particular flavor is relatively comfortable.

As a phrase, "I don't understand" is a starting point. Then maybe you think about a solution, or maybe you collect more data. But you start to develop a solution or at least a way to manage the problem. At least, I think that's the right idea.

I don't really know.

Minus Firearms

I woke up this morning, and I did not get myself a gun, nor was the blue moon in my eyes. Whatever happened overnight, I had not turned into Tony Soprano. That's just as well for everyone, including Tony Soprano. Still, I felt like I had the weight of the world on my shoulders.

It's a matter of scheduling. My college reunion is past, though it still shines brightly in the rearview mirror. Halloween is now over, too. I have a half-full bowl of leftover candy on the kitchen table. These are candies that neither the missus nor I will eat—because I buy only that kind. That way, there's still some left when the costumed children come calling. I must find somewhere for it to go. It was less of a problem when I showed up at work every day: Put anything on the reception desk, and it was gone by lunch. Things you found beneath your sofa cushions, chocolate-covered rivets... anything.

I have been out of sorts this past week. I put a pair of shorts in the washer, realizing it will probably be the last shorts I wear until 2019. That's one of the things I regret about autumn. I've been forced into long pants, socks, and jackets (because the dog wants to be walked at dawn), and not those alleged three-season jackets either—jackets with heft and purpose.

But autumn has many compensations for the change in attire. One of my neighbors has been burning wood in his fireplace; the aroma (and sometimes the smoke itself) blankets the area. That's a wonderful smell, and I enjoy it. The day also shifts. The dog and I took the second walk just after noon today. The jacket was on, but the sun was warm, not broiling, and afterward we both settled in for much-appreciated naps.

Autumn also has events—"happenings," as they used to call them. Halloween was just the start. Next up is Election Day. I have always thought Election Day a big deal, but I know people who try to ignore the whole thing. Ignoring Election Day is, well, ignorant. I'm not going to go off on a big get-out-the-vote speech, but the importance of that should be extra obvious this year. When I read the newspapers, the actions of some policy makers seem contemptible, cowardly, and horrifically expensive. Policy makers these days appear to have a strange fascination with solutions that exhibit such characteristics.

After Election Day comes Thanksgiving. You can tell it's getting close because Christmas items start to seep into the stores. I enjoy Thanksgiving, I really do, but it involves preparation. You have to skulk around the grocery to wait for the first delivery of turkeys. That's the only delivery that has turkeys small enough to feed two people and a dog for less than a month. Then there are the side dishes: the whipped sweet potatoes, the green beans, my mother's stuffing, which is a banquet unto itself. Those are standards. But then there's the cranberry sauce. We have tried a number of recipes over the years, and some were okay. There was the year where we mixed the cranberries with other things and poured a little orange juice into the amalgam. That was pretty good, but it takes extra steps for a meal that already requires several hours and pairs of hands to prepare. I grew up with the cranberry jelly, the sort that sits on the serving dish just as it came from the can, with the ridges still embedded in it. I like that kind.

After Thanksgiving, of course, comes Christmas. I will get through all of that with a little grace and probably more enjoyment, but we are in the planning stage now, where every bump looks like a mountain range. Sometimes it's more tiring to think about things than to actually do them, because you carry with you all the things that might go wrong. Inevitably, some things will go wrong, but not everything, and we live to fight another holiday season.

Anyway, I woke up this morning, and I did not get myself a gun. Instead, I walked the dog. That is more in keeping with my current frame of mind, and the house smells better when he can sojourn outside. Walking the dog at dawn is easier in the fall, simply because dawn comes later. A few extra minutes of sleep can make all the difference.

The stars were out when we left under a still-darkened sky. Over there was the Big Dipper, which is the only constellation I know. I am astronomy-challenged. But there were lots of other stars, too. They are large balls of burning gas shining across unimaginable distances. They speak of and may contain existences that are beyond our imagination. The night sky is both wondrous and humbling. There was a celestial light of particular brightness—I supposed that it was a planet, Venus perhaps. Then I noticed that it was blinking and moving far more rapidly than the others—an airplane headed into Hunter then. So much for philosophy.

The stars were mostly gone by the time we finished our walk. The sun hadn't appeared above the trees, but the light from the east had erased them. The trees stood out in dark silhouettes against the lighted sky, like one of those luminist paintings. Yesterday, there were clouds floating toward the light; today, there were a few very high ones, showing soft tones where the light hit them.

Man and dog, we walk the same route almost every day. I have an inkling of what he gets out of it. I watch the ears go up, hearing things I cannot, and the nose to odd patches of the underfoot, smelling the comings and goings of creatures I cannot detect. There are mailboxes to be marked, and no bit of fallen Spanish moss will go without him indicating his passing.

But I wonder if he has an inkling of what I get out of it—sometimes I wonder if I do. But after this particular walk, all the burdens of the autumn seemed to drop away, or more properly, they seemed to be put into a proper context. Spring feels full of possibilities, and summer is the time for making those possibilities realities. Autumn is when we realize what all the frantic activity means in the greater scheme of things.

It's a good time, autumn.

Fog

In Chicago, according to Carl Sandburg, the fog creeps in "on little cat feet." In Savannah, it waddles from the ocean, in an alligator's crawl. And then the alligator sits and rests.

Recently, I was on my way to the studio and decided to sit in one of the smaller squares. The fog had erased the sky and faded the tops of the buildings. It was close to dusk, so it was darker to begin with. From my vantage point, I could look down one of the short blocks south of Liberty. This street is pretty typical for downtown, with a row of Colonial town houses, each with a staircase leading to a second story. The fog obscured everything above the second-story windows. A few houses were decorated with lights for the holiday, and the bulbs glowed in the mist. It was quiet. I bet the people south of Liberty value that quiet.

I had overcome most of the holiday to-do list, and those things left undone could probably remain so. Oh, there was still the dinner to prepare and some presents to wrap—those would get done. I usually make some plans that are more gorgeous in the abstract than they turn out to be once attempted. Those things that seemed to be a good idea at planning time would remain vaporware. There was a little more baking to do and one more holiday event, but yes, things were mostly under control.

But this was one of those days when the north wind had decided to go elsewhere, and so had the rain. It was a little chilly, but not bad.

I felt something germinate in my mind as I sat in the square, a sense of something good. I couldn't describe it, but I sat there waiting for it to grow. When I got up maybe a half-hour later, the sense had sprouted, but I still couldn't name it. I passed a restaurant as I headed to the studio. This particular restaurant specializes in what they call plant-based dishes, and they have a magnificent torch outside that throws a flame perhaps ten feet into the air. The torch is enclosed in some sort of transparent structure. I wondered if this is to keep some malefactor from sneaking up and broiling a kabob when nobody is looking. Probably not. There's probably a good reason for the casing.

The following day, there was another touch of sunshine, and then the fog rolled in again. This time, I walked along the river, accompanied by the randomly obedient dog. The dog walks are the highlight of his day and sometimes mine. This is not a dog walk in the sense of a purposeful march. We meander. He sniffs at whatever he feels is worth the effort, and I stop so he can complete his review. He is a big fan of chewing on goldenrod leaves, for whatever reason, and grounded Spanish moss seems to stimulate his bladder. Whatever. It's dog time.

While he searched the trail for goldenrod or maybe Spanish moss, I looked upriver toward the city. At that point in the river, there are a few small buildings and maybe houses and a curve just after the giant storage tanks on Elba Island. The fog veiled the tops of the tanks before thinning out lower, and some of the buildings were dressed in their holiday best. The small structures had colored lights, so I decided they were residences.

And there it was again, that same feeling.

Some people find the holiday spirit in family and friends. Some people find it in gifts. Others find it in church. I find it in holiday baking and other communal expressions. But since I am essentially a solitary person, I find it most often in walks with the dog and exploring and photographing the landscapes and skies around Savannah.

My gift this year was the fog. It allowed me to look at the familiar street with the town houses and see it for the first time, at least that way. The fog gave an extra dimension to the river, and I arrived where I started, as Eliot once intoned, and knew the place for the first time. And when I looked up at the Cathedral of St. John, the mists seemed to give the lights an extra glow—a nimbus maybe. Those things were always there, but the fog revealed them to me.

The other gift was the leisure to see. I've taken the time to let the fog show me things unseen. I've taken more time this year to notice how nature's activity offers opportunities to view familiar landscapes differently when we walk in the morning and the sun is just over the horizon or when the light hits the tall pines and turns them into Maxfield Parrish paintings with brilliant colors and contrasts.

So that sense of good I felt while sitting in the square was about the gifts of fog and leisure, of seeing and taking the time to see. When the holidays are over, I'll go back to my busyness, just like everybody else. But the holidays give you the inclination and the time to look again at the things you take for granted the rest of the year.

And that may be the greatest gift of all.

The Desk

I have a paymaster's desk; I like the style. But style doesn't really matter.

If you have a desk, it is an accessory to your conscience. The pile of things on top of it is a physical manifestation of your failures to respond, file, or otherwise clear it.

I sat at my desk early on Christmas Day.

"We have left undone those things that ought to be done," my conscience intoned mournfully. The pile in the center held bills, mostly insurance notices. There was a letter from the city thanking me for my services, the result of my resigning from an advisory group. It was a nice letter, but I couldn't remember any services I had performed. I supposed I should reply nicely.

There was a spoon from the prior eve's indulgence and the empty cola bottle that meant I had started my day. Perhaps these qualified as "we have done things we ought not to have done." Over on the right lay a book I had used last week and hadn't reshelved, an undistributed Christmas gift, and a magazine that I hadn't read yet. They were perched on top of the in-box, which remained full of pre-Christmas filing I hadn't done yet. Then there was the persistent shoebox with papers to be shredded—the papers that declare parts of me that I don't want leaving the house in one piece. There's the pile of "things that require mature consideration," which were waiting for me to achieve mature consideration. It happens occasionally, but not right then. Also a stack of business cards longing to be entered into the computer address system, before I forget the task or the person and pitch the card. And an array of Post-its full of data that would probably have the same fate, too.

The computer is no help. My computer calendar told me it was Christmas Day—all day. The fact that it's "all day" takes up an extra line. Really? I was hoping that this "all day" would be sometime in March or another time when the desk is clearer.

Maybe you are murmuring "First World problems" at this point. True enough, but still wide of the mark. The correct term is "bourgeois angst." I am as bougie as I can be, for the same reason that I am many other things—it works for me. My needs are modest, so I have attained as much wealth and power as I need. Wealth and power are like brandy; too much will assuredly make you sick.

If you must put it in terms of worlds, poverty and fear are third-world problems and frequently also second-world problems. We of the First World add guilt to the mixture. We have made our way by being proactive, flexible, and thought leaders in our chosen fields, to use business terminology. What that means is we worry about stuff even when it's going well. Is it going well enough? Will it go well tomorrow?

"We have left undone those things that ought to be done," that's the bougie motto right there. And if we aren't doing things for ourselves, we're doing them for others or for the future. All of that is part of our culture. It's in our politics, our religions, and our histories. It's the keystone of Western civilization, and it affects all of us, even if we don't pay any attention to politics, religion, or history. I know people who have demonized the plastic straw and are working very hard for its eradication. And I know many, many people who are trying, each in their own ways, to make those Second and Third Worlds less fearful and impoverished.

Bourgeois angst gets things done. Some people live without it, of course. Sometimes people inherit or make obscene amounts of money and attain the power that money confers. The angst drives the rest of us to count the cost of the things we do and to keep an eye on what it means for the future. Sometimes those with more wealth and power than I have forget that. That's the sickness that I am talking about. They develop their little philosophies without regard to the cost or the future.

Of course, sometimes they don't. There are many foundations out there, funded by the overcapitalized, for making the world a better place. The people who fund these efforts may outnumber the ones who don't. But that just makes the ones who don't seem sadder and sicker.

I don't have the problems of overcapitalization, and I don't ever expect to have them. What I have is bougie angst—it comes with the territory. The idea that I need to get things done is central to me, and it probably makes me a better person. And that means paying the bills and refiling the books and maybe even recording the business cards before I decide that I know too many people anyway and throw the clutter into the trash.

Sitting at my desk, I looked at the calendar again. It was Christmas Day—all day. There were things to be done: presents to unwrap, a large meal to cook, bases to touch with the people we know. The bills and books and filing would have to wait. Christmas Day would be busy and demanding without them.

Like most other bougie things, angst must be managed. There must be time and resources to deal with a problem. Getting all emotional and guilt-stricken takes up time and doesn't generate any resources—so that's a bad idea. In the end, I decided to leave the desk in its primal state. In fact, I've been chipping away at the piles ever since.

"We have left undone those things that ought to be done," and that's okay. For now.

Frost

Now, where was I?

Back in November, I was in the middle of doing things, and then all of a sudden, it was time to cook a large turkey-centric meal. Then it was time to get ready for Christmas and have Christmas complete with another large meal. Then it was time to disassemble Christmas. I did all of that. What was I thinking before the holidays arrived?

I looked around the house. Several waves of paper had washed over my desk, and I have fought them back to the point where I can see wood again. There's no help there—the ideas have been scrubbed away. Over on the table, several books sat stacked; they might provide a clue. But then there's my corner on the other side of the house, and I haven't sat there since turkeys loomed over my future.

My corner is over by the bookcases. It consists of said cases, a reasonable light, and one of those stressless chairs. The chair is white and comes with an ottoman, also stressless, I suppose. Well, it was when I bought it. It is now well aged and well used, and if it isn't quite white, it is still pretty stressless.

Other residents of my home refer to this chair as the "fermentation vat." Like many of the observations in my home, that may have some justification.

I sit there when considering the problems of the world or reading some important book with insights on life today. The last one I remember told me how to solve a murder in Provence if I were a village policeman. If I ever become a policeman in southern France, that will be a great reference.

But my memory is not photographic now, not that it ever was, so I went over to the chair to remind myself where I was pre-holidays. A book of poetry sat on the shelf that's slated for reading in progress. It was *North of Boston* by Robert Frost, and a folded Post-it marked a page of interest.

That's not unusual. I spent part of my life in New England, and Frost is a favorite poet when I read poetry. He captures the New England frame of mind, does Robert Frost. Okay, let's see which poem I was reading. Oh, it was "Mending Wall."

> Something there is that doesn't love a wall,
> That sends the frozen-ground-swell under it,
> And spills the upper boulders in the sun;
> And makes gaps even two can pass abreast.
> The work of hunters is another thing:
> I have come after them and made repair

> Where they have left not one stone on a stone,
> But they would have the rabbit out of hiding,
> To please the yelping dogs. The gaps I mean,
> No one has seen them made or heard them made,
> But at spring mending-time we find them there.

Well, that's true enough.

Here, if you dig in the dirt, you will find nothing but sand until you hit the water table. If you dig in New England, it won't be long until you run into chunks of granite. The farmers there unearth the granite and use it to build dry stone walls because there's nothing else you can do with it. And walls are hard to maintain. Frost was lucky if he had to mend walls only once a year.

But I understand that—mending walls is hard work. And if you aren't a granite-chunk-handling New Englander, it can be expensive, too.

> We wear our fingers rough with handling them....
> There where it is we do not need the wall:
> He is all pine and I am apple orchard.
> My apple trees will never get across
> And eat the cones under his pines, I tell him.
> He only says, "Good fences make good neighbors."

The "we" in this case includes the neighbor who owns the adjoining property. This verse describes two kinds of New England minds clashing: Frost, who says that the wall has no function, and his neighbor, who says it's the principle of the thing.

> Before I built a wall I'd ask to know
> What I was walling in or walling out,
> And to whom I was like to give offense.

But the neighbor carries on. We all know people who have convinced themselves to do things even when those things don't really work or don't do anything we really need. And it is irksome, or worse even, when love of some abstract involves effort or expense on our part.

Frost certainly isn't happy.

> He moves in darkness as it seems to me,
> Not of woods only and the shade of trees.

After I left New England, I lived in Virginia. There is far less granite in Virginia, so the early farmers built rail fences. You poke two or three lengths of tree trunk crossways into the ground and then run a cut sapling between this triad and the next one. You've probably seen these on Civil War battle-fields. But even that is expensive and hard to maintain. And while herd animals like cows and horses aren't known for their cleverness, they frequently find their way around or over the barrier.

The walls don't work all that well.

Well, it's a good poem and a true one. There's a lot to think about there. But I can't remember why I was so interested in it before the holidays. Maybe I'll just read the newspaper instead.

Grapefruit

This was the week of the Great Bridgeport Fruit Harvest.

I moseyed out to the back of our property and looked at the grapefruit trees. This is not a long or difficult mosey; the dog gets there in five bounds. I just don't go out there that much in the winter. But this day, the temperature was in the low seventies, and the sun shone through the clouds enough for a good survey.

Both of the grapefruit trees are at the fence line, nestled com-fortably among the overgrown azaleas, towering live oaks, and persistent smilax vines. There are a few scrubby palms there, too. I suppose I should do something about all that overgrowth, but I don't, aside from slicing back the smilax every so often. Beyond the shrubbery lie the backyards of the neighbors who face the next street down. These neighbors are perfectly nice people, with full lives and rich insights, but I'd rather look at overgrowth.

There are two grapefruit trees. One is shaded by the other and produces only fitfully. The other is the star of the show. This harvest, the first thing I did was pick grapefruit. In my yard, that means scooping up the ones that have fallen to the ground and putting them into the organic garbage. These are not edible. The next thing was to get the polesaw and try to knock down the rest. The tree is about thirty feet high and produces its fruits starting at about fifteen feet. I think that's rather sullen of it, but my mind and the mind of a grapefruit tree do not match up—at least I try to avoid many similarities.

After much shaking and cursing, I harvested around three dozen. This was a successful harvest, mostly because I did it without beaning the dog or myself. I left the tree with about the same amount. This was not being considerate; my polesaw reaches only to twenty feet or so.

So now I have three dozen grapefruit. Here are two fun facts about grapefruit.

First, grapefruit have a limited shelf life. After a while, you have to refrigerate them, and if you do that, there's no room for actual food, much less the bowl of cranberry sauce left over from Christmas and other such precious artifacts. Three dozen grapefruit have a fairly large footprint.

Second, three dozen grapefruit are about twice our annual consumption and maybe more. I can eat grapefruit only with a drum of antacids close at hand, so I don't. Other resident people have them occasionally.

I could give them to neighbors, of course, but grapefruit in January is about the same as zucchini in August. If we see someone walking up the driveway with zucchini, we activate the intruder alarm.

I could make grapefruit wine . . . you remember the Steely Dan lyric about shoeless revelry amid FM radio and grapefruit wine. I even looked up the recipe. I could make twenty-three liters of grapefruit wine with my yield. That's somewhere around six gallons. But you have to buy unimaginable amounts of sugar and a carboy to hold it, and that seems like throwing good money after bad. And I would have a carboy of something I don't need rather than a fridge full of more solid versions of things I eat.

In short, there are no good alternatives. So I am announcing that I have a grapefruit crisis in my backyard. I already have too many grapefruit, and there are more on the way. And when they come, they'll just fall to the ground and rot. Insects will come and feed on them. The seeds of some of them may even germinate and create new grapefruit trees. My mind reels at the catastrophe produced by more grapefruit trees.

Here's what I need: I need a wall to keep all those grapefruit from falling onto my property. Not just any wall, a great wall, maybe the greatest wall ever. The wall will be on a slant, so when those rotting grapefruit fall, they'll travel down the incline and fall into my neighbor's yard instead of mine.

Now my original idea was to have my neighbor pay for it. But she doesn't appreciate the seriousness of the crisis. Here we are in the middle of grapefruit-apocalypse, and she doesn't want to pay for the wall. Too bad. Shortsighted.

So I am going to petition the Chatham County Board of Commissioners for money to build the wall. This is clearly a countywide emergency, and we all need to be aware of the perils of unregulated grapefruit tree growth. Do we want Chatham County to become a wilderness of grapefruit trees? Of course we don't.

This is such an important issue that, should no funds for walls be found, I will ask the Chatham County government to shut down. Yes, I know, the schoolchildren can't use the bus, and the brush won't get picked up, and maybe even some much-needed road repairs will have to be delayed. But those things aren't as important as preventing the grapefruit trees from taking over Savannah. That only makes sense.

Romance (Paul Simon's "Congratulations")

I just played a Paul Simon piece on air, partly because he made the news by announcing he will stop touring. He turns seventy-seven this year; if he doesn't want to tour, he shouldn't have to. But the other part is to remind you that we are now close to Saint Valentine's Day. If you acknowledge that with flowers or candy or such, the end of your buying season is close enough for you to take action. But the song "Congratulations" may be a counterweight to the online flower vendors, store decorations, and those really sugary hearts with fortune cookie-type inscriptions.

What is love anyway? Has anyone got a nice, neat definition? Will that definition apply to your partner, your cat Snuffles, your favorite cousin, the salad dressing at that Italian restaurant down the street, and Olympic luge? I suspect not, even if you say you love all these things.

It's like many other collective terms, like patriotism, faith, fortitude, and progress. There isn't one satisfactory definition because what you mean depends on the context. You think about Snuffles and Olympic luge in different ways. To make it even more complex, every other person has those context issues, too, and their definitions probably differ from yours. There is no one satisfactory definition because the emotion has more facets than a disco-reflecting ball, just in one person. In more than one person, the term threatens to become meaningless.

When I see the usual Valentine's decorations, I think of a couple I knew in college. They spent perhaps a semester and a half mainly gazing into each other's eyes. I can report that they both went on to live rich, satisfying, productive lives—just not with each other. I don't know what happened. As involved as they were with each other for nine months, it didn't work for them.

Not that I was immune to that sort of situation. I have an ex-fiancée who told me, "You are a goat, not a sheep." I think she meant that I seek my own way. At the time, I thought it was a compliment. I had noticed (and valued) some goatish tendencies in her. I was just bright enough not to mention that, but I did pick it up. As it turned out, extreme goatishness was not a quality she wanted in her life.

When two people attempt to merge their lives, they run into the clashing definition problem. Because they are trying to merge lives, they run into it nearly every day. This is not hearts and flowers; this is who takes out the garbage and what movie shall we watch. That new car smell is off the vehicle after you drive it home. You are into the maintenance phase.

Perhaps one of the most toxic phrases in all of English starts with the words, "If you loved me, you'd..." And by the way, that phrase is not based on gender. It comes out of male mouths as well as female with the same dolorous effect.

Can a man and a woman live together in harmony? Or any other combination, for that matter? Possibly. It depends on the people. It depends on what those people expect of each other and what they expect of themselves. It depends on what they expect of the combination. I doubt you can either lose yourself in the combination or expect the other person to do that and have it turn out well.

When I sit at my computer, I have a lasting fondness for Microsoft Office 2007. We've been together for eleven years now. I know what to expect of it, and it does the things I want it to do pretty well. We're comfortable with each other. Microsoft stopped supporting Office 2007 last year; that means that getting things done became harder. Mostly, there's a complex conversion routine that serves no purpose I can determine, but it takes time to sweep it away. I continue to use Office 2007 anyway. Much of that comfort is that I have learned how it works and some things I must do to make it work, whether I favor them. Where Office 2007 is concerned, I've curbed my goatishness.

And that's just a computer program. The complexities of dealing with a combined life with another actual person are far more numerous and difficult. Candy and flowers go only so far. I will do something in observance of Saint Valentine—probably. But that's a temporary thing. Before and after the celebration, I will continue to take out the garbage, perhaps even on the day itself. You've got your definition of love, and I've got mine.

Old Folks

I'm a boomer. That is to say, I became air-breathing after the dual tragedies of World War II and the Depression. My parents survived those terrible times. You might expect that the times left their mark, and they did.

My parents wanted their kids to be clever enough to endure the trials they themselves did. Yet they were unwilling to see their kids go through the tribulations that provide those smarts. This is the eternal problem of parents in changing times. So they told us about their times. A lot. We kids, of course, lacking experience of any sort, could only grasp bits and snatches of what they were trying to say. That meant that any conversation that started with the words, "When I was your age . . . ," became less a teaching moment than an anesthetic.

My father was particularly eloquent on the subject. In addition to everything else, he survived an unscheduled four-month stay with the German Wehrmacht. Wehrmacht hospitality facilities for prisoners of war were never that comfortable and, at that particular time, definitely not so comfortable. His survival skills were pretty well honed, and after that experience, he examined every chunk of luck for a hook.

We the children of that era developed the attitude that those hard times of our parents would not return, and we were right. Not because we were such great prophets, but because the adults of the time were determined not to let those times come back. But my father never really believed in lasting good times—he'd had too much experience with bad ones. I would tell him that things are different now, and he would only shake his head and mumble. He was stuck in his era.

I'm a boomer, and so are many of the people in my circle. We share experiences great and small. We are all too aware of the predicament of age. One of our fellow boomers, Paul Simon, wrote rather acutely about it while we were still youthful—imagining us years from then quietly sharing park benches in our seventies.

We do not share park benches quietly today, at least not as much as we used to. We thickly populate the realm of good works and beneficial institutions instead. That's good for them, and it's good for us, too. But we are still creatures of our age and time.

We sit in fluorescently lit classrooms and conference rooms and community centers, rather than on park benches, drinking tepid, overpriced coffee from paper cups. The vendors have discovered that, if you put the same things in coffee that you used to put on ice-cream sundaes, the coffee's temperature and quality don't matter as much. We examine budgets, the foibles of our peers, and how whatever we are doing would be a tremendous success if only . . .

Occasionally, the "if only" gets around to "kids today." If only kids today were more interested in what we were doing, we'd be doing much better.

This may be followed by somebody picking apart the tastes, habits, and general state of being of kids today. The speaker will be assured of nods and embellishments by the rest at the table, possibly followed by reminiscences. Sometimes the kids today consist of everyone under the age of fifty, according to the speaker.

I remain silent. While working, I attended too many "if only" sessions where the presiding member would grumble "it is what it is" and steer the group back to more useful discussions.

Because, however it was back then, it's different now.

Because, just like we were, kids today are shaped by the context of their times. My points of reference and theirs are entirely different; they never had to live with the Kennedy and

King shootings, the war in Vietnam, and the rest of the things that created the context for our era.

I am also aware that I have no idea what that context is for kids today. I don't even know what they call themselves. We've gone through Generations X, Y, and Z, as well as the Millennials.

Have we reached actual equations yet—Generation πr^2 perhaps?

My problem is that I am stuck in my times, just like my father was. There is much going on of which I am unaware, and some of that will shape the next bunch.

And if you don't like it, well maybe you should be handing them a better place.

If you are one of those who likes to recite the tribulations of your times, rest assured that Generation πr^2 will have their own.

Having as a society removed the Soviet threat, we proceeded to turn on each other. Right now, politics seems to be handled on the basis that the other guys are mortal enemies. This promotes the agenda of the fringes who want violent solutions against mortal enemies. The attempt to keep policies in the hands of adults has had its losses. And the elders are fully participating. Some of them are leading the charge.

We are all shaped by our experiences. Sometimes they inform us, and sometimes they haunt us. They stick to us like pinesap, and each succeeding year deposits another layer. Eventually they immobilize us. We become hardened and immune to clear signals that times have moved on and some experiences don't apply to the present anymore. We become flies immersed in the amber of our own background—warm to the touch certainly and objects of some curiosity, but irrelevant to what's happening now.

And if you are younger and reading this, your turn will come, too, just as my father passed on the characteristic to me.

Boy, those old people today, huh?

Writing, Again

Shall I make Gabriela pregnant, or shall I get a haircut? I finally opted for the haircut. It's less complicated.

If you are writing a novel, you are faced with choices like this all the time. The haircut was more soothing and was probably necessary, but it doesn't get the novel written. On the other hand, there are no new words for the novel. Well, pregnancy was a bad idea anyway. The novel is supposed to be a thriller, and pregnancy shouldn't be that thrilling, at least not as a process.

When you write a novel, you are somehow playing God. You create environments, characters, and situations. Of course, they have to be exciting—or at least interesting—if you want the book to be read, but if you can only relate to exciting, that's okay. If you write your creations well, however, you start to understand that supreme beings have a messy job.

I am perhaps two-thirds of the way through mine. That means my characters are well developed, maybe too much so. I like some, I have an appreciation for others, and I invest my inner demons into a few of the rest. A famous novelist, who wrote a series of books about the same characters, once said that you get to a certain point and the characters write the book for you. That's probably overstatement. I can remember some books in that series where the characters could sue for nonsupport.

But the characters certainly do constrain you. Part of the fun is coming up with situations that your characters have to handle. Less fun is writing up a situation and feeling your characters peering over your shoulder. Sometimes they laugh and point, sometimes they snort, sometimes they just shake their head. "I would never do that," they whisper in your ear. And the worst part is that they are almost always right.

I'm not a good enough writer to include characters I don't understand. Is anyone? So I have to go into them in pretty fine detail. Sometimes, they have to come from inside me. My characters are based on my experience. Some of them are composites of people I know or knew, and some are partially me. Many of them are, even some of the less likable ones. Humans are capable and adaptable, and there have been moments where I have reacted to a situation with less than sweet reason. I channel all those times when I wished I could have had some plastic explosive handy—one of my characters has a nasty habit of blowing things up.

So you get to know your characters because they are partly people you know and partly you and maybe somebody you read about. And you bask in the glow of these magnificent beings you have created. But then you remember all those writing courses you took and books you read, and they all say the same thing: Kill your darlings.

Well, maybe. If it makes your story better, invite that guy who blows things up into a chapter. But only if it makes the story better, and then you must decide which darling to commit to the ages. It all depends on which messy disappearance will make a big impact on the plot.

Inevitably, you will run across some plot detail that you don't know anything about: history or culture or maybe psychology. A character who actually blows things up probably has different marbles than you do. Then it's time for research. Research is a little like painting. Half the time, the trick is to know when to stop; otherwise, you are going down a rabbit hole. Personally, research fascinates me. I know half the neighborhood bunnies and their burrows on a first-name basis. One of my minor characters had been in the Marxist Guatemalan rebellion of the 1990s. I researched the war extensively and justified that by writing about what I had learned. After I had penned about five pages, I remembered that my story really doesn't involve the Guatemalan civil war. Then I remembered another adage from the writing books: Your trash basket is your best friend.

All these things are solitary activities—or seem to be. But while you are busy creating your world, the one in which you actually live isn't waiting for you to complete a paragraph. Hair must be cut, groceries must be gathered, and the freight cars that block President Street must be waited out. (Now that the drawbridge will be a thing of the past, can we get an overpass for the freight yard?)

I have banded together with a small group of other writers, and we review each other's masterpieces. We live by the Golden Rule, tempered with the need to correct mistakes and gently point out everything from ant holes to caverns in plots.

I'm perfectly well aware that this is an excessive amount of time to spend on fictional beings. Is this egotism? Maybe—it certainly isn't money. My chances of winning the lottery with a single ticket are better than my chances of living off the proceeds of the novel, unless I am critically ill when I receive the check. Fame? I'll buy another lottery ticket against that chance. Recognition? We are still in the extremely unlikely range, and that's okay. There's a certain segment of the population that only recognizes authors if they are drunks, addicts, or the stout plowmen from the funny farm.

In the end, egotism doesn't work well either. The personalities that I create not only constrain the writing, they guide it. They don't write the book by any means, but they certainly guide the plots and the scenes. I guarantee you that the book you finish isn't the book you set out to write.

Fiction is really a photograph of a set of people: The shutter opens with chapter one and shuts with the last word. Like real people, fictional characters ebb and flow through your life, and like real people, you only know them for the interval that you spend with them. The difference is that you never really have to think about a character's entire life span.

Even in my unremarkable life, I have seen examples of bravery, fortitude, and humility that have stunned me. Sometimes it's been in major situations, and sometimes it's been in situations where the pain and endurance affected only one person. Human virtues, when exhibited, don't wait for earthshaking events. Maybe a part of fiction is to celebrate those virtues by stuffing them into people made of words.

Calendar Weather

I will be watching the snow fall on Miyajima for the month of February.

I only discovered that this week, when I flipped the page of the calendar. The beginning of February has been busy in the Bridgeport homestead, and I only got to the flipping of the calendar this week. The diary exists on the side of the filing cabinet by my desk and is anchored by a bent paper clip, which is fixed to the top of the filing cabinet by the weight of the printer that sits there. I suppose that having a paper calendar and a filing cabinet mark me as irretrievably out of touch, and for all I know, maybe the printer does, too. But you live in your world, and I live in mine.

February's picture is a woodcut print by Kawase Hasui. Hasui was a brilliant artist who lived mostly in the first half of the twentieth century and produced pictures for calendars, or at least that's what he got paid for. He was like Norman Rockwell, who made his living as a magazine cover artist. Both produced far greater works than their salaries. Hasui retains all the charm and interest of the medieval Japanese woodcut printers, and he adds a Western sense of perspective, incorporating the third dimension.

In this particular piece, a pine tree dominates the left side of the foreground, its needles cradling a fluffy snow. In the left middle, further back, stands a wooden shrine. It looks like one of those Japanese stone lanterns that people put in gardens, except it is about eight times bigger and sits atop a latticed pedestal that looks to be taller than most people. Dead center is the shrine itself, a red-orange gateway. Off in the distance, snow-covered mountains provide the background. The sky has darkened, and small flakes of that fluffy snow fall on the whole scene.

Hasui was particular about portraying bad weather: He could do sleet or blowing blizzards, but this is a soft snowfall. Hasui knew snow.

The shrine is located on the island of Itsukushima—whose nickname is Miyajima—just off the coast of Hiroshima. That matters because the shrine itself, that red-orange gateway, is built on tidal soil. At high tide, the only way to walk through the gate is to don scuba gear. Hasui has pictured it at this point, and it stands in the obviously chilled bay.

There must be a great story behind a shrine in the tidal flats, and there is. Part of the Shinto religion is deference to gods who rule over chunks of the environment. In the old days, the gods were considered to be as capricious and unforgiving as those in ancient Greece and with the same powers for exacting a terrible price for angering them. If you provoked Hephaestus, the Greek god of blacksmithing, you would find either a hammer or an anvil the size of the Tybee lighthouse traveling your way. The Shinto gods operated in a similar manner.

The Itsukushima Shrine was first built in the sixth century, but the current design comes from the twelfth century courtesy of the warlord Taira no Kiyomori. It was dedicated to the daughters of the storm god Susano-o no Mikoto. Miyajima, by the way, means "shrine island," and according to practice, neither birth nor death should occur on the island. The heavily pregnant and terminally feeble leave or never enter.

We don't follow animist religions here as a rule, and we tend to be patronizing about them. They seem to be part of "crude" cultures that haven't discovered the book of Revelation, 4G, or orange-level alerts. We think of them as relics of "low-performance" cultures, isolated from the rest of the world. If somebody is running around the jungle nearly naked, with the time to carve fright masks and dance ritually, we think that's an indicator of their inferiority.

But the Japanese are as cultured and well connected as we are. These are the Japanese who design and make better electronics and autos than we do and who turned trade into an art form.

The Japanese have demonstrated a particular flexibility toward religion. Somebody who knows more about Japanese culture than I do said that the Japanese tend to be more Shinto when young, Christian in the middle years, and Buddhist in old age.

I wonder if there isn't something to that. I'm not suggesting that anyone make formal changes of religions as they mature, but each of those religions have great appeal during the maturation process. For example, it seems to me that a culture that follows Shinto precepts will be a bit more careful about the environment—not because they think the god of the willows is going to whack them, but because they have a due regard for the importance of nature. The Japanese have had their environmental disasters, but far fewer than you'd think. Today, Japan has a substantial number of tourists from China who revel in the clean air that is becoming unavailable on their home turf.

If you see religion as a way of life supported by rituals, rather than just a set of rituals, the picture becomes a lot clearer. Just about every form of organized religion contains bits of wisdom that are useful in our everyday lives, and no organized religion can meet those everyday needs by itself. We each develop a set of ethics that applies to us, drawing on wisdom wherever we find it. Ethics have their basis in religion and, maybe for some of us, multiple religions.

None of that has any bearing on Hasui's woodcut, of course. In the old days, our calendar makers would usually put a picture of some South Pacific isle on the page in the hope that the image would help you weather the month. But I live in Savannah now. Here, after I get through looking at Hasui's picture, I will go outside where the jonquils bloom, the clover is already growing rapidly, and some early azaleas are in flower.

Creatives

Getting to the broadcast studio this week required a stop at the gas station. As the nozzle gurgled its way through the contents of my wallet, I wondered if entertainment was a commodity. You know, like gasoline or a dryer or a double mocha latte, half skinny. For me it is, but many other people require more from their entertainers than they do from their dryer manufacturers. We want more insight into our creatives.

I recently heard the music of a man by the name of Stanton Lanier. Mr. Lanier is almost local. He lives in Atlanta, and judging from his Web site, he is probably a Very Nice Man (and you can capitalize that). Both his music and his life are inspired by deeply held religious beliefs. He's no dummy either—he has a chemistry degree from Georgia Tech and an MBA from the University of Georgia. None of that really bears on why I play his music. I just like the music. But there are many people who would insist that those who inspire us live a blameless life.

In the past, I have played music for listeners of WRUU from other sorts of people. Reviewing the list I see drug addicts, alcoholics, suicides, and a variety from the categories of "unhappy" and "maladjusted." Some of the better composers and musicians, for example, had tremendous problems. But the music they produced touches all of us. It really doesn't matter to me. I play music—I don't pass judgment on people's lives.

When I'm not playing music, sometimes I read books. If musicians span the range of virtue from angels to degenerates, authors tend to find niches that nobody else ever envisaged. There are too many examples to bother with, and the same thing is true for painters.

This streak of perversion runs counter to our usual expectations. Most of us expect people who create to be exemplars of humanity. We have the same expectations of actors, athletes, and even politicians. They are not exemplars. They are merely a reasonably typical sample of humans. If they become successful, however, then they feel entitled (and we, in turn, often entitle them). An entitled person rarely raises the tone of his or her dealings with others. The whole point of being entitled is more focus on the self and less on others. How many notables have wound up snarling, "I'm nobody's role model"?

But creatives are a special case. In fact, the general oddity of creatives has become recognized. There are other people, and not a few of them, who expect that creatives will be defective in many ways—the better to pursue their art or music or whatever. Anyone who is creative knows that, and even in the most minor sense, creatives make it an excuse to focus their lives on themselves and their creative impulses.

This is a form of entitlement and may be worth it if the resulting literature or art or music lives on. Unfortunately, there are many creatives whose artistic vision is myopic—it doesn't extend past their noses. Artistically worthwhile or not, the people around them might not find their myopia so charming. Some creatives, for instance, are noted for their somewhat cannibalistic relationships. That can be wearing in your living room, even if it doesn't perplex the world at large.

There are people who can deal with that mindset, and they become advisers or even members of a posse, assuming the creative is successful enough to make it pay.

Everybody knows about this narcissism. What people don't know about are the creatives who are and remain perfectly nice people—or at least are able to function in society as well as the rest of us. As many psychotics and addicts as there are among creatives, there are rather pleasant creatives, too. There are actors who visit children's hospitals unaccompanied by file crews, artists who take care of disabled parents, and creatives of all sorts who go into teaching and enjoy it.

Of course, what Joni Mitchell called "the star-maker machinery" works against that grace shown by the nice creatives. The star system pampers top performers and starves the rest. A big part of that machinery is public relations. But those public relations contraptions don't work very well unless the public cares about divorces or binges or financial ruin. And the public does.

My attitude creates some problems, given that I am part of that star-maker machinery. (One of the smaller cogs, certainly...)

I play music on the radio and interview people I think deserve notice. Some of them are already visible—I played Keith Jarrett recently. If they don't want to tell me about their drug problems or innermost traumas, that's okay. I prefer it that way. I focus on the creations, not the creators.

In a little over a year on the radio, I've played close to six hundred tunes. That by itself takes a certain amount of effort. But playing music is more my taste than mining and reporting lurid stories about the composers and performers.

The only thing I know about Stanton Lanier is what I see on the Web. He put it there, so I'm sure it reflects a self-image. But whether he is worth my radio time and yours isn't in the details of his life—it's in the music he produces.

Looking ahead, I'm going to do more interviews. I've penciled in artists and teachers and musicians, many of whom are combinations of those things. In some cases, their lives include doing many neat and pretty altruistic things. But it's their creations that move me.

My Generation

A friend passed on some back issues of *The New York Review of Books*. I scarcely ever read the articles, but I like to look at the ads from the academic presses in New York. (The actual book reviews are written by intelligent people about books by other intelligent people, and they often make me feel somewhat abashed. Once I was invited to a gathering where most of the other attendees were from the African country of Gabon. "But it's okay," said the inviter. "They all speak French." I don't, so it wasn't okay, and the presumption that I did stunned me. Sometimes that's how the *Review* makes me feel.)

Anyway, I went through the pile and thoroughly enjoyed the advertisements. Academic presses fascinate me because I know what they charge for books and I know what they pay authors. There's quite a difference, and I'd love to see why. This time around, however, one of the articles caught my attention. It said, and I am quoting here: "Certain years acquire an almost numinous quality in collective memory—1789, 1861, 1914. One of the more recent additions to the list is 1968."

After a brief stop at Google (and Oxford Languages): "nu·mi·nous, *adjective*, having a strong religious or spiritual quality; indicating or suggesting the presence of a divinity."

I read on.

Why? Because, my goodness, they might be talking about *me*. I was not only alive in 1968, I had reached the age of mobility and high education, though those things had not yet affected my sense. (There are observers who will tell you that it has remained so.) Not only was I there, I was living in Washington,

D. C., at the time, which was a hub of many of the things that happened.

When you were growing up, did you imagine being at the Constitutional Convention in Philadelphia or watching the armies amass at Manassas or the Marne? This article was saying that my era was as much of a watershed.

It's a long article, with four numbered chapters. That makes perfect sense because the author, Professor Jackson Lears of Rutgers, reviewed not one book but ten. Professor Lears is a near contemporary, so many of his insights are informed by actual experience as well as the printed word.

It's also a good article, with many clever observations, and I'd love to chat with Professor Lears sometime. But at the bottom line, a book review is supposed to answer the question of whether I should buy a given book. In this case, the aggregate cost of the ten books shot over $300, and I'm opting against their purchase. I did mention the price of academic books.

But it's odd, finding an article on books that examines the time when you were alive. The narrative looks like an account of the Treaty of Ghent or the Third Crusade. Wait a minute—stop the autopsy. I'm not dead yet. I'm an eyewitness to some of what happened, and I'm not sure the article has it all right. The generalizations about the era seem misplaced.

I have no doubt that the ten authors did their research and writing. One of the authors wrote about urban guerrillas in Cleveland, and aside from the airport, Cleveland and I never met. But the article tries to capture the mind of the generation, and those characterizations don't come close to encompassing everybody.

I didn't think or act the way that some of the authors depict. That may be because the authors are attracted by more radical views that may or may not lead to mayhem of various sorts. I am not. In the midst of everything that went on, my activities weren't worth a footnote.

Professor Lears rightly notes the transition from the idea that the country could do anything with the proper insight to the idea that the country was a barrier but the individual could do anything. That was a pretty radical change, and it resulted in some of the narcissism that showed up a generation or two later. In the movie *The Big Lebowski*, a taxi radio starts playing a song by The Eagles, and the hero growls that he hates The Eagles. I don't agree, but The Eagles' music returns to individual self-absorption. The music of the years before The Eagles covered communal self-absorption. For an old radical like Lebowski, that was a bitter turn.

Professor Lears returns to that concept of "numinous" a number of times, the notion of a religious or spiritual quality pervading life. I'm not sure about the religious angle. Religions are far better organized than that time's mindset respected. People in those years had become suspicious of organization, any form of organization. But a spiritual quality, certainly.

Preceding years didn't have that spirituality because people were devoted to group efforts, mostly initiated by the government: to go into the Peace Corps, to go to the moon, to promote and improve civil rights where there were none. But in 1968, the government was involved in enterprises that were both dubious in spirit and flawed in execution. That was obvious to some in the beginning and, by 1968, painfully obvious to many. People fell back on their own resources, the things they could manage themselves, and the focus became individual.

The study of 1968, or any other year, is useful if it teaches us something. Otherwise, books and studies become cheap drama, a sort of gratuitous peep show. If 1968 is the equivalent of 1861, I wonder if future generations will hold reenactments of, say, the battles in Chicago outside the Democratic National Convention. I'll guess that won't happen.

So what did we learn? We learned that governments, even ours, indulge in ideas that we personally think are unsupportable. We learned that governments execute flawed plans, sometimes merely to justify their commitment to the bad idea. And how many times has a bad idea, poorly executed, resulted in something beneficial? Has it ever?

The year 1968 and those that followed taught us lessons about dealing with a national administration that is fundamentally adversarial to the things we believe and acts in ways that do not reflect the history or mindset of the country. And when those years had passed, we hoped that we'd never have to use that knowledge again.

But no life is without disappointments.

Divination

Stockbrokers, weather forecasters, economists, and analysts of all sorts—we spend immense amounts of money, attention, and effort on them to try to predict the future. It's a big business. We do it even on a personal level. Two of the more personal ones appeared this week: One was the turn of the Chinese New Year, with the astrology that accompanies it. The other was a prediction, based on the reading of the Bible, that the East Coast would be flattened by a tidal wave.

Someone who knows more about astrology than I do tells me that astrology is not about divination but about possibilities, forces within people, especially those affected by universal elements and events. But the astrological sources I referenced seemed to place a lot of emphasis on divination.

On February 5, according to the Chinese lunar calendar, we entered the Year of the Pig. The pig is the last zodiacal animal before the cycle starts again. The legend is that the Jade Emperor decided that each animal would take its place according to when it arrived at his party. The pig overslept and so was given the last slot.

But divination is more complicated than that. The animal sign combines with other elements so people can differentiate each pig year. The year 2019 is the Year of the Female Earth Pig. In this case, the dominant environmental element is yin earth. The sign indicates farmland next to a river, bringing water into the equation. As a matter of fact, water is a strong element, and therefore this will be the year of the muddy pig. There is the danger of too much water on the flatland, with the possibility of property loss.

That's not an uplifting prediction here in Savannah. Much of our land is not only flat, it's rather concave and full of marsh grass and the assorted animals and insects that go along with that. Many of them are uncomfortable neighbors—we really don't feel like inviting them in.

This sounds rather dire, but many predict this year will be dire. A neighbor of mine, well versed in another set of rather more Western beliefs, has been predicting a tsunami in April. I don't know that Savannah has a normal tsunami month, but April wouldn't be my first guess. Just in case, stock up on waders now. The National Weather Service says March will bring a deep Arctic invasion of the United States, with temperatures in some places forty degrees below normal. Maybe get a parka to wear over your waders.

But getting back to the Chinese zodiac, the trend I just reported is an overall general one, as seen from an altitude of twenty thousand feet. What it may mean for you personally depends on what year you were born. I hit the air in the Year of the Dog, so I need to parse the reading for the year with my birth year.

Fortunately, the ancient arts are well covered by the Internet. Being modern, we can get loads of information without crossing anybody's palm with coins or bills or anything else. But like everything else on the 'Net, there's a certain amount of information overload as well as misinformation—and that leads to confusion, if not outright contradiction.

One seer whom I consulted predicts that it will be a perfectly spiffy year, to include riches and reaching career goals. That sounds a lot more hopeful than running into a fifty-foot wave on the way to pick up the dry cleaning, but I have my doubts. My career goal was to stop having one, and I achieved that a few years back. Careers tend to be labor-intensive, and my interest in having a career nowadays is somewhat minimal. I have no complaints about the one I had, especially now that it's over, but that doesn't mean I want it back. So that prediction is overtaken by my lack of concern about goals with regard to careers.

Another tells me that Years of the Pig are when pleasure and the avoidance of conventions come together. In my younger days, that would have had great effect on my morale. Now I think it means napping more and shaving less. But again, I started that some time back. This soothsayer also instructs that this is a good year for investments and for keeping an eye on my lymphatic system. (If I were to act as I once did, I can readily understand that. However, I don't think that more naps and less shaving will overtax my "lymphs.") This month and next month will be perfectly dandy, but the month after is unlucky, and that starts on April 5. That would include tax day and, of course, the impending tsunami.

But wait . . . birth years have elements, too, and I am a Fire Dog. Fire Dogs must avoid fatigue this year. I try to do that, heaven knows, but I am on fatigue's regular route these days.

I consulted many other sites, and they either confirmed these findings or contradicted them. But they all tell me that dogs are skeptical, so maybe I'm just not seeing what is in plain sight. We'll see. That's a very dog thing to do.

I tried to look up the tsunami prediction and didn't get very far. It's based on a manipulation of Bible readings, somewhat predictably Isaiah. The BBC did a report on it some months back. It requires a volcano in the Canary Islands to explode and fall into the ocean. This creates a mega-tsunami, with water hitting the United States anywhere between thirty and three hundred feet high. One source says it will come as far inland as Richmond, Virginia. The most pessimistic site had some information I couldn't access, because a pop-up blocked the article with the offer to be anointed. As my parents tell the story, I already had that box checked many years back upon baptism, so I gave up on reading further.

This is a rather offhand approach to disasters, but risks are always with us. For many years, I lived in the Washington, D. C., area when the cold war was ongoing. My particular place was in suburban Virginia, not that far from the Pentagon. Had the cold war become hot, I would have been one of the first to have my incinerated atoms hurtling into the upper atmosphere. Had I been at home rather than in my various workplaces, it might have taken a few more seconds until it was "game over."

I lived in that area at the turn of the twenty-first century. Some of my neighbors were positive that the year 2000 would turn every computer malevolent, and hordes of the hungry and desperate would invade our vicinity. One couple in particular stocked up on survivalist gear and muttered darkly about nobody trying to visit them on January 1. I didn't see them much after that, save for the garage sale they had on camping equipment in February.

I will give all this divination data due consideration. On the offhand chance that the volcano in the Canaries stays where it is, I'll start preparing taxes—and I'll think twice before doing anything that will agitate my lymph nodes.

And as far as it being the Year of the Pig, well, anyone who reads the newspapers could have told you that.

Spring 2019

The marsh in spring

Purebred

The North Sea comes to mind today. That's the body of water that washes onto northern Britain, the Low Countries, Germany, and Scandinavia. As seas go, it is sullen at best and unapproachable at worst, rather manic-depressive in maritime psychology. But fish like it, and that makes all the difference.

From what we know, the earliest settlers filtered into the north as the ice cover retreated. They discovered that the growing season was short and the winter long. Keeping yourself fed could be a problem. That's where the North Sea enters into the equation. Despite its psychological problems, the North Sea had fish, and it didn't ice over, like fresh water or even the Baltic Sea. It didn't take settlers long to start floating around the edges of the North Sea.

Over time, humanity advanced—that is to say, it became more organized, and it built better floaters, things that might survive the unstable nature of the seawaters. Humans started to make intentional voyages to trade, perhaps to conquer, or maybe just to find bigger fish. Whatever the reason, people began to float around the North Sea fairly consistently. In any group, there are always those who decide they can get a better deal somewhere else, and sometimes they're right.

Humanity may have advanced, but the North Sea has stayed pretty much the same as it's always been: a violently changing and capricious puddle. Intentional voyages sometimes didn't allow for the moods of the sea. People who wanted to go to Denmark could wind up in Scotland if the sea decided to act up and if they didn't sink to the bottom.

Every area around the sea, whatever the population, was blended with a strong admixture of somebody else's people, because they traded there or because they were looking for a new home or because that's where the North Sea decided they would go.

If the North Sea decides you should go west around the north end of Scotland and then south, you end up in the Irish Sea. The Irish Sea is perhaps a younger brother of the North Sea. It has the same basic attitude, with less room to avoid shoals and rocks. I spent one of the worst nights of my life on the Irish Sea, on a ship that looked both large and stable at the dock. On a very rough night, it seemed neither.

The populations around the North Sea became more organized to the point where they decided they could comfortably distinguish between homeboys and outsiders—us and them. This distinction was, well, bogus and continues to be for any population in and around the North Sea (or any other sea, for that matter). Homeboys used things like language and religion to make the distinction, and the taste for conquest remained alive and well in some.

Which brings me to today...today is Saint Patrick's Day. Saint Patrick grew up somewhere in Roman or post-Roman Britain and was captured by Irish slavers. After a spell as an animal herder, he somehow returned to Britain and took Holy

Orders. He sailed again to Ireland in due course and made his mark, to put it mildly.

We think of the Irish as Celts, many with bright red hair. But the ethnographers tell us that Celts were dark-haired. And the Celtic culture seems to have arisen on mainland Europe in a broad swath from Austria to France. Ethnographers have been fighting over where the red hair came from for years—the best guess is that it stems from Pictish invaders from Scotland. You can also find native redheads in North Africa, Kazakhstan, and among the Ashkenazi Jews. Apparently, there are advantages in pale skin and red hair in colder climates. Some scholars have even stated that the Neanderthals were redheads. Immigrants—every last one of them.

Despite these diverse origins, the Irish, like everyone else, have developed their own culture and sense of civilization. We celebrate that on Saint Patrick's Day, too. Furthermore, the Irish have not only received immigrants, they have been hardy travelers as well. There are people who will tell you that Saint Columba's monks visited the New World in oxhide boats well before the Vikings drifted into Nova Scotia.

The Bridgeports, as far as we know, arose a bit farther north and east than the North Sea. But because they came from one of those North Sea countries, we suspect that there's a healthy amalgam of people from other places, at one time or another. On my mother's side, there is a dollop of Irish, and that dollop is mostly from the west, somewhere around Galway. But even in Galway there was diversity. Religion was a sharply defining characteristic in that area: There were Galway Catholics and Galway Protestants. The Bridgeports came from both of these traditions. In a younger day, I chatted with some of the immigrant relations, all of whom seemed relieved to have left that conflict across the water.

So the Irish, who were themselves great immigrants, absorbed immigrants from a lot of other places before they became immigrants.

Some people look at Saint Patrick's Day celebrations like Savannah's and call them commercial and inauthentic. Sorry—these celebrations are very authentic. The people who swirled around the northern seas brought many different things with them, but the one thing they all understood and cherished was beer. Beer was the one thing everyone could agree on. In celebration of the Irish, have a glass on this day. And don't for a minute think you aren't entitled because you don't believe you are Irish. You may be more entitled than you know.

Surviving Saint Patrick's Day

Spring is not the time for complicated thinking; it's the time to feel the sun on your face. So I'm just going to talk about a variety of things.

We are in the middle of the sweet season in Savannah. It comes here earlier than in most parts of the country. The temperatures are pleasant for most of the day, and plants are starting to grow again. The ancient Romans had a festival for these days—they called it Lupercalia. They sacrificed small animals in the hope for health and fertility. Here, we call it Saint Patrick's Day, and we sacrifice beer.

Down at the Chippewa Square art gallery, we artists emerged from St. Patrick's Day with a busted window, which is irritating, but there was much less volume of trash in the square than last year, and that's good news. With the trash gone, the square is very appealing.

But many other places have appeal, too. The azaleas are in full bloom everywhere, and the flowering trees, usually white, contrast nicely with the electric colors of the azalea blossoms. Out by Rancho Bridgeport, the marshes are starting to green, and the normally scruffy-looking bushes have some brilliant blooms. The azalea bush out front of our rancho has one branch that extends about two feet above the rest, and I have been meaning to trim it back. But now it has some flashy violet florets, and I can't bring myself to do it. Small white and yellow flowers grow in some of the lawns, and many of my neighbors will not mow until they are through blooming or another excuse arises.

It would be foolish not to take a day off in the sweet season, and I am going to do that next week. The Metropolitan Opera, you see, is staging Wagner's *Ring Cycle* this year. Three of those operas are long, even for opera. Next week, the Met is doing *Die Walküre*, which is the story of an all-powerful god with nine teenage daughters and a wife with strong moral values. As you may imagine, complications ensue, and they take some time to explain and resolve. Even if the characters don't dawdle, those explanations and resolutions will consume all but about ten minutes of my radio time, so I will feed the dog earlier and abandon the studio. The Met will complete the *Ring Cycle* in April, and we will need to make schedule adjustments on those weeks, too.

Speaking of agendas, I see where the voters of Skidaway Island decided against incorporating as a city and did so by a wide margin. That appears to be a wise decision. I don't live on Skidaway, so I don't have a horse in that race. Perhaps cities should enter life the way newly minted graduates must—the first requirement is that they pay their own way.

Skidaway's primary tax base is residential and small commercial, and the costs of another layer of government will fall on them. Since many of the Skidaway residents live in The Landings, already subject to communal fees, the extra burden might not be worth the cost. Tybee has made it work, but Tybee has the beach, which draws nonresident dollars into the community.

Lastly, Brian Renner is one of those people who manages to run things well and be nice about it, a trick I never learned. Brian and I have been talking about music, and I've contributed a tune or two to his *Beyond the Liner Notes* show on Fridays. He's asked me to cohost the show, and I've accepted. Brian plays a wide variety of music, so I get the opportunity to be noisy, which I enjoy. I'm not sure that we'll ever get to the "Baby Shark" song, but we'll go beyond the contemplative playlists of *When the Moon Sings*.

So now I cohost *Behind the Liner Notes* with Brian and *Listening to Literature* with Leigh E. Rich. WRUU lets me run the board myself on *When the Moon Sings*.

Thank you, WRUU. I'm having fun.

Wagner and Clare

Next week, if you tune in to WRUU, Siegfried—having dissed Wotan in act 2—will be treading through the ring of fire to find Brünnhilde asleep on the rock and wake her by kissing her. Don't let that ring of fire confuse you—this is Richard Wagner, not Johnny Cash. Anyway, Brünnhilde will renounce the world of the gods (remember she is Wotan's little girl), and the two of them will wander off hailing "light-bringing love and laughing death," and that's a quote.

So with that lengthy Wagner opera from the Met, *When the Moon Sings* will start a half-hour later next week—after somebody from Buildings and Grounds certifies that the ring of fire is indeed extinguished. The maintenance staff also must give the floor a quick mop because ashes can be slippery.

In wondering if we could get in on that "light-bringing love and laughing death," I talked to the program's Philosophy and Life Enhancement Division. They told me that we'd find it hard to associate ourselves with that thesis. I see what they mean. So please, if you are in the mood for light-bringing love and/or laughing death, tune in earlier. We here at *When the Moon Sings* mistrust the wattage of love and the giggles of death.

Turning to watts of love, Sidney Clare was an American lyricist. He wrote "On the Good Ship Lollipop" and "Ma, He's Making Eyes at Me," among others. But his most enduring lyric was "Please Don't Talk About Me When I'm Gone." He's right—it's impolite. So tonight my thoughts turn to azalea blooms. They are still here, but they are starting to fade, and next week may be too late to talk about them.

They are starting to fold up and go away, these azalea blooms, even if the bushes themselves stay around all year. Azaleas are useful plants here in coastal Georgia. They shrug off the humid heat, they tolerate the nutrient-poor soil, and they grow quite happily in shade. They require next to no care, and unlike many of the other plants that share those characteristics, they won't try to eat your garden or your house.

Azaleas are practical plants. They grow calmly, spread slowly, and generally try to be pleasant—or at least civil. They are the green equivalent of Canadians, I suppose, at least in reputation. About the only real problem is that troublemakers sneak in beneath their cover. If you have a reasonably large plant, you must watch for sprouting Virginia creeper or smilax.

Isn't that just the way? You find something stable and useful that solves problems, and the next thing you know, all sorts of sneaky things are going on underneath. It's like the stock market or cable TV. But you expect that from people, not plants. Maybe plants are just rudimentary people.

So we have our useful, stable, predictable azaleas. Thorstein Veblen said that "thrift, which is nearly inseparable from the cow, is a standing objection to the decorative use of the animal." Most of the year, azaleas seem a little bovine, but not now. At the first sign of spring, they dress for Las Vegas. Azalea blooms are electric and high wattage in color. It's hard to think of an electric white, but azaleas meet the description. If they glowed at night, Savannah might be Las Vegas.

Azaleas grow together. Oh, there's certainly some pushing and shoving, but two plants can be right next to each other and grow without strangling their neighbor. Wisteria vines from the same plant will try very hard to strangle whatever is in their reach, but azaleas don't work that way. That means you can have brilliant pink right beside high-voltage puce or any other color you want. And all the colors seem to match up well.

So far I haven't told you anything you don't know. But maybe you didn't know that azaleas can be lethal. Develop the habit of chewing on the leaves and you may "off" yourself. Azalea pollen, stems, and leaves contain a neurotoxin that causes various symptoms, none of which is recommended by the program's Philosophy and Life Enhancement Division. Symptoms include diarrhea, perspiration, dizziness, changes in consciousness, passing out, double as well as blurred vision, hypotension, and bradycardia. I had to look up bradycardia—that's a slow heartbeat, but anything with "-cardia" on the end of it is something you don't want to mess with.

As a matter of fact, if you eat honey produced by bees that have been hanging around azaleas, the honey will have the same neurotoxin, with the same results. In Turkey, they call it "mad honey." Pliny, the elder one, tells us that an army invading Turkey was defeated because they ate mad honey. Some people in Turkey produce mad honey intentionally because they think it enhances sex. I'm not sure how diarrhea and passing out would enhance sex, but that's just me.

Azalea blooms start in coastal Georgia, but you can follow them up to Augusta where they will be at their height for the Masters golf tournament. If you want to be rabid about the whole thing, you can pursue the blooms both north and west as the weather warms. They have azalea festivals in New Jersey, Texas, Oklahoma, Missouri, and even Oregon—and probably many places in between here and there. There is supposed to be quite a nice one in Muskogee, Oklahoma, which may be why the "Okie From Muskogee" in that song didn't smoke marijuana. He had a jar of that honey in the toolbox of his pickup.

Azaleas grow all over the world. Many species are Asian, but some are native to North America. They do grow in Germany, and maybe when Wagner wrote about "light-bringing love and laughing death" it was spring and the blooms were in season. Maybe he fixed himself a nice hot cup of tea and put some local honey in it. That would explain many things.

First Beach Day

Savannah has reached the point in the year where weather prediction is nearly impossible. Unlike much of the East Coast, we have no mountains to funnel the fronts from the southwest to the northeast. Sometimes weather comes that way, but sometimes it comes from due south, from the north, from the southeast, and so on. Later in the year, the Bermuda high will establish itself, and the variation becomes much smaller. Most days, it will be too hot and too humid, and some days, it will be rainy, too hot, and too humid.

My parents spent the end of their lives in southwest Florida. We would watch the thunderstorms rise over the tomato fields, consolidate, and then move off. Some of those storms stop over Savannah on their way up I-95. But that's for later. Right now, we have had a week of brilliant sunshine, cloudy sunshine, a monsoon with a tornado watch, and stiff gales from the southeast that swirl when you least want them to.

On the warmer and sunnier days, I feel the beach call to me. Maybe it's the sea that calls, but I am much too maladroit to actually sail it. This is not a prediction: I have, over the years, proven my incapacity to sail with a number of spectacular and probably comedic incidents. They were without fatalities, or they have been so far. (It's like electrical work around the house—there are some things that you just don't want to mess with.) I have seen waterspouts come toward my boat, calm days turn agitated at a moment's notice, and unexpected waves slop over gunwales that are supposed to prevent that. My impulse was to hide in the cabin, and in each case, there was a resolute captain in charge who allowed me to do just that.

I may be a resident of the marshes, but I am without any particular desire to wander out into them. Marshes generally don't have a cabin to hide in.

But the beach . . . that's a different thing.

Today, the beach is windy, with a northeast breeze that creates whitecaps far out to sea. The sun is bright, and unprotected skin bears watching. The breeze lulls you into a sense of security that the sun ambushes. The temperature is somewhere in the low seventies, another luller. Another twenty degrees, and you'd automatically slather on whatever mixture of 10W-30 and coconut grease the drugstore had at discount. If you turn the color of corned beef, you've left it undone for too long.

Lunch is at the grill on the other side of the parking lot. This is a salad day. If I go too long without salads, there are consequences. The northeast breeze blows bits of salad off my plate. I can deal with it.

A flight of pelicans soars slowly overhead into the wind. This time of year, the pelican flights are more populous. Perhaps these are migrators, the ones heading north for the summer. They won't make much headway today. Flying into the current they barely move at all.

Beneath them, the palm trees around the grill shiver with the airflow. The grill usually attracts pirate birds, which are rusty-looking, crow-like creatures. They perch on the umbrella tops and swoop down to steal unattended food, especially the sweet potato fries with molasses. I understand that they are a sort of grackle, not that it makes any difference. They could be finches or hummingbirds or East Coast condors. They are still pirate birds. They are absent today, but they don't care for greens anyway, so I would be safe.

I hit the grill early, and by the time I am ready leave, people are waiting for tables. Lunch is late for many of the folks around here, so I go in advance. I do not come here for the press of humanity.

At this time, press they do. It is time for me to be somewhere else.

The beach has changed over the winter. The northern end is blocked off. Tybee is building the future home of something or other; I haven't gotten close enough to the sign to discover what. Whatever it is, it requires a forest of large cement posts. A parking garage, maybe?

On another visit, I will probably sulk about that—it barricades the part of the sand I like most. I can't go to the trouble to sulk today.

I check my skin under the bird-free umbrella. It is the color of potted meat product, an improvement without discomfort. Summer is still ahead.

I do take a few photos. The surf is breaking in odd sweeps today. The images probably can't capture that, but electrons are low-cost compared to film. Sometimes low-percentage shots work out. But this is not a photo expedition. A photo expedition is when I get up before the alligators or the sun. Sunrise can be spectacular, but the colors and textures often come out before then. People don't usually arrive until later.

Men are supposed to be resolute. There are cattlemen, rocket men, and, of course, seamen. Each of these goes out into the unknown and experiences the wonder and danger of those environments. Lacking the skills and training of these notables, I am a beach man. My bravery extends only as far as pirate birds and stiff northeast breezes.

So, yes, right now I am a beach man with skin the hue of potted meat product. Later in the year, when the Bermuda high establishes itself, I will turn into an air-conditioning man, with a habit of hibernating until the sun touches one horizon or another. But to find me now, it would be best to look under the blue and white striped umbrella.

Yet there is something about the seaside that appeals to me when I can see it in a more or less natural state. The same is true of the marshlands. You can see some beautiful and amazing things there, and you can do it from a ringside seat. We will be a sadder people if we lose that.

Lannisterism

Does art imitate life, or does life imitate art? I know a fair number of artists, and there's no particular agreement even among them. Landscapers and portraitists seem to favor the former; more abstract types may prefer the power of the mind over the real.

The answer is, of course, that it depends. "It depends" is the answer to almost every question. The minute you try to summarize or generalize a situation, you are leaving out circumstances that may be critical to the individual situation. It's true in business, law, romance, and everything else we try to do. If you have ever been a teenage boy wondering what girls like, that's the right answer. Unhelpful as it seems, it's the only real answer available. Any other answer is a counter-generalization. Generalizations regarding half of humanity have exceptions, and not a few of them.

As I write this, a number of my friends—real and electronic—are hyperventilating over the latest episode of *Game of Thrones.* (One of these friends has set aside the voyages of the starship *Enterprise,* at least temporarily, and that's after two decades of absorption). In the latest televised installment of

Thrones, there was a battle, and a very confused battle it was. Some viewers have complained about muddy lighting and jerky photography. We who understand battles through remote electronic viewing expect a battle to be crisp and well-focused. Sorry, real battles are confused and sans sharp imaging. The survivors of D-Day tell very different stories, depending on where they were. A massive number of soldiers over a large field are going to have different experiences, and weapons throw up dirt and confusion. The professionals call this the fog of battle. Sharp pictures and cohesive stories aren't usually available until well after the conflict.

For those of us who don't follow the *Thrones* series, it is based on George R. R. Martin's novels and involves a mythical kingdom where several noble families contend for the crown. None of these people are running postindustrial democracies, so they grab for the crown in pretty medieval fashion. From a philosophical standpoint, the contenders and their supporters would be considered mostly morally compromised. They push the envelope even by medieval standards.

Several incidents are drawn from reality, such as "The Red Wedding" episode in which a wedding is an excuse for a massacre. That episode is based on a few events in Scottish history. So, sometimes, art imitates life. The episodes where a dragon incinerates an army or the zombie army comes calling are probably less factual. But even when drawn from history, this is entertainment, so these people are doggedly nasty all the time. Even in medieval days, nobody was that bad all the time, not even the Borgias or the Medicis who had a reputation for being mean and nasty. "The Red Wedding" is partly based on the seventeenth-century Glencoe Massacre, which was considered poor form even then.

According to a reliable source, there have been 2,339 deaths in *Thrones* over seven seasons. True, that number includes random bears, wolves, and dragons, but not that many. Many of the humanoids killed come back as a version of zombie—which does very little to elevate their moral character, although it does require them to be killed again. Also true, one major character came back as a non-zombie. But we just began season eight, and the death toll has already risen.

Now, art imitating life is okay for most people, though art that dwells on the seamier aspects of humanity usually has a smaller audience. On the other hand, some people, mostly moralists, get agitated when they think life may imitate art. They see moral decay in video games, on the 'Net, in cap pistols, and in situation comedies. Faced with the inevitability of adults watching this stuff, they plead with us to shield our precious children—many of whom act like the objectionable material and worse—from witnessing this moral decay.

I'm no moralist, generally. I think children see and process more moral decay than their well-meaning parents are aware of—and most often from those very same parents. Life tends to be something other than antiseptic. Our times have seen the utter failure of great moral crusades from Prohibition to the War on Drugs.

Forbidding entertainments to children is an easy fix, because it doesn't affect the adults who advocate for such amusements. But I cannot see how making *Game of Thrones* an adult-only pleasure would accomplish anything. I have noticed that the general character of the country's politics has taken a plunge in the years that *Game of Thrones* has aired. I wonder if the current crop of pols see themselves as Lannisters or Starks or Boltons. They are certainly acting like it, figuratively. Some of their followers have gotten more than figurative—the synagogue in Pittsburgh, the church in Charleston, and now the synagogue in California. In short, I am not concerned about the effect of the show on children, but it seems to have had a sad effect on adults. I wonder if we should make the show children-only and forbid adults to see it, or at least plead with our supposed leaders to stop acting like children.

But, no—moral crusades have failure in their DNA. People will start selling episodes on the street corner. Lawless elements will charge premium prices for a view of the "Loot Train Attack," and addicts will pay them. Pirated copies will flood the country from foreign lands. We will catch and jail the street hustlers, and the episode kingpins will remain free.

So does art imitate life or does life imitate art? I think it's cyclical—they nourish each other, for better or worse. Are the current politicians a symptom of *Game of Thrones* or a cause? Well, maybe both. It all depends.

Screwup

Casa Bridgeport is, as I have mentioned before, on the islands. It is not one of those places along the edges with deepwater access, eight bedrooms, and eight baths. It is inland, among tall pines and all the noxious vines that grow up their trunks and random insects that shelter underneath. The Bridgeports do not have the burden of overcapitalization.

I left Casa Bridgeport for the radio studio at a bit after four o'clock last Saturday afternoon. I drove through wind and rain and got there with more than ample time. Just before the program started, a tornado warning came across the Emergency Broadcast System, and I mentioned it on air straightaway.

After the show, I went home and found that the cable was off. Usually that doesn't bother me, but when it came back on, I learned that a tornado had touched down. It hit the Savannah Yacht Club, proceeded up Johnny Mercer (a route I use every day), tore apart the detailing operation in the parking lot of the garage I use, ripped part of the roof from the Goodwill in the shopping center that sees me at least twice a week, and blew itself out in the empty lot where the feral cats live.

All of that is part of island living. Tornados happen here, and this won't be the last. Everybody knows that. So we have a system to warn people when these little weather events happen. And this was a little event—the winds in the tornado only managed a little more than one hundred miles per hour, and the funnel that hit the ground wasn't exactly huge.

So here's the problem . . . the system didn't work. Oh, the Emergency Broadcast System worked, and if you happened to be watching TV or listening to the radio, you knew about it. But the sirens didn't sound. So unless you were plugged in electronically, you didn't know about it. And if the power had been cut, you wouldn't have known about it.

Things always break down at the worst times, right?

Except, when the investigators looked into it, they found that the computer server that triggers the siren was down—for scheduled maintenance. It was down for scheduled maintenance, folks. It wasn't broken; it was just off-line.

It was off-line for our little tornado. If the tornado had been the size of the ones in Oklahoma, the server would still have been off-line. If the tidal wave the seers had predicted for April had come just then, the server would still be off-line. If somebody had launched missiles to incinerate Savannah as a warning against America's weird international posturing, nope, nada, nix. No sirens. No warning. Because the server was off-line. When people learned that the server was off-line, the first thing they did was get mad at the National Weather Service. But I worked with the Weather Service a few times and saw dedicated, intelligent people trying to do a mainly thankless job. So I didn't get mad at them.

But this, this is a screwup, and it needs to be fixed. And it won't take that much to fix it.

If you've worked with computers, you know that systems that have to run twenty-four seven need maintenance just like any other system. A long time ago, computer engineers figured out that backups—servers that take over when the main server is down—provide coverage. I can go online and get a thoroughly capable server for three thousand bucks. I understand that the National Weather Service isn't exactly overcapitalized either, not in today's political climate, but it's a $3,000 fix. And that's only if your engineers can't figure out how to switch the siren functionality to another server that's up and running, which they probably can.

When I left the house, Ms. Hampden was asleep in her chair, and the dog Stink was dozing in the living room. When I got back home, they were where I'd left them. I'd like to think the sirens would have given them a chance to crawl into a closet or something to survive a tornado that was close to my home.

But the sirens never sounded. And they wouldn't have sounded even if this had been a great big thing. Because a computer server was down for maintenance.

C'mon, guys.

This is a screwup.

Fix it.

Obituaries

One of the habits of retired people is watching which players leave the stage.

That's because they mean something to us. The younger me didn't pay much attention to that because the people leaving the earth really didn't mean anything. There might have been some vague sadness, and maybe for a family member more than that, but we really couldn't connect departing with anything we knew. It's different now.

This week, at the age of ninety-seven years, Doris Day passed away. Through the 1950s and into the 1960s, Doris Day was America's sweetheart, a movie star who oozed sweetness and goodness. Then, all of a sudden, she wasn't. It wasn't anything she did. People just started to listen to bands that featured guys in beards playing bongos. The world had become more sophisticated, and the Eisenhower era fairy tales didn't sell anymore. I once listened to a hip radio DJ become a little unbalanced because his station had contracted with a studio to plug a Doris Day movie. I don't know whether she kept up with the times, but her scriptwriters surely didn't.

Doris Day's life, of course, didn't follow her movie scripts. One of her managers swindled her out of millions of dollars. With the help of her son, savvy in these things, she got some of that back, but nowhere close to all of it. The periodicals in the grocery stores and pharmacies printed unflattering pictures and swore she was destitute. She wasn't.

According to a marginally reliable source, Doris Day's net worth at the time of her death was in the hundreds of millions of dollars. She devoted much of retirement life to animal welfare. I think that's kind of neat.

Also this week, I. M. Pei left the stage, at age 102. Mr. Pei was a brilliant architect. When Savannah gets around to constructing buildings that look postcolonial, the architect in charge will probably be influenced by Mr. Pei's ideas.

If you've been to Washington, D. C., the East Building of the National Gallery of Art is his work, and so is the renovation of the Louvre in Paris. I know the East Building well. It is at once a stunning structure to behold and a glorious place to display art. There are intimate spaces for showings of smaller works, and there are grand spaces for bigger things. The East Building devotes itself to modern art, much of which is outsized. The gallery handles large works beautifully.

Mr. Pei did many other things as well. In our near-neighbor town of Augusta, he designed the Chamber of Commerce building, Bicentennial Park, and the James Brown Arena. He designed Mesa Laboratory in Colorado and the John F. Kennedy Library in Boston.

Pei's designs also helped several cities revitalize their downtowns. Unlike many architects of his time, he worked to make his buildings fit with the surrounding landscape. Each building is a creation of the function of the building allied with the area surrounding it. Frank Lloyd Wright established a school of thought similar in mindset; his buildings reflect acknowledgment and integration with the encompassing environments. So, too, I. M. Pei tailored each of his building to its location. There won't be knockoffs of Pei's work, or if they are, well, they'll look cheap and derivative.

According to another semi-reliable source, Mr. Pei's estate was in the neighborhood of $150 million.

Tim Conway also passed away this week. He came to our attention in *McHale's Navy*, which was a fairly standard military service TV comedy of the early sixties. He did a number of other, more forgettable series after that but came back to stardom when he joined *The Carol Burnett Show*. Carol Burnett gave Conway the latitude to improvise. He did so brilliantly, and the video sites on the 'Net are full of films of his comedic antics producing spontaneous laughter from other cast members, especially Harvey Korman, and causing them to divert from script. The films are still funny. If you are curious, search for the "Elephant Story."

In his later years, Tim Conway developed a range of health problems and required much medical attention. Still, his worth at the time of his death was around $15 million.

And then ... if you tried to use Route 80 today coming off the islands at about eleven o'clock in the morning, you were stopped cold at Skidaway Road. That was for the funeral cortege of Kelvin Ansari. After a long stretch in the military, Kelvin Ansari joined the Savannah Police Department. The other night, somebody robbed a patron coming out of a barbershop on Bull Street. Sergeant Ansari answered the call. The suspect was supposed to have left the area. He hadn't. He jumped out of a car blasting away. He killed Kelvin Ansari and wounded another officer.

Kelvin Ansari was much younger than the other people I have mentioned, and while I don't know anything about his financial affairs, I'm fairly sure he didn't leave millions. In fact, there are a few organizations, one being the police department, accepting money to help his family.

In their own ways, Doris Day, I. M. Pei, and Tim Conway tried to keep us entertained. Sergeant Ansari tried to keep us safe.

I am used to seeing injustices. After all this time, I know something about the way the world works. But when I look at those financial statements, something still bothers me.

Does it bother you?

Transportation Choices

This week concluded May, and that's fine with me. May is supposed to be a milder month, even in Savannah. It's the end of the social season before the weather becomes a convection oven. Well, all the events over the last two weeks might as well have taken place in August. People put on their finery and opened the door. There was the weather, like a long-lost relative, one you'd intentionally misplaced, bellowing "Guess who?" and making the other guests uncomfortable. We've hit one hundred degrees or more the last four days, and the forecasters are optimistically predicting the high nineties for the rest of the week... just like they did for the last four days.

Savannah took the horses off the street this week. In Savannah, one of the pleasures is taking a horse-drawn carriage ride around downtown. Well, not right now. The alternative? Enter the pedicabs. I understand being cycled around by a sweaty, grunting SCAD postgraduate isn't the same thing as enjoying a ride in a horse-drawn carriage, but the licensing people make sure that none of the pedicab drivers has a permanent fur covering. There are many other ways to get around, including a ghost tour where you ride in an air-conditioned hearse.

In this weather, dogs, like horses, should be left in the shade to drowse. That assumes, of course, that they want to. My particular dog, the oddly but appropriately named Stink, drowses in the air-conditioning as a matter of course. Outside is exciting for him until he actually goes there. This results in a certain amount of pestering during the day, especially when temperatures are at their worst. Cruising the backyard by himself is not his first option, so granting his wishes involves going out myself, which is not my first option.

Earlier in the week, I decided that maybe he didn't understand the problem. So about 11 o'clock one morning, the latest I could manage to go, I took him to the Whitemarsh Preserve.

The preserve sits close to my home. It is a multi-acre lot bounded by three roads and a substantial marsh. It is unimproved and heavily wooded. I'm not sure how you could improve it—you could develop it, certainly, but the result would not be an improvement. At one point, somebody tried: In the middle, there is a cleared field and two cement slabs that look like foundations. One of the trails is wide enough to accommodate a car, so maybe. The slabs remain unbuilt upon.

In addition to that main trail, there are lesser trails winding through the forest. They meander and dip and wander rather aimlessly. These are maintained by a trail bike association—maintenance being laying them out in the first place and then keeping them clear of limb-fall. The association also created logs, up and along which you can ride your bike, and occasional benches, probably so you can repair whatever broke when your balance wasn't up to log-riding. I cannot say, and I do not judge. They are doing a fine job.

My interest in riding bikes disappeared about ten years ago and has not returned. It will not return this time of year, if it ever does. However, bike trails are also fine places to walk dogs when the bikes are elsewhere, and that's most of the time.

And so the faithful dog Stink and I went to the preserve. We have walked most of the trails, Stink and I, so this was not an adventure. I am no woodsman, but if a plot of land is bounded by three roads and a marsh, you have a good chance of coming out someplace where you can find your way. And if your feet start to get wet, you made the wrong choice.

We have avoided one trail until now, and that is the Fart Swamp Trail. The reasons are probably obvious. Now, I didn't make up that name—somebody else did. Trail bikers have a mordant sense of humor, I suppose.

The morning was hot. The afternoon would be a good bit hotter, which was why we were out in the morning. I decided that Fart Swamps are probably densely wooded and free of other traffic, including humans, so we started down the trail. Signs pointed in one direction or another. Fart Swamp, they said. Like most of the other trails in the woods, this trail was anywhere between one foot and four feet wide, with tree roots cutting across underfoot. The surface was dusty sand for the first sixteenth of an inch and hardpacked beneath that.

I admit to sensing a certain amount of heaviness in the air as we started, but that might have involved anything, not just methane. The day was still, the sort of still you get only in the South when some high-pressure system drops its anchor on Atlanta and stays there. Even if there had been a breeze, the forest canopy would have deflected it. But I was right about the lack of direct sun and other people.

We wound around on the trail for about twenty minutes—trail bikers have the same lack of love for direction as deer or cattle. The heat was accompanied by dryness, discouraging large mosquito hatches, so murdering mosquitoes took much less time than usual.

Finally, I saw a wooden sign with no arrows. Fart Swamp, it read. It did not point in any direction. This was it.

The Fart Swamp, including its odor, was indistinguishable from the rest of the overgrowth. There was nothing that differentiated it from its surroundings, and there was no unusual odor. I was disappointed. I expected a better show or, at least, a smellier show. Perhaps the dryness eliminated the usual odor. On this day, the name was misleading.

Briefly, I considered lighting a match, but undetected methane might still be there. Singeing the dog and myself would not improve the day. We retreated to the road and then back to the air-conditioning. After we'd been home for a while, the dog got into some odd dish of food that my wife had left at dog-level and then sat under my computer desk.

Be careful what you wish for, for you shall surely receive it.

Summer 2019

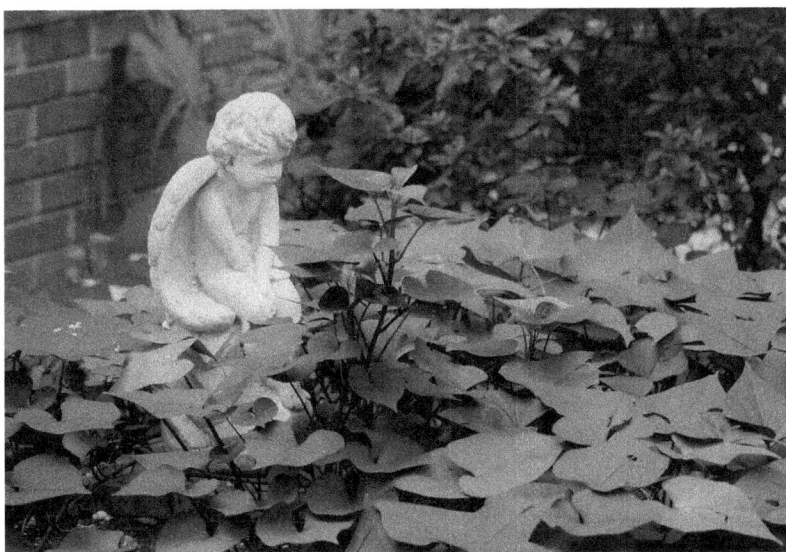

Protein

I looked at the living room window this week.

Not out of it, *at* it.

Looking out the window is, well, just not an option. Water has adhered to the outside, either as a mass of stationary droplets or running slowly down the pane. In other places I have lived, that meant spring had arrived—the sun had melted the snow mass, and soon the ice would leave the rivers and lakes. But we in Savannah are still waiting for the ice to form on the rivers and lakes, like all the other years we've waited and it hasn't happened (not that we'd appreciate the phenomenon . . .). In Savannah, mist is not the arrival of spring, it's the arrival of summer.

Last week the heat arrived, with several days over one hundred. But it was not up to our normal swelter; the heat didn't buffet you to and fro like one of those heavyweight punching bags. There was a missing element—humidity. This week, however, the humidity entered the ring swinging as the temperature dropped and the seven-day forecast called for scattered thundershowers. They faithfully appeared when I was parked too far from the entrance of wherever I was going to stay dry. And these were authentic Southern showers, the kind that the North saves for showy displays, like the ones at Niagara Falls. Now we have both heat and humidity, and we are ready for summer.

With looking out the window being off the table, Ms. Hamden and I watched a bit more television this week. We watch a lot of nature programs, to the point where we can tell what's going to happen. If the killer whales show up, the seals with the shortest attention spans are going to walk that rainbow bridge. If the leopard seals are swimming around, you can kiss a number of penguins goodbye. Herring in their thousands are decimated by birds, fish, and mammals alike, and don't get me started on anchovies.

The world, as given us, is a predatory one. Everything in our world makes a living by feeding on something else. There are those of us humans who have a problem with that, but I am content to go with the flow on this one. Like it or not, we are not that far removed from our environment, and consuming only inert vegetables results in a sooner collision with inertia ourselves. Besides, the inert don't taste all that good.

In recognition of our world as presented, I visited a steak house this week. I live east of the city where steak houses are as common as ice on the lakes and rivers. This one is new, and when I got there, I found my pal Chris running the place. Chris is as affable as ever. Over the years, I have encountered him as he managed breakfast places, barbecue places, and just about everything else. This time, it's steaks.

The steak I chose was the smallest one and still twice the protein I usually consume. It was served with a salad, some potatoes, and the veggie of the day, which turned out to be a sautéed mixture of some sort of squash, zucchini, and onions.

It had been cooked so you could still taste the squash and zucchini, which I don't find attractive.

I generally don't eat steak out; steak is a do-it-yourself product for me. The grill, the seasoning, and the timing have to be just right. But this time, the cook was Chris, and I thought he'd probably do the right thing. I was correct. The steak was perfectly cooked, wonderfully seasoned, and more tender than most of the lumps of tofu I have encountered. I will remember that steak fondly. The sautéed veggies will go in the place where I usually keep memories of sautéed veggies, and I will be careful to close the lid tightly so the critters don't get into it.

Of course, the idea that we do predatory things because we live in a predatory world can be carried too far. At the beginning of the last century, some thinkers decided it was okay to plunder, hoodwink, and steal because animals do it that way. That was called social Darwinism. It was a misrepresentation of Darwin's theories, but it was a pet theory of monopolists. There are still people who bully, bluster, and lie with unconcealed glee, and you don't have to look far to find them.

Social Darwinism isn't that popular anymore. Neither is phrenology—the idea that the dimensions of your skull determine your personality—or eugenics, which says that your heritage automatically decides what you feel and do. Those ideas popped up around the same time as social Darwinism from a similar misreading of science.

Darwin said those who adapt survive; he wasn't impressed by sharp of claw and red of fang. We humans have been first-class adapters. Still, in our basic needs we are anchored to the basics of our world. Our genius for adaptation has helped us satisfy those basics, not change them into something less disturbing.

A number of people I know, and they are thoughtful and interesting people, have decided that feasting on animals is somehow unethical. They suggest that animals are sentient and plants are not.

But as we know, even plants have their levels of sentience. I recoil in horror from newborn bean sprouts that have been sliced off in their prime. I refuse those soybeans that have been mangled into an oozing mass, then fermented with rice wine and sesame oil. Saint-John's-wort, deprived of its seeds at the very moment they should be creating the next generation of Saint-John's-wort, only to be ground up and baked with similarly harvested seeds of other plants to make five- or twelve- or fifty-three-grain bread—how can you defend that? Mushrooms and other fungi, the noble clump of kale, and zucchini without number, all sacrificed for your base instincts. How dare you?

It all depends on where you draw the line. You can be predatory on plants or on animals; the choice is yours. Humans have adapted to consume whatever is available. Many years ago, Robert Ardrey pointed out that we are "risen apes, not fallen angels." We cannot survive on noble intentions. We must eat.

I draw the line at what tastes good. Steak does. I never met a zucchini that did, no matter how it's prepared, and I've given up the search.

In all seriousness, what each of us does is up to each of us. If fermented bean curd is your thing, eat it. I am not looking for converts, I am simply looking to go my own way. I ask that you do the same.

Rambler '64

With age comes wisdom. Most adages out there are only partially true, if at all, but that one is pretty solid. Hang around long enough, and you start to get an idea of how things work. You still may not like what you see, but you understand it better.

And what do you do with this wisdom? You store it away in a leaky container that is overstuffed with other things that don't make any difference anymore or never did. I cannot remember where I left my glasses, but I perfectly remember the jingle for the 1964 Rambler. A sprightly tune it was, with banjos and a very folksy feel. Everything else I remember about the 1964

Rambler has dissipated. We were not an American Motors family, and we were certainly not a new car family, so there was little need for Rambler info, jingle or otherwise. Location of the spectacles I had just three minutes before would be useful, but that's been overwritten by the banjos.

In computer terms, the active memory is fine, but storage is outdated and overfull. So it's probably okay we have machines for that now. You can store away both wisdom and 1964 Rambler jingles. Guess which one will get more hits if you make them public on social media?

Once upon a time, we were taught that we use tools and animals don't, and that makes us different. That was before we found monkeys deploying sticks to snack on termites or sea otters whacking mussels on sharp rocks to crack them open. We further found animal moms and dads teaching the skills to the kids. So maybe the difference is that we have a machine for that and sea otters don't. That, and we have plastic.

Of course, poking sticks into termite residences does not compare to deciding whether the prime interest rate should be raised or if one should fix or replace a balky air conditioner. Tell a sea otter he or she is twelve points behind in the latest Ohio polls and that sea otter will remain unmoved. We take a different view.

Humans differ from animals in that we have a more precise idea of the future and a better grasp of analogies to get us there. We work on analogies, we humans do. Analogs allow us to compare our current predicaments to past ones and perhaps find a solution from that past. In addition, we can document those solutions and let others in on the secret.

The problem is that analogies are not always applicable and frequently just plain wrong. Your remembered situation may not match the current problem, and the differences may make your particular solution a bad choice. To wit: I used to follow newspaper columnists. One of them would leap to Burke's *Reflections on the Revolution in France* every time Congress considered a bill that displeased him, as if a proposal to raise the minimum wage were the same as the Reign of Terror. History has many things to teach us, but there's so much history out there that it's easy to learn the wrong lesson.

To implement the future we envision, we need data. Envisioned futures require planning and consideration, with frequent reviews and replanning. Planning almost never can envision all the consequences of any action. It uses logic.

Reality frequently blows raspberries at logic.

Machines don't work with analogies. They work with precision and logic based on presumably mathematical certainties. We have reached the point where we can introduce analogies into the programming.

Of course, for that to work well, you have to make sure that the machine will use the right analogy, which in turn means knowing what the right analogy is in the first place. Good luck with that. If you happen to miss with your selection of analogies, your mechanical answer will be wrong but with extreme precision.

So why do we work with analogies? Because the universe isn't even close to mathematically precise, at least not the parts with which we live. Our environment is a swirl of colliding, competing, and coordinating factors, and predicting which set we are dealing with at any given time is not an easy task. That's just the natural world. Add on all those human-based factors, and because there are so many of us now, you have too many variables to predict much of anything.

Once upon a time, Americans had a reputation for being exceptional. That was based on working with frontier land—huge stretches of virgin territory that people could develop without regard to human-based factors. The people of the frontier acted with vision, hard work, and a sense of community to overcome natural forces and elements, and they did a good job. They were hardly moral exemplars, but they got the job done.

The problem is different nowadays. Frontier values in a settled land create disruption and, frequently, casualties. People created casualties on the U.S. frontier, too, but the victims apparently didn't seem to matter. It was left to us today to moralize and deplore those depredations while shaping a framework for living together across three thousand miles of contiguous land. So, too, the Soviet Union was an exercise in frontier values, with a casualty list longer and wider than any American activity during the nineteenth century. Frontier values in settled lands create enormous numbers of victims. The frontier is gone and maybe so is American exceptionalism. We have proven no better at adapting to the problems of population than anyone else.

The answers to that problem that I see floating around all seem to have flaws, no matter how firmly or belligerently stated. Belligerence and correctness don't appear to overlap much. The answers all seem to regard human life as secondary to their grand philosophy, a twentieth-century mistake that we have more than enough evidence to abandon. With that said, I don't have an answer either. I will not stoop to a grand philosophy. What have you got?

The advanced age that generated my wisdom also becomes a factor. If I don't have an answer, I don't need one—my horizons are limited. Longer-term problems will be solved or not, without my participation. There's a certain sense of relief in that.

After the Fireworks

Next week is Independence Day, and we will celebrate it in my neighborhood as usual. That means we are treated to the "rocket's red glare" starting around the first of the month and will still have occasional expenditures of gunpowder-launched vehicles until two days after the holiday. By the last evening, fireworks and agitated messages from pet owners will cease until New Year's Day. I don't send messages about the noise and residual carbons. My dog Stink regards rocketry as a mildly irritating form of thunderstorm and goes back to sleep after a grumble or two following the first fusillade.

Anyone who pretends to have oratory skills exercises them on Independence Day, and I'm not going to do that. For one thing, I think that just about everything that could be said about independence has already been uttered and probably will be again. So my reflections are not on the achievement of independence but what came after it.

When a revolution succeeds, whether it's political, philosophical, or scientific, the next question is: "Now what?" More revolutions fail than succeed, and a successful one is a significant accomplishment. Governing on a revolution's principles is an even better trick—many pivot to the outlook of the more bloodthirsty. We didn't do that.

Governing on new principles only works when the principles can be translated into reality. Even Christianity had its uncertain moments. The apostles and disciples whom Jesus left behind had the same uncertainty as any revolutionary, and they were not exactly united in their approach. Must one be Jewish to be a Christian? James thought that might be the case; Paul was adamant that the two were separate. The involvement of Titus, a Greek, laid the foundation for separate faiths.

Is the religion based on good works or faith? Again, Paul and James advocated different approaches, and the whole matter became an issue anew sixteen centuries later.

On Independence Day, the colonies in the New World declared themselves to be self-governing. Then the colonists had to win a war to be independent of a foreign power, England. But the work was not yet done. After the former won that war, they had to deal with the problems of self-governance: what it is; how it's done; how war debts are paid without money; what to do with an unpaid and restive army; how to integrate the needs, ideals, economies, and governance of thirteen sensitive and querulous colonial governments (let alone the other populations that preceded them).

Once the war to secure independence ended, there was a big celebration, and everyone felt good. Once the celebration ended, the real work began. The Articles of Confederation were just that—a pact among neighboring lands, with no sign of a republic and barely any central government.

Perhaps not surprisingly, it started to fail and rapidly. Eleven years after independence was declared, the Constitutional Convention produced the U. S. Constitution. Benjamin Franklin, when asked about the form of government, purportedly muttered, "A republic, if you can keep it." The Constitution was the first step in attempting to keep it.

And that's when the true value of the leadership began, to my mind. We mostly avoided guillotines, firing squads, palace revolutions, and great ideas. We did what we needed to, and we kept what worked.

Amazingly enough, the leaders of the constitutional fix were among the same bunch who led the colonies to independence in the first place. That would be George Washington, Alexander Hamilton, John Jay, and James Madison. And you can't forget Robert Morris, whose trading empire kept the country afloat financially during and after the Revolution, and he did himself no favors in the bargain.

Mainly through the efforts of George Washington, the army got paid. Pro tip: Unpaid armies after revolutions do nothing to promote the public welfare. Give somebody firearms experience and training and drag him through nasty, dangerous times, and he'll want to be compensated for it. If you can't or won't, it only causes dissention, and he's already armed, right? In the centuries before, armies were told to disband, go home, and wait for the check. They developed a nasty tendency to do none of those things.

The first task was to fix the Articles of Confederation, a vague set of notions that provided no guidance or funding for acting like one nation. Madison realized that the Articles of Confederation were the governmental equivalent of a 1983

Yugo—no amount of patching was going to make it work right. So much power was given to the states that the central government was often crippled. Madison spent the 1780s crafting a replacement, getting buy-in, and doing what had to be done for ratification.

"A republic, if you can keep it"—Franklin understood the importance of maintenance. We always have a big party on the Fourth, but to keep the country going, we need to maintain the vision and the sense of the Founders.

That means we have to pay attention to what's happening today. In general, we've been lucky again. While our presidents have frequently not been of the same caliber as the Founders, only rarely have they surrendered to ideological purity or blatant self-interest. The whole idea of governing is to stay away from these things.

Up above, I dismissed much of Madison's work as consensus-building, but that's a catchall phrase for hammering out details to make the result acceptable to as many people as possible. It's a grueling, difficult, and frustrating process, and Madison gets full marks for having pulled it off. On Independence Day, I think as much of Madison as I do his colleagues. And I can see the results of not building consensus; they aren't nearly as attractive. That lack of consensus seems to be a basic tenet of human nature—and not just on the governmental level. I don't know if there's common ground between pet owners and skyrocket wranglers, but I witness the grumbling from each group for days after the holiday.

Independence is a fine thing, and we rightly celebrate it. But independence and all those other things we expect from our country require not only acquisition but also maintenance. The daily problems must be managed, lest they become threats to precisely those values that started the Revolution. I will remain silent on the quality of management I see right now.

But the Fourth of July is reason for a good party on a warm summer's day. Enjoy it.

Armstrong and Cernan

At the end of this month, the fiftieth anniversary of a pretty significant event will whiz by: the walk on the moon. I haven't acknowledged it because I really don't have anything to say about it. But in the last few days, I have been consulting with some of my contemporaries—people who were also around when it happened. We watched snatches of it on our televisions, and it was somewhat breathlessly narrated by Walter Cronkite, and Walter didn't lose his breath about many things. We felt pretty good about it. The country had done something special. But it didn't last. We went back to whatever we were doing soon after.

Were we a bit jaded about the space race? We had been doing things in space for twenty years by then, and mostly doing them well. People had listened to the voice of Shorty Powers tunneling through the crackle and roar to describe the exploits of astronauts like Gene Cernan, and we expected success at that point. Because it's NASA, and NASA doesn't do shoddy, right? But no, we weren't jaded—these were wonderful things the country was doing.

Had the moon landing happened in 1964 or 1966, we still might be having parades about it. Neil Armstrong and the rest of the astronauts might be an even bigger deal than they are today. But it happened in 1969.

In 1969, our country was at war overseas and at war with itself. The cause was Vietnam. The year started with some North Vietnamese attacks on the anniversary of the Tet Offensive. In March, the air force began to bomb eastern Cambodia, and by April, there were 543,000 American troops in Vietnam, with some of them coming home in boxes. Thirty thousand were killed or wounded. By the end of the year, we had yet another battle called Hamburger Hill. It wasn't even safe beyond the combat zone: In January, an explosion on the aircraft carrier *Enterprise* killed twenty-seven and wounded more than three hundred.

Back home, there was the widespread conviction that we weren't doing the right thing. Lyndon Johnson had not run for president, and Hubert Humphrey had been beaten by Richard Nixon because many voters thought that Nixon would get us out of the war—he said so. By 1969, there were substantial doubts that he would, even if he could. Students took over the Harvard University administration buildings, soon to be followed by similar takeovers at several other academic institutions. The generation that was supposed to fight the war was the one most convinced that it was wrong.

Overall, 1969 wasn't such a terrific year. There were the Manson murders, Chappaquiddick, the trial of the Chicago Eight, and My Lai (the first pictures were published in November). By November, President Nixon had given up the pretense of getting out of Vietnam and gave his silent majority speech. As if silence represents consent.

My personal situation wasn't any improvement on the general one. All sorts of people had all sorts of plans for me, irrespective of my own. Naturally enough, they conflicted with each other as well. Whatever one did next was going to be judged wrong by somebody. It's a great lesson about relying on yourself, and a cruddy way to learn it.

I missed Woodstock—that was in 1969, too. I was otherwise occupied, and the thought of a trip to Upstate New York to sit in a field for a few days with a massive number of other people didn't thrill me. It still wouldn't. I have seen recorded scenes of Woodstock, and some really great music came from it. I would have been the one to catch trench fever.

So it's too bad that the moon walk happened in 1969. It was a great achievement, and it looks even better from the perspective of now. I hope we have some sort of commemoration that celebrates it as it should be celebrated. The one in 1969 wasn't that sparkling because of everything else going on. If you want a whiff of what this "everything else" was like, listen to Simon and Garfunkel's tune "7 O'Clock News/Silent Night." That came out in 1966, but by 1969, things were worse, not better.

It takes the shine off national celebrations when a government declares war on its own people, and that's what had happened in 1969. It takes the shine off many things. Schoolkids were encouraged to plan out their lives; they still are, for that matter. For those of us who actually did, 1969 was often a catastrophe. Our planned trajectories were all interrupted by the war—I know mine was. But I was lucky: I found my feet and went on. Many of my contemporaries didn't. I can put faces on a few names on that wall in Washington, D.C. I can think of a few who suffered from the aftereffects of that year, people I met some years after it was over. I can name a few people who never really recovered from the trauma of that time.

I don't really have any personal complaints. Like I said, I found my feet. But I get agitated and unhappy when I think of the consequences of that year on people I held in high regard and still do in many cases. I remember what it's like when you are forced to view your own government as an adversary. It's not a comfortable feeling, and seeing it happen again isn't my favorite spectacle either.

Neil Armstrong left the stage a few years back, but his achievement still stands. For that matter, some of the NASA folks who helped put that whole mission together are still around. If there ever was a team effort, that was it. Thank them. Maybe by the centennial—that would be 2069—you can live in an atmosphere where you can celebrate it properly. Neil Armstrong deserves it. Gene Cernan deserves it. And you deserve it.

Birthday Reflections on Stupidity

In the very near future, I will have a new number to recite when they ask me my age. At some points in life, that's a major development. But my age has a fairly large digit in the tens column, so a change in the ones column doesn't mean very much unless the new number is a zero. That zero causes morbid reflection sometimes.

Being older, I should expect to be wiser. But there is a misprint in the instructions somewhere: As I have gotten older, I have gotten wider. I am not alone. I wonder if the misprint wasn't in the original adage.

This whole business of wisdom is elusive anyway. Having a fairly extensive track record to examine, I don't know how much wisdom I've dealt with, but I have more than a passing acquaintance with stupidity. There are two varieties: the self-generated sort and the sort we import from others. Most of the time, when people talk about stupidity, they are talking about the things we see in others. But the truth is that other people's stupidity is just additive to the substantial freight we personally tote around. It seems like an unnecessary burden on top of the stuff we generate ourselves.

Some of the personal kind is just mischance, which is another way of saying "not paying enough attention." This is the "Who put that tree root in my path?" sort or maybe scratching your head with your car key while you wonder why it isn't in the ignition. These are usually temporary problems with easy fixes, and hey, everybody does it.

On the opposite of the spectrum, there's the "hold my beer" variety. That's where somebody does or says something very visible and daring, and it doesn't work out for reasons the speaker didn't consider. Failure is usually spectacular, sometimes injurious, and nearly always filmed by somebody else. Forget about forgetting about it. Some TV shows are dedicated to these entertaining failures. You may already be a star.

I commit the first sort pretty regularly and the second hardly ever. My sensors and skills were never better than average, and age has dulled them. Stardom has never been an ambition, and daring physical feats have never seemed desirable or even possible. I leave that sort of stupidity to the far more capable. The real secret to personal stupidity is wandering beyond your capabilities. All learning curves start at the bottom, and to become accomplished at something, you are going to make rookie mistakes. You will wince at some of them later.

But nobody's an island, and only the luckiest of us makes it to peninsula. Humans are group-formers, like most primates. True, we are not herd or swarm beasts—although advertisers and politicians frequently can't distinguish between the two—but we are social animals, and that leads to the collective form of stupidity.

As declared by the Web site called Despair.com, none of us is as dumb as all of us. We have meetings and conferences in groups because, in theory, that's how you establish consensus where everybody agrees on something. In practice, meetings and conferences often consider a wider variety of factors and still come up with the wrong conclusion or frequently no conclusion at all. You also have coordinating committees that have the charter to reach no conclusion. They are there to stop any action that any member will hate, and they are remarkably effective at that, even when the idea is a good one. Paralysis is a frequent result of meetings. Against that, nobody in a meeting ever asked somebody else to hold their beer.

Group-formers are different from herds or swarms. Herds and swarms have one alpha beast. Groups establish hierarchies, otherwise called organizations. Everybody has a status, but some have more status than others. Baboons snarl and fight with each other to establish status.

Humans use other methods. Sometimes.

Most organizations have subtle and sometimes invisible hierarchies, and of course everyone is looking to improve his or her status. That affects meetings and conferences as much as the matter that is supposedly at hand. You have seen that as often as I have.

So group stupidity comes from an infinite variety of causes. It's easy to get frustrated with it, especially if you see the iceberg on the port bow and the rest of the committee doesn't. But the alternative to group stupidity is the individual sort, and that can be worse.

Unfortunately, bosses and customers are human, too. A lot of them reach their positions by paying attention to their surroundings and adapting, but there are always those who insist on channeling their inner brilliance rather than paying attention and adapting. Inner brilliance almost always collides with survival and never wins. Practitioners of inner brilliance call this bad luck...outsiders call it karma.

So let us give one cheer for stupidity! It leads to wisdom in people who pay attention. It leads to anger, frustration, maybe even belligerence in people who don't pay attention. If you really need me to comment on the choice, I'd go with wisdom. It's easier on your nervous system.

New Month on the Calendar

For the last month, I have been looking at pine trees in the rain. They are not Savannah pines: They have the traditional conical shape, not the mushroom form of our longleaf pines. They reach up into the sky as high as ours do, though. The buildings in the foreground are not Savannah either. They are painted red, and the eaves of the roof curve gently toward the sky. The place is Nikko, in Japan, and the woodblock print depicting it was created in 1929. In front of the buildings, a man wearing a yellow slicker and some variation on galoshes, along with his traditional broad Japanese sun hat, splashes through puddles.

Nikko is in the center of Japan, a mountainous region many miles north of Tokyo. It is mostly parkland and forest preserve and may still look like that now. I hope so. It is a cool and peaceful scene, and I turned the calendar to the new page for August with a tinge of regret. The illustration for July moved me.

I love pictures like this because they give you a sense of place and the idea that the place is special. I get the same feeling walking down Jones Street or in Chippewa Square or out at Fort

Pulaski. We have special places in this city, and it's one of the reasons I live here. Since we are a tourist destination, I am not alone in finding and enjoying those places.

Besides turning the calendar page, I spent the week delving into the life and work of one of Savannah's famed writers. I hadn't encountered this author before, so it was a deep dive in preparation for a radio discussion yesterday. That included reading critical analyses of the author and his works by people who are paid for such things. The ones I read were mostly positive, and the reviewers stretched their psyches to see profound lessons in every semicolon. Critics are like that—they love or hate things extravagantly. I wonder if being manic-depressive is a prerequisite for the job.

I couldn't help but notice that some critics used their essays to take shots at the city, like saying the author began and ended his life here but he didn't stay because, well, you know how Savannah is. Since his life was varied and somewhat difficult, the critics found it easier to chide his birthplace than to note that he went to Harvard and spent much time in England. I didn't notice any sneers about those places.

One review states that the author was "living with his family in the teeming heart of Savannah, a city still under the spell of the lost splendor of an earlier American greatness." That creates a picture of our city, right? Okay, let's look at that. The family lived on East Oglethorpe Street. That would be Oglethorpe between Bull and Broad, where a quarter of the land area is consumed by the colonial cemetery. Have you noticed East Oglethorpe teeming with anything? I haven't. It's a major east–west street, and nowadays, it separates tourist Savannah from the rest of Savannah. All the teeming is done down by the river several blocks away. Maybe if there's a parade or something, but otherwise, no.

The second part of that is equally puzzling: "under the spell of an earlier American greatness." In colonial times, Savannah was a major port (and, well, still is), but about the same time

Milledgeville was the state capital. I don't know of anybody who remembers those times, do you? I would agree that Savannah is far from the most progressive community, but nowhere else for hundreds of miles in any direction is either. Savannah isn't "great" and probably never was, but then it never pretended to be. Maybe that's one of the reasons it's a comfortable place.

Another critic referred to the city as "crumbling." Sorry, that fails to paint the right picture either. To read these people, you'd expect to see an ancient coliseum, probably somewhere around Johnson Square, from which the early planters and merchants pilfered blocks to build their colonial residences. Savannah isn't Rome. It never was and has no ambition in that direction.

Savannah has its problems, heaven knows, and those problems aren't small. They are both acute and chronic, and other communities in other areas solved those problems sometimes twenty or more years ago. They concern the structure and infrastructure of the city, the mindset of many of the residents, and the likelihood that someday, in some future year, we may be as pitiful as these reviewers paint us. But we aren't there yet, and there are many people working hard, this very minute, to prevent that from happening. We are not the ruins of ancient Jericho.

Savannah has a powerful magic, a sense of place that draws people from all over the country. Two million people show up for Saint Patrick's Day—not the most decorous of holidays—and other, quieter folks visit at other times of the year. Despite those pressing problems to which I alluded, plus the occasional hurricane and other assorted disasters, there are people who don't wish to live anywhere else.

As I mentioned, the author lived much of his life elsewhere. Many of Savannah's other notable residents did, too. Johnny Mercer did not run Capitol Records from the second story of a walk-up in City Market. Bucky Dent, Miriam Hopkins, and Stacy Keach all made their marks on the world in other environs. Those seeking fame and fortune go elsewhere.

What interests me is that the author, having lived in many places, some of them glamorous, decided to live in Savannah after he tired of them. He retired to Savannah, and comfortably, for several years. This was not any apparent nostalgia, as his first experience here did not end happily.

But I see the broad night sky over the marsh, the fog seep through the town houses in winter, and squares that seem to be lit for an evening performance of *A Midsummer Night's Dream*, and I wonder if he saw them, too.

I'll bet he did.

Anfechtungen

Anfechtungen. The word is German, and it came to my attention in a large book devoted to comparing the religious philosophies of Erasmus and Luther. According to the author, *Anfechtungen* is an existential trial sent by God to test the soul. Luther was subject to *Anfechtungen* in many parts of his life and described it as cosmic angst, when God the Father, God the Son, and the Mother Church seemed to conspire against him.

Luther was born in Eisleben, which is a bit west of Leipzig in north central Germany. Eisleben was known for mining and not much else. Luther's father was a man of middling means who leased coal and copper mines, and his parents—as Lucas Cranach's portraits of Luther's father and mother attest—made for a rather severe-looking couple. So Luther was born in the fifteenth century in northern Germany, in a town whose name translates into "ice life," to a severe-looking coal miner and his wife, and went from there.

Psychologically, *Anfechtungen* is driven by fear. Prior to leaving the Roman Catholic faith, Luther spent hours in confessionals subjecting every one of his actions to critical analysis and suspecting that they were all motivated by sin. He was a member of a monastic order that encouraged this self-examination, but the order had never encountered such a serious communicant. According to the book I was reading, Luther, suspecting that he had forgotten a sin, rushed back to one of his confessors after one of his longer sessions. "God bids us to hope in his mercy," commanded the confessor. "Go in peace." Another confessor more acutely commented, "God is not angry with you; you are angry with God."

There's the second piece of the puzzle. What starts out as fear usually becomes anger at some point—or at least is accompanied by anger.

Theology aside, I think we've all had moments of *Anfechtungen*. The first case usually hits in the early teen years, when we discover we have a place in the world whether we like it or not. And we usually don't like the place we have naturally and need to work on improving it.

The idea is that fate is picking on you, which is a rough equivalent of *Anfechtungen* in English. In some cases, fate *is* picking on you—some people find themselves in irreconcilable situations. But the reality of hopelessness happens much less often than the delusion of it. In the early teens, the clash of deeply held convictions with the realities of life, in addition to everything else that goes on then, requires navigation but is not generally a lost cause. Time adjusts the situation, usually for the better.

Psychologically, the church fathers are a fascinating lot. Luther seems to attract much attention. In 1958, the eminent psychologist Erik Erikson wrote a book called *Young Man Luther: A Study in Psychoanalysis and History*, which attempts to clinically profile Luther. The book caused a stir when it was published, but most people who have studied Luther and his life have been less than enthusiastic about Erikson's tome.

Historically, Luther dealt with his *Anfechtungen* by adjusting his beliefs to fit the situation, and as it happened, his ideas resonated with many people in his place and time. Once he had developed his philosophy, he went about his life using it as a blueprint, which curtailed the fear and anger that once plagued him. He did so with the perseverance of someone who had grown up with the coal miners of Germany in the Middle Ages, in a town highlighting the ice of life.

If there is a point to the story, that's it. Anger and fear may be motivators, but strong emotions are really bad approaches to solving a problem. They cloud judgment and cause overreaction. Acting from fear and anger leads to flawed solutions, which just make the problem worse.

So my personal enthusiasm for *Anfechtungen* is pretty limited and probably less than the enthusiasm I witness in many others. *Anfechtungen* seems to be the prime motivator in many of the political developments as of late, and that includes politics at all levels, from neighborhood to national. It appears in interactions in nonpolitical organizations as well. If you see an idea that is outstanding in its fecklessness and misdirection, anger and fear are typically the driving force. In the political world, people usually press their ideas by infecting others with the fear and anger. Sometimes they succeed.

The second part of my impatience with the concept is that it takes time and energy away from problems that are more pressing and more in need of a solution. People full of fear and anger see only the problem (or some semblance of it) that makes them fearful and angry. They seem to feel that any sacrifice is worth solving that particular problem. Historically, when they have made those sacrifices, they have found that the solution spurs worse problems. Ultimately, it's a matter of perception. If you see things as existential trials sent by God to test your soul, that is what they will become.

Lucas Cranach, the artist who painted Luther's parents, also depicted many religious scenes. One is a portrait of Christ crowned with thorns. This is not a serene Christ, as so many of them are. This Christ is weighed down with pain and perhaps knowledge of his physical fate. He seems to be asking the question that must be answered before anyone else decides that they are subject to *Anfechtungen*:

You think *you* got problems?

Dead People

This morning, I read a chapter of Jane Jacobs' book, *The Death and Life of Great American Cities.* I'm doing that for a reason. Aside from that reason, it's a good book, and I'm enjoying it. Then I started to listen to music. I've been on a jazz kick lately, and I listened to a collection Wes Montgomery and Milt Jackson put together as well as some Grant Green and Jim Hall, too. I wrote an e-mail to a friend, and I used a quote from William Faulkner to help make a point. Then it struck me: I spend an awful lot of time with dead people. Worthy as all those people are, not one of them is still with us.

Dead people are easier to deal with. For one thing, you can be a little pickier about those with whom you associate. Dead people don't send you bills or tell you that you must lose weight. Furthermore, you can be pickier about how you deal with them. Several authors I enjoy led lives that were, quite frankly, dumpster fires. But I don't have to deal with their addictions or incivilities or personal phobias. I only have to deal with their writing. And don't get me started on painters...

Best of all, dead people don't send idiotic things out on the 'Net. Several people do quote dead people, but they usually get the quote wrong or apply it in some way that the author never intended or envisioned. After all, video games were developed after Benjamin Franklin was long dead, so how could he have said that video games cause gun violence?

Dead people don't send e-mails either. There's a bank executive in Quebec who has a proposition for me based on my last name, and he wrote to tell me so. Strangely enough, he didn't bother with my name in the salutation. He only called me "My Dear." If you don't keep up with these things, scammers are using Quebec phone numbers for callbacks—not that I will return their calls (legit banker or no). But I might give his contact information to the lady from Chile who tells me her dead relative has an offer I can't refuse.

Chilean relatives aside, those who are no longer with us are more easily managed. You get to choose when you deal with them, and you do other things if other things are more pressing. And dead people don't expect you to deal with crises—or perceived crises. When you walk in your front door, no dead person will collar you and ask if you know what your son, daughter, dog, giraffe, or stock did today.

Our relationships with the deceased are different from those with the living. We go to them for information, entertainment, wisdom, and such. Those things can come from the living, too, but not nearly as often. We seek to understand our current situation by looking at the past; with the present, we can only hold our own. There is no historical record.

Now, Ms. Hamden and I live in Savannah. In Savannah, the dead who are purported to wander around from time to time have become part of our arsenal of tourist attractions. I'm not sure why the customers flock, but flock they do. If somebody wants to hang around after dying, I'm not sure I want to have anything to do with that person. There are, apparently, other viewpoints. I've eaten in a number of restaurants that supposedly experience frequent paranormal events. I have never seen any, but from the quality of the food, perhaps they all occur in the kitchen.

I once spent a few hours on assignment in a brewery. Really. I was doing photography for a commercial venture. The resident specter, who I understand is named Toby, apparently hangs out in the billiards room and shoves customers or spills drinks. As if there aren't enough live people doing the same thing! In any case, I spent an hour in the nearly deserted basement, which though nicely appointed, was still a basement and somewhat dark. I would have expected to encounter Toby there, but he did not appear. Outside, the day was blazing hot, and the brewery had the air-conditioning going full blast. Much of it seeped into the basement. Maybe Toby doesn't have an overcoat.

The dead are all around us. We live in their houses, occupy their jobs, and take their ideas and extend them to whatever situation we find ourselves in. Our ability to use the concepts and artifacts of the past and build on them creates civilizations and separates humans from every other living thing.

We learn from the dead, though what we learn and how we learn it are always saddled with doubts. Does all this really apply to us now? We can't really tell until it's over. We are all faced with managing our lives, individually and in groups. The experiences of those who have gone can inform our decisions, even if they can't provide us with set answers. And most of the time, they can't.

So dead people don't usually disturb me, but sometimes they do. For example, there was a fifteen-year-old soccer fanatic and a twenty-five-year-old graduate student in a cancer care program. The soccer fan lived in El Paso and the cancer care student in Dayton. They were mowed down, along with many others, in meaningless shooting sprees. Their spirits don't disturb me, but the way they died does. What's even more disturbing is that their deaths aren't isolated incidents—they've been preceded by those of primary school children, high schoolers, outdoor concertgoers . . . and so on. These dead people became that way as part of mass shootings, an issue that we as a society still haven't addressed.

After I finished the chapter in Jane Jacobs' book, I paid some bills, made a few medical appointments, did some chores at the request of my legally sanctioned housemate, and picked some vegetables for dinner. Then I completed some inventory work for a friend. Those things require dealing with the living, and while they went without incident, I didn't think they were as rewarding as the first part of the day.

So with those things done, I turned on the music. Django Reinhardt was playing and then Miles Davis and John Coltrane. I picked up the Jacobs book and read another chapter. I spend an awful lot of time with the dead.

The Purpose of Life

I had a little extra time this week, so I decided to examine intellectual trends in America. I didn't restrict myself to the intelligentsia or even to those who think they are the intelligentsia. Their explanations would require more time and quite probably reveal the same results. No, I looked at broad social trends.

More and more, we seem to be asking oversimplified questions—questions that are so all-encompassing that no answer will be wholly correct, if there are any answers at all. Now, we're all used to oversimplified answers. That has been the hallmark of government when anyone dared to ask a question. American democracy encourages question-asking, so we see an awful lot of oversimplified answers. That said, even oversimplified answers are hard to come by.

Case in point: Some time ago, I wrote to a congressman when a bill on Internet neutrality was being considered. That's something I'm interested in. When I received a reply, it told me that he was a fine American and took most of a page to do that. After reading the thing three or four times, I saw a word sequence that hinted how he would vote, which was not on the side of the angels. As it happens, I know several other people who have written him about various issues. They've shown me his responses, and I've found out that he doesn't like handouts, he stands behind the military, and he's troubled by the drug problem. Unfortunately, none of that had any anything to do with the questions that were asked.

That's not just a data point, that's a trend. I first noticed it when somebody decided that ketchup is a vegetable, thus meeting dietary standards. But the real indicator came later. We once had a secretary of defense who used his press conferences to ask himself oversimplified questions, for which he then provided oversimplified answers. Whatever the press asked was merely a cue to decide which oversimplified question to ask himself.

I once worked for a man who had done advanced work in psychological studies. Neither he nor I was employed in anything remotely related to psychology, and very few sessions with him wound up with anyone feeling better about themselves. But he was a clever and articulate man, and psychology was very much a part of his tool kit.

He once told us that the most honest answer to any question is, "It all depends . . . " But he was an exception. He thought about an answer. We've gotten used to answers that require little or no thought.

It seems that, since we've gotten used to sloppy answers, we've started to ask sloppy questions. That's important, because a sloppy question makes a sloppy answer inevitable—garbage in, garbage out. A carefully thought-out and well-constructed question won't necessarily get a response equally well constructed, but hip shots only result in hip shots in return.

As an example of a sloppy question, let's use one of the fundamental ones. What is life? Okay, now the challenge is to come up with a meaningful definition that fits you and an amoeba. Outside of bio-generalities, no answer comes to mind.

Most people who ask that question are really asking, "Who am I?" Well, that's a lot simpler.

I can't remember who said it first, but the last time I saw the idea was in the movie *Dead Poets Society*. In brief, we are all worm food. Well, okay, that's part of what we are. But no one is inert enough to remain merely worm food. Not while still alive, anyway.

Then there was the song, way back, that claimed "you are what you do." That's not a complete answer either, but it spruces up the worm food response a little.

Then there is "you are what you eat." This carries the implication that the kale and parsnip crowd is superior to the curly fries crowd . . . at least it does to the kale and parsnip crowd. I can't say. I have very occasional cravings for curly fries, but I have never once pined for kale.

The question of what we are is related to the question of what our purpose in life is. There are quite a few answers to that, too, and they are all equally unsatisfying. The latest answer is that the purpose of humanity is to create plastic. Well, we do that, but it's not something that I ever indulged in personally. If that is the purpose of my life, I am a failure. (If it is to ingest and inhale plastic, well ...)

As I mentioned, oversimplified questions deserve oversimplified answers. If my only purpose were to be worm food, I would have retained all the food I've eaten and processed. I'd probably weigh even more than I do now. But no, I have spent decades running around with the energy that the food gave me.

If I am what I do, I wake up a new person every day. Sure, there are similarities, but it's never quite the same. If you compare what I do now with what I did, say thirty years ago, the difference is pretty dramatic. My level of activity is trending toward early childhood levels, but part of that is being smarter about what I attempt. I now take naps without even being told.

If I am what I eat, that ignores the processing that goes on after you eat. We convert whatever it is into biochemical elements that we can use. Imagine thinking that the essence of your being is tofu or a double caramel macchiato, skinny, of course. "[T]here is always a well-known solution to every human problem—neat, plausible, and wrong." Thank you, Mr. Mencken, for that quote.

Perhaps the real answer is that we are all those things. We are what we eat, we are what we do, and we have a high potential to become worm food at some point. What happens before that depends at least partly on what we pursue. And what we do changes as the day progresses—and the month and the year.

So who am I? Well, it all depends ...

Depressed

This was a blue week at Rancho Bridgeport. Not that there was a particular reason. Oh, there was a flare-up in medical visits for all three of us—people and dogs our age live with potential catastrophes as a matter of course—but when you are a little blue, you find plenty of other reasons to cause depression. But this was just a mood. The weather played a part, too, arranging for rain whenever I even thought about walking the dog, and that was more of a priority this week.

The dog is too fat. We knew that going into his appointment, and we have taken measures, as they say in corporate America and movies about the Mafia. His extra pounds, unlike mine, are pretty well distributed, but he is still overweight. This is secondary to his inclination to sleep when he is not walking or eating. If I suggest he go into the backyard unaccompanied, he looks at me pityingly, then flops down and snores. But walking this week involved either dodging showers or getting soaked. We did both.

On the other hand, driving involved platitudes. We have a splendid new electric sign on the islands heading east. This is a good thing because now you might be alerted when the highway to Tybee is congested or flooded or whatever happens on Highway 80—and a lot happens on Highway 80. But when there aren't problems, the sign maintainers are stuck for what to display, so they put up inspirational messages. You know the kind: "Drive carefully" and so on.

For the past several weeks, there's been a display about watching for turtles. I like turtles well enough, more than they seem to like me, but the sign is at a point on the highway where the road is six lanes and speeds are limited to fifty miles per hour. Anyone hypervigilant about turtles is liable to cause casualties among the humans. Turtles are probably going to be on their own, despite warnings. When you are down, even that thought becomes a downer, too.

Little things pile up on bigger things. I changed the towels in the bathroom. One was in the wrong grouping. The bathroom linen was a resplendent burgundy save for that one bath towel from an incongruous set—a darker, kind of a sullen grape jelly.

I ran my fingers across the nap; it had the same absorptive characteristics and feel as sandpaper. Had I been in a better mood, I'd have changed it.

In such times, if personal things aren't going so well, a change in focus might help. Looking at the wider world sometimes gives you a better perspective on your own little complaints. But I am not one to respond to cute kitty pictures, and these days the wider world seems as dismal as my own, if not worse. The newspaper and other media are not purveyors of hope. The management of wider matters seems as inept as mine, if not worse.

For me, there's always been a refuge in music.

If you pick your own music, you can avoid songs about dead girlfriends or Great Lakes shipwrecks or some of the less inspirational thoughts of those who use "metal" as the suffix for their music category.

I chose "You Are the New Day" by the Kings Singers. It's a great choice—uplifting without being soppy. It came out in 1980, when global warming was less pressing and U. S. citizens shot each other in multiples with less disturbing regularity. But every era has its problems, and in 1980, we were more concerned about frying each other with bombs and freezing survivors with a nuclear winter. The song starts well enough, but then you get to a verse about humanity's unique ability to end it all.

True enough, we can certainly still irradiate each other into subatomic oblivion, but that didn't really solve my mood problems.

I turned off the music.

Over the history of humankind, we have developed strategies for depression. They usually lean on some sort of diversion. The more common ones involve food, alcohol, sex, drugs, or overspending, singly or in combination. They all have two problems ... they are beyond my means and interest, and they don't work. Singly or in combination.

Eventually, you come home, and the problems are there waiting for you. Problems have an amount of patience that would make a sloth blush. But I was stewing. I went to the kitchen pantry because food was my one convenient option.

I found my answer in a can of stewed tomatoes. Now, I would no more open and eat a can of stewed tomatoes than I would fix myself a wasabi and gin, but the concept triggered an idea.

You stew tomatoes to preserve them. They can last years that way. Maybe stewing over problems works the same way—it just preserves them.

For me, problems require action—not just a run in the woods, but actually trying to solve them. It was the call to action. I put on my big boy pants, summoned the dog, and we went for our walk. Ten minutes into that walk, the sky opened, and we came home soaking wet.

Temporarily ignoring the trail of water we left through the kitchen, we made our way to the bathroom, where I dried myself with the purple towel and then dried the dog. He enjoyed the raspy texture much more than I did. The towel ended up something more than damp and well matted with beige hair, because one or both of us sheds in the summer. No finger-pointing. I deposited the towel in the place where we keep imminent laundry and replaced it with a burgundy one. Now the bathroom linen was uniformly burgundy, without exception. I faced the dribble of water in the kitchen with a determined glare and a sponge mop.

That's what I call progress.

The Nut Business

Now, at the end of August, there's a change in the air.

The dawn walks are accompanied by the chug of yellow buses driving around picking up the scholars. School is back in session and has been for a few weeks. The waiting students have reconnected with each other and poke at their cell phones or talk into them. There are always a few incapable of speech or finger dexterity because the early morning is too much to cope with and too early for communication. I am one of those.

The beauty bushes or chinaberries or whatever they are that grow in the woods have sprouted a good number of berries; they have turned from green to a deep violet or even purple. The spring and summer plants are turning brown. The lawn in front of my house is still surprisingly green, with only a few parched patches, since it's been a good year for rainfall. The birds, identifiable only as "little brown jobs," are amassing in large flocks, the better to head south.

And, of course, the change in air includes changes in the air. The temperature is dropping slightly and reluctantly. Cooler breezes sweep our way from the ocean. Thunderstorms that arise in the middle of the Atlantic become massive and circular before heading our way. There's one close by now. Most of them will miss us, but I checked the gas-powered generator just in case. We are just too dependent on electricity.

Summer is going, and autumn hasn't quite arrived. It's the bipolar season: We'll have a few days of one, and then a few of the other. People farther north get obsessive about when spring arrives, but we focus on when autumn is here—no more Atlantic uproar, the influx of monarch butterflies, the day when the lawn sprinklers fall silent.

Change is constant. This week, I actually watched a baseball game on TV. Well, I watched two innings. The last time I watched a game, the pitting of these two particular pitchers would have been an incredible duel between two acknowledged masters. But time marches on, and pitchers age rapidly. One of them threw ninety balls in a little more than three innings, and the other had nothing but trouble and disappeared after allowing eight runs in two innings. And so did I.

Things change naturally, but since we are increasingly interconnected, things also change when somebody has an idea and it seeps into the lives of others. And this is where our common human trait of fallibility comes in. Humans hunger for change, and nature doesn't.

Let's say somebody comes up with a great new method for grinding filberts. I don't know why, since I've never cared for filberts that much and can't eat them now, but let's just say they did. Since it's a great idea, the other filbert grinders will adopt it sooner or later. All is well, so far. But then, somebody will adapt it to manufacturing peanut butter. It doesn't work quite as well with peanuts, but it's an improvement over current methods. Soon the peanut butter manufacturers have bought in. Then somebody adapts it to another field. Again, it produces an improvement but with some downsides. This goes on for quite a while because it's the new management technique. Sooner or later, a manager will tell his employees that they are going to adopt filbertology as a management scheme, and the employees, who manufacture parts for nuclear reactors, will simply roll their eyes. The idea has been pushed past its natural limits to something bizarre and unsustainable.

I saw this happen with data mining. Data mining can provide businesses with great insight about how they operate. It can even result in cost savings. But that assumes the data exist in the first place. Managers who wanted to get into data mining but didn't have the data to begin with started to slap together vague approximations to use in place of actual data. The result was both expensive and misleading. But the idea was new and shiny and lasted until the next new idea came along.

Pushing ideas past their logical boundaries is nothing new. I found this 1950 obituary by Philip Tomlinson in *The Times Literary Supplement* on George Bernard Shaw, who practiced his craft starting in the late 1800s:

> He was no originator of ideas. He was an insatiable adopter and adapter, an incomparable prestidigitator with the thoughts of the forerunners. Nietzsche, Samuel Butler (*Erewhon*), Marx, Shelley, Blake, Dickens, William Morris, Ruskin,

Beethoven and Wagner all had their applications and misapplications. By bending to their service all the faculties of a powerful mind, by inextinguishable wit, and by every artifice of argument, he carried their thoughts as far as they would reach—so far beyond their sources that they came to us with the vitality of the newly created.

Sometimes the idea isn't so hot in the first place. Our powers of abstraction sometimes exceed our capacity to determine what is real. Our logic works only as well as the things we can foresee, and nobody can foresee everything. Worse, delusion can be sustained by logic.

If we were all good Vulcans, like Mr. Spock, we would look for additional data when things weren't working well. But we are human—we hire clever and capable people to make the existing data look better than it really is. That's the basis of advertising, marketing, a wide range of consultancies, and so on. Finding the shade of lipstick that suits a particular pig is a billion-dollar industry. If we are reading fewer novels today, it's because we have narratives poured over our heads every day, and more and more people are going into fairy-tale shock.

Any industry that attracts the clever and capable also attracts second- and third-raters, people whose narratives are so incredible that no one believes them. And sometimes fate gives them maximum exposure. Fate in this case might include the media—and the things the media themselves broadcast to their believers. Castles in the air look insubstantial to nonbelievers and cause doubts about the soundness of the construction crew.

When that happens, humans generally hunger for change.

And there's change in the air at the end of August.

Autumn 2019

Another One

Michael Ende wrote a fantasy novel called *The Neverending Story* in 1979. I don't know much about it, but I know that's what we live—a never-ending story. When our taste and capability for life erode, other characters, probably younger, pick up the theme. Stories end when authors get tired of them. Life itself does not.

Even though the story hadn't played out when I started to put this talk together, I'm going to tell it. It's life.

Over last weekend, the weather outlook for the upcoming week turned dismal and scary. On Monday, we were ordered to leave the area. I had compelling reasons to stick around, so I ignored the order. That said, I live in Zone A, the most hazardous, so I arranged a place to stay in Zone B, which is still in the evacuation area but a better situation if the worst happened. Then I did all the battening, buying, and recharging you have to do if it's bad but not the worst. I was hoping very hard that the hurricane rotating toward us would shift itself east, because I had skin in the game.

People have little indicators they use to predict the weather. The indicators aren't scientific or especially accurate, but people use them anyway. In the North, people read the *Farmers' Almanac* and watch the amount of fuzz on the fall caterpillars. If the caterpillars are especially fuzzy, some people decide that the winter will be harsh, so they buy an extra pair of thermals or have their boots relined or whatever.

I started to look at minor indicators here in Savannah. On the minus side, Monday was gray and sticky—not particularly hot, but moisture-laden. It felt like somebody had sprayed a thin aerosol of honey over the city. Also on the minus side, every public official south of Charlotte was urging all of us to flee, and the news was full of disaster-related stories. I won't even trouble you with what was on the Internet.

On the plus side, the weather service I use said that we would get lots of rain and winds of thirty-five miles per hour. They stuck to that forecast throughout the day. That's not conclusive—no set of weather guessers gets it right all the time—so I looked for other indicators. Over a midday while, the Popeyes on Victory Drive had waiting autos spilling onto the roadway, presumably for that chicken sandwich. No mere hurricane was going to keep those folks from their lunch. In our immediate area, three bars and two liquor stores declared they would remain open no matter what. One of them is right next to a marina. The convenience store on the corner said the same thing, but they make that a habit. If somebody detonates a nuclear device near us, the convenience store will still be open—though they will probably just leave the peanuts outside, rather than cooking them the usual way. I continued to batten, buy, and recharge.

When I checked the weather early on Tuesday, we were out of the cone: The hurricane would not slam into our part of the coast. That was heartening, but still not conclusive. Official weather guessers aren't right all the time either. I continued my disaster routine. But the sky was blue, and the air was light; again, nothing to bet the ranch on. The Popeyes was now deserted as was most of the rest of Victory Drive. I expected that. Drainage in Thunderbolt is a tricky business, and Victory can gather lots of water from more disorganized low-pressure systems.

Wednesday, the dog and I took the morning walk late, getting in just before the first bands of rain arrived. The best-guess forecast had the winds at forty-eight miles per hour, which is tolerable. As storm preparation, one of the weather sites I monitor recommended that we stay inside and read a book. I don't know if that's good advice, but it's a set of directions I can follow. I decided to stay home, Zone A and all.

Having done everything else, I was down to the fine-tuning. All dishes were washed, and most clothes were washed and dried. I cleaned the bathroom, too, though I'm not sure why that would be storm preparation. It was just something else to do. When my scullery-maid mood left, I tried to watch TV. I tried hard. When I tuned in, the baseball games were either rained out or foregone conclusions. The usual sitcoms and nature shows were on, but they didn't appeal. One channel had the Northern Iowa football game and another a Houston Texans game—from two years ago. The TV, which is new enough to nag, told me that I had saved four days of electricity by not tuning in until then. I decided to go for the record. However, the power stayed on, so I hunkered behind my computer screen.

Unlike most weeks, Thursday was hump day plus one.

The sustained winds stayed in the twenties, the rain fell, but not extravagantly, and aside from major hits to random twigs and Spanish moss, all was well.

Our traditional power outage came at two in the morning and left at eight, which inconvenienced very few people. The hurricane was north of us, and everything else would be a postscript. I took the dog for his morning walk, which was late, wet, windy, and short. The weather was bad enough that he was satisfied, even with short. The things that hit the roof of the house rolled right off it, as opposed to crushing anything. I was grateful.

I must also be grateful for the stormwatchers and emergency planners who put such time and effort into keeping us informed. I will mention the Chatham Emergency Management Agency specifically, though many others contributed—from professionals to neighborhood clockers and watchers. You all did good. This time, many of them erred on the side of caution, but that's okay. There have been recent times when the weather fully lived up to their anticipation.

I am also marginally grateful to the state's governor for coming to Savannah (after he told everyone to leave) to inform us that the federal government, and especially the president, had our best interests in mind and was watching every hurricane-tracking wobble. I had thought the president was focused on the storm situation in Alabama, so that was reassuring.

Time flows on. What happened is far easier to deal with than what might have happened. What happened is real. We were lucky. The people farther south weren't as lucky, and some people north of us might not be either. Our reality is very little worse than it was at the beginning of the week.

Let us be grateful.

Fake Weather

Heaven knows, I try to keep my thoughts at a higher level, especially the ones I talk about here. In real life, that is to say away from the microphone, I have no more success at it than anybody else, but that's not for broadcast. I gave up on trying to keep my thoughts elevated this week.

My work experience was with corporations, large and small, and involved working for and in competition with other organizations, large and small. I am a veteran of bureaucracies. Believe me, there is bureaucracy in corporations of thirty-five employees, and it follows the same patterns as in bureaucracies of a hundred thousand employees. So I have seen numerous examples of doing the wrong thing for inexplicable reasons.

People in that bureaucratic situation develop the hide of a rhino when it comes to the illogical. The illogical happens for reasons that they don't know about, and if they call out each instance, they become exhausted and get earn a reputation of not playing well with others. It's not a good way to start a career or maintain it, but it's a dandy way to end it, especially before it starts. And by the way, the people toward the top of the pyramid live with the same fallout as the people at the bottom of the pyramid. But people in the middle of the pyramid are especially vulnerable. They're accountable not only for the people who work for them but also to the people above them.

If you're in the middle of the pyramid, strange ideas abound in those who work for you and those you work for. If you think the people who work for you have strange ideas, wait until you meet the people you work for. They have worked hard and prospered, and most of them are driven, sleep-deprived, and dynamic. They have some vague ideas about what you do, and some very specific ideas about what you ought to do. Those may or may not match the realities of your situation. They don't want to hear that the idea they gave you is stupid. They especially don't want to hear that if the idea was wished on them by somebody to whom they report, whether it's a customer or higher management.

If you've ever worked for an organization, you know this predicament. It's a characteristic of profits, nonprofits, universities, churches, professional organizations, political groups, motorcycle gangs, Scout packs, and playgrounds. It always has been. Imagine you are a captain of a Greek ship. The commander tells you to gather your men because you are going to sail off to Turkey to settle a dispute with the Trojans over a failed domestic arrangement. Worse yet, imagine that you have gone through that and now have to implement some of Ulysses' singular ideas about getting home. Did you ever wonder how many of the original crew of the starship *Enterprise* made it back home? Oh yes, there will be blood and not always figuratively. It will be no better in the future.

But there are chinks even in the hide of a rhino, and some fly is bound to find it. Let me give you an example.

I did contract work for many organizations, both private and governmental. One of them was the National Weather Service (NWS), so I'm familiar with it. People who work for the NWS are sharp cookies. The general public doesn't have enough information or techniques to accurately predict the weather everywhere, all the time; that's what the NWS is supposed to do. NWS forecasters get as close as they can by using tools that are pretty good (most of the time) and keeping a trained eye on weather situations. They are especially good when it comes to violent weather.

I'm familiar with violent weather, very recent really violent weather. So are you. We were spared, but only just. During the Hurricane Dorian episode, I watched a variety of sources, and all used NWS data, though they may have interpreted it differently. The emergency management agencies used it, too, and their problems extend way beyond whether to stay home or join the traffic jam to the west.

The weather forecasting job is hard enough, but somebody at a more executive level embroidered the NWS forecast to include places that weren't threatened by Dorian. That caused some panic in the other places, and the NWS folks had to either contradict an executive or make things up. The NWS people know enough about organizations not to contradict an executive, but they weren't going to broadcast pretend weather either. Why? According to one estimate, Dorian cost Savannah $150 million without hitting us, to say nothing of the fear it propagated.

When asked for a correction, the mistaken senior executive reiterated his mistake, making an amateurish amendment to an official chart. The forecasters in the affected region were told to shut up, and the U.S. Department of Commerce, which supervises the NWS, anonymously insisted that the senior executive was correct, because your boss is never wrong, now is he?

This time, the media elected to follow the story, and there's been pushback within the department. I have no idea what conclusion the investigations will make, nor how long it will take to reach it.

But the cards are stacked against any criticism of the executive. Because he's still the executive.

The particular senior executive who made that mistake has a standing problem with interpretations of what he does. Whether the reports are accurate, he bleats that it is all fake. There are those who confuse "inconvenient" with "phony."

Fake news is one thing. We see it all the time on the Internet, where people either ignore or don't know the rules of journalism. It's especially potent when people don't check their sources. Readers of standard news sources expect that facts will be checked. Readers of obviously spun facts don't care.

Facts and data can be interpreted any number of ways, so there will always be some discussion. But weather, weather is based on the best, most accurate and available information we have, much of which is based on actual data from the past. Right or wrong, it's a set of facts with which we all have to live. So it is surprising that the very people who complain the most about fake news have given us a whole new category of fake news: fake weather.

Real Weather

My neighbor walked up to me as I stood in front of my home. I was looking at my lawn and wondering why any mole in his right mind would think there was anything to eat there. But moles apparently have the same incidence of mental illness as any other species.

"Did you see the forecast?" he asked.

"Sure," I said, because I had. September is when oversized circular storms blow in from the mid-Atlantic. We live on an island. We pay attention.

"Supposed to get down to the low seventies tomorrow." He grinned from ear to ear.

If you don't live in Savannah, his joy may seem slightly misplaced. But we care. Both of us get up early, if possible, before the school buses. He tends his yard, and I walk the dog. The dawn temperature is what counts. Later in the day, it will be too hot to do anything more strenuous than pop a top; it's the dawn temperature that counts. Yes, the midday temperatures are backing off, too, but not fast enough to matter. In most places, the focus is on the highs in the summer and the lows in the winter—here, we do just the opposite.

A very nice lady I know just returned from spending the summer in England. She grew up there, somewhere in the Midlands around Manchester. It was a wonderful time for her, replete with old friends and relatives. "We left the door to the cottage open," she marveled. "No heat and no bugs."

Her attitude and mine might part company over the weather. I have been to England several times and visited various places from Cornwall to the Scottish border. I can count on a closed fist the number of times I was tempted to leave the door open. You might, if you've decided to age a side of beef in your living room. For me, English weather is brisk at best. I was once tempted to take off my sweater, but that was in Dover beneath the cliffs. The usual English weather goes roaring above the cliffs there. They even have a few palm trees.

As a child, I lived several hundred miles north of Savannah. Either because of the location or because I was a child, I was a sun worshipper—we all were. The *beau idéal* was a summer day, with the sun shining brightly overhead. If you give kids a box of crayons and ask them to draw a nice day, that lemon yellow crayon is going to come out sooner or later to construct a vague circle somewhere near the top of the paper.

Children quickly become absorbed in their own lives, and the weather becomes inconvenient at most. That's all right. As they mature, the weather transforms into tangential—somewhere between not troublesome and causing extra effort and aggravation. There are things to learn and things to do. Even the people who stand in front of the camera in the middle of a blizzard and tell you how snowy it is have to learn other things before they can do that. Jim Cantore of the Weather Channel had to spend much time indoors before he became the harbinger of doom.

But even in the middle of a busy life, the weather is there, and sometimes for the better. I once spent a Thanksgiving on Cape Cod, the farthest I could go with a limited budget and a car that ran every now and then. The peninsula was largely closed and deserted, which is Cape Cod at its best. The temperature stayed in the low seventies for most of that trip, even though colder, more hostile weather to the east churned up the sea on the ocean side. My companion and I visited cranberry bogs, sat and watched the evening mists gather over the waters, and ate out of cans more than once. Thanksgiving dinner occurred at a restaurant specializing in turkey breast that's been stabilized chemically, the sort you got when the army cook ran out of creamed chipped beef on toast. But the weather was magic, and it was one of the best Thanksgivings ever.

Of course, it can go the other way. While growing up, I was once evacuated from a house by rowboat. We left from a second-story window. We had gotten through the first part of the storm fairly well, and then the eye of the storm passed over us. That's an odd feeling—it's still windy, but the sun shines and you get the impression that things are going to be okay. Then the other part of the storm hit. Things were not going to be okay.

Today, the weather becomes more of a factor at certain points in my personal day. The noble dog Stink and I have seen many a sunrise and more than a few sunsets. The light is different at those times of day—it's yellower, and the distinction between lit and shaded turns dramatic. Even if you go out before sunrise or after sunset, the trees create spectacular silhouettes in the pale light. At twilight, you see flittering among the trees—these are not spastic birds, but bats looking for mosquitoes on which to snack. (I've never been a big bat fan, but I understand more of their value now that I live here.)

Those days when the sun doesn't shine have their advantages, too. The evening mists have nothing on the dense winter fogs that roll across Tybee. The pier disappears into the gray, and the waves come crashing in unseen and without warning. The usual glut of people is elsewhere. It's a different feeling.

Here in Savannah, we have a different relationship with the sun: It is not always our friend, or even our enemy, as it might seem in places farther south. That ambiguous relationship leads us to appreciate times when the sun is not a factor.

When I come inside, I deal with the inside things that have made up most of my previous life. Let's see, at the computer here, I find that an organization I belong to has one more "like," that an acquaintance thinks The Beatles are "marvy," that there's a new way to construct Gantt charts, that somebody is missing a package and somebody else found a ring in the grocery store parking lot, and that Windows 10 has problems, new ones.

Excuse me, I'm going to go outside for a while.

The Sorry State of Propaganda

It was an exciting week at Rancho Bridgeport for reasons that aren't of interest to anybody else. But in the midst of everything, the people who don't know my political leanings got in touch with me. I am pretty up-front about where I stand, but some people don't pay attention or don't care. Which is why I'm not one of their guys—they don't pay attention and they don't care.

First, their party got in touch with me. I'd been selected, personally selected, mind you, to answer a survey on national events. I would gladly have written several essays to answer their questions, but this was one of those mark-the-answer questionnaires. And, of course, none of their answers even came close to my opinions. The choices ranged from stupid to vile, with several stops that combined the two. I don't know why I was personally selected to receive their mail—I have a history with the other guys, and it's freely available to anyone who looks. Apparently, they didn't pay attention and didn't care. Of course, they also asked for money. Maybe that was the primary goal of the missive.

Then I got an e-mail from a woman I met several years ago and haven't seen since. We established that she leaned the other way at the time, but maybe she's forgotten that. There was no text to her e-mail, just a string of graphics that had been siphoned from the 'Net. Because I earned my degree in a specialized form of political science, I have pored over both Nazi and Communist propaganda posters in pursuit of understanding. Let me tell you, the best efforts of the German and Russian creators had nothing on these guys for breathless deflection of reality.

But there are differences. The propaganda specialists of the last century felt they were educating the ignorant masses and kept their work at a very basic level. Keeping your work basic also allows you to oversimplify issues, which is handy if you are going to replace knowledge with enthusiasm. In Cambodia, people were shot if they looked like they might know something. But the educating-the-ignorant aspect of propaganda may have worked to some degree. The shining idealisms of the twentieth century cost about three hundred million counted deaths and who knows how many uncounted ones.

Here and now, the problem is different. Not that many living Americans are so poverty stricken and proletarian that they have been left completely uneducated. They may not have paid much attention to their education, but that's different. Of the ones who did pay attention, their views have been shaped by their life experiences. You aren't dealing with *muzhiks* here, and the pretense of education doesn't work anymore.

So anyone who sends basic-level propaganda posters, no matter how these are sent, is doomed to failure if the aim is to influence me. To be even the least bit effective, propaganda has to be plausible. No matter how long and loud you proclaim that the sky is green, nobody will buy in. So the trick is to keep the proclamation simple and more reality-adjacent than not, so that your words may be interpreted, and kindly, by people who have bought into it.

We fought a few world wars against opponents that had masterful propaganda, and then a cold war with another. In all cases, our adversaries were motivated by complex philosophies that were long on creating a future and short on dealing with the problems of the present. They managed to do this while the problems of the present were killing people left and right. In fact, they decided that the people of the present were really just stairsteps to the future and really didn't matter. A nation that deals with its own people on that basis is liable to have the same attitude toward you and your people.

In the second global skirmish, the clash of heedless systems of belief in Europe caused fourteen million deaths by conservative estimates, just counting the Eastern Front. The number of wounded may be ten times that, and anguish and hardship were nearly unavoidable in that region. People were convinced that they needed to pick a side, no matter its deficiencies. How many of the dead fought and died for a cause that they were not especially attached to? That's unknowable.

If the twentieth century has taught us anything, the idea that there are only two ways of looking at things proved to be both false and fatal. Those lucky enough to survive the Second World War had to rebuild their lives in ruined surroundings; some even wondered if the dead were luckier. To our everlasting credit, we helped the nations we could with capital, technology, and advanced concepts—the Japanese built their current industrial dynamo based in part on American concepts brought to them by the American military government. How ironic that American companies only embraced their own concepts sporadically and when convenient. We won the war and the quasi-conflict that followed by being practical and paying attention to immediate problems.

When I look around the United States today, I see that people believe that there are only two ways of looking at things, and each person is pressured to join one or the other of them. Each side has multiple founts of propaganda, and the propaganda is both as useless and as aimed at emotion as in the previous century. Some of the stuff from the people I normally favor is as dumb and self-serving as the other side. I am told it is necessary because the other guys are doing it. It's taken on the trappings of a sports team. One is supposed to love the Washington Redskins even when they are a terrible team (and sport a racist name). And since I do follow the Redskins, I can tell you that they haven't been a good team for some time now. That's okay for sports—it's not okay for things that matter.

And things that should be done, and must be done, aren't getting done because of the us-versus-them mentality. That's another irony: Having resolved the bloody impasse in Europe using untold finance and blood, we now strive to create exactly the same atmosphere. I can't tell you what will happen, nor how to resolve the problem. But I can tell you that we will be poorer in this climate.

Charisma?

I wonder if we've progressed socially much further than the cave people. Obviously, we've progressed technically, but I wonder if our interactions with each other are any more sophisticated. I wonder if the impulses that led cave persons to whack other cave persons over the head with a club are any different from those of people who walk into grade schools while carrying assault rifles.

Our interactions have to be somewhat more sophisticated because we deal with more people in a week than the average Paleolithic person did in a lifetime—and far more often. Keeping our interactions sorted out takes more time and energy. But that's a very small difference. The Paleolithic peeps had the same life span as vinyl siding, so you can't compare them to the graybeards we have today. Cave dwellers had a mindset more in line with high schoolers.

It's all speculative, of course, because we don't know that much about cave persons. We don't even know that much about ancient Egyptians. But the Hellenes, the ancient Greeks, left many records—inventory lists, oratorical transcripts, poetry, and speculations on the nature of who they were. And some of it is as nuanced and sophisticated as anything along the same line today.

We use a lot of Greek words in modern English, and we overuse them in some cases. One of my favorites is charisma. For the Greeks, it meant the gift of grace, the attractiveness that leads other people to follow the possessor. The word has evolved: For the medievals, it meant that God had favored the possessor. Then the social scientists started to work on it.

The social scientists first divided it up into two categories, because social scientists can't seem to work without slicing things up like they would a salami. They recognize personality-based charisma and divinely inspired charisma. Either way, it remains mysterious to them. They began to call it the X factor. The term "X factor" became commonplace. (This was a fair number of years ago, of course.) Today, we associate the X factor with conjoined twins who play dueling banjos with their feet and other such contortions for a panel of B-minus celebrities who are supposed to be judging talent. But social science is where the term got its start.

So charisma is the power to have people buy into your act. I've never had any, so I couldn't say. Part of that is because people have never quite understood what my act is. That's okay.

238

I sometimes have some personal confusion about the matter myself. I am one of those retirees who still doesn't know what he wants to be when he grows up. I'm beginning to wonder if I will grow up or if there's any point to it this late in the game. Being a grown-up looks like work.

But back to charisma. Social scientists are fond of questionnaires because they let you do science without being particularly social. You can ask questions that you couldn't keep a straight face asking in person, and you don't have to watch the reactions of your interviewees when they hear what you want to ask.

A social science questionnaire might go like this...

Question one: Do you have charisma? (That's an important one; otherwise, they are compiling a whole lot of data that doesn't matter, which is even less fun than asking the questions out loud.)

Question two: Is your charisma personality-based or divinely inspired? (The questionnaire will probably provide checkboxes here, because writing anything as an answer will just encourage other answers and likely ones that won't fit the convenient categories that guide the creators.)

Question three: Which divinity inspired your charisma? (Again, the questionnaire would probably have boxes, one for each divinity. It also would probably instruct you to "Check all those that apply," but "Other" would not be among the choices—that would just ruin the sample.)

I could go on, but a questionnaire is obviously not the right answer. People who have charisma don't really know why other people buy into their acts, and asking them won't provide any information at all. Anyway, I can't quite see Joan of Arc or George Washington treating that questionnaire with any seriousness.

The questions, you see, are misplaced. You shouldn't be asking the charismatic, you should be asking the people who buy in—the adoring public. I suspect the answers would be pretty diverse, and if any social scientist put "I don't know" among the options, that would be the majority answer. Over the years, interviewers have asked that type of question at Elvis shows and Beatles concerts; the answers they've gotten have been emotion-laden and data-free.

But my point is still the same. It's not that charismatics are doing anything special; it's that people are buying into the charisma of charismatics for some reason. The source of the charisma is not the charismatic, but the people buying into it. You might as well ask a 1965 Mustang why it's a classic car.

The Greeks understood that, too. They had a word for people who believed in their own charisma: hubris. There are several definitions, but hubris essentially means drinking your own bathwater.

The term is derived from the Greek word for outrage. According to my 'Net sources: "Hubris often indicates a loss of contact with reality and an overestimation of one's own competence, accomplishments or capabilities."

The Greeks didn't care for hubris much. They thought it was a challenge to the gods, something that would cause your own downfall. They called that downfall nemesis. Christians call it pride.

Too many times, we've seen seemingly charismatic people crumple into heaps of dust. We've seen it with actors, singers, talk-show hosts, or anybody else who is in the public eye. Oh, and politicians, too. Nobody leaves the earth without being wrong occasionally, whether he or she admits it.

Tweets

Right now, each one of us has more power to communicate than Thomas Jefferson or Franklin D. Roosevelt or William Faulkner ever had. Our electronic gizmos are fast, efficient, and accurate. When Jefferson wanted to thumb his nose at Alexander Hamilton, it took him a month to do so. He'd dictate the nose-thumbing words to a secretary, who would make

a clean copy. Jefferson would sign it, and then they'd package it and give it to somebody who had a horse and was heading to New York.

All that meant that Jefferson would weigh his words carefully, because it took time and effort to get the message to Hamilton. Was this to be a simple nose-thumbing or a full-scale one with wiggling fingers? Would he use facts, opinions, irony, or invective? You must remember that Jefferson knew Hamilton before *Hamilton* became a major Broadway hit—so he was less impressed than we are now. Even in Roosevelt's or Faulkner's time, what you communicated in writing was carefully thought out if only because it might come back to haunt you. Each one of those men responded with well-considered words, some of which live with us to this day because they are inspirational.

In theory, having fast, efficient, and accurate gizmos means that we have more time to weigh our words and to consider the consequences of what we say and how. If you communicate via the 'Net, you have the time to consult with others who may be able to add to your narrative and provide a useful perspective. If you are in Statesboro, let's say, and you owe a reply to somebody in Chicago, you can talk to people in Reno or even other people in Chicago before you reply.

This should make us all better informed, our arguments more nuanced, and our messages able to express what we mean more clearly.

Don't you just love theory?

In practice—which differs from theory more than the theoretical prefer—our marvelous communication capability gives us the opportunity to pass on raw, ill, impulsive impressions in near real time. That has the same consequences that verbal raw, ill, impulsive impressions always do: It causes conflict. The speed and access of our communications also allow us to spread stupid or malicious rumors using the same digital avenue that facts travel and without anyone checking the source or accuracy. More conflict.

Texans, at least those familiar with the bars in Texas, know that there are certain phrases you use when you want to start a fistfight. They call them "war words." You can't get through a session on social media without running into some of them. On the computer or the screen of an iPhone, there's no requirement to back up words with fists. A wide range of people find that liberating and as encouragement to use more of those "war words" and ill-thought-out phrases. I haven't been inside a Texas bar in ages, but I suspect they've updated their "war words" based on things they saw on the 'Net.

I don't have any particular love for Texas bar fights—or bar fights anywhere else. I've had opportunities to indulge and refused them every time. But a bar fight is active, if futile. Sitting in front of a computer and airing your woes to the world isn't active It's passive. The futility is built in. It's the same as doing nothing, except now all your electronic friends know your hot buttons. Don't think they won't push them if the opportunity arises. This makes a Texas bar fight look almost justified. At least it's good exercise.

If you are sitting in your home, in front of a screen, safely sheltered from any consequences of "war words," even conflict can be entertaining, I suppose. Isn't that what television is all about? But social media communications get into distinctly non-entertaining areas: resentment and whining. Resentment and whining are what people do when they can't or won't fix whatever it is that they are whining about. Of those two causes, "won't" accounts for a much greater percentage than the whiners and sullen would have you believe.

If you have something that bothers you, putting it out on the 'Net does nothing. Zero. You haven't *done* anything about it. You might find other people who have the same complaint, but more likely, you will find people with some other complaint that they will now feel empowered to air because that's what you did. It's a great way to discover all the unhappiness that people are too polite or too cowardly to talk about face-to-face. If that's actually what you wanted from the 'Net, congratulations.

Again, going back to theory, the 'Net was designed to empower the user by providing information and communications to sentient beings who would use it in a variety of productive ways. That empowerment is still there if you choose to use it that way. But the 'Net also works well for people who just want to whine or resent something.

Passivity—doing nothing with no intense thought—in an active world has its uses. It seems to be what Aristotle had in mind when he talked about his ideal life. Well, maybe not entirely, but Aristotle and his world of contemplation never really came to grips with who would wash the dishes and take the garbage out. It's still an active world—even two millennia after Aristotle—and that level of passivity is still unreachable.

In an active world, creating what you want counts for something; in a complex one, working with others to create a common vision does, too. Complaints about other people's creations do not count for anything. Business manuals say that ideal employees have a bias for action. Life says that those who do not have that bias get a smaller say in the outcomes.

So to achieve something and be recognized for it, you first have to do something to reach that achievement. This is true for six-year-olds, and it's true for world leaders, too. But then you don't have world leaders posting their whining and resentments on social media . . . or do you?

All Saints' Day

This week, I started to think about All Saints' Day. All Saints' Day is on the first of November. It's the day on which we are supposed to commemorate, well, all the saints. It's like Memorial Day for the fallen in religion rather than the fallen in war. In fact, in Great Britain, remembrance starts on All Saints' Day and ends on the second Sunday of the month, which is called Remembrance Day and more or less duplicates our Memorial Day. Now, if you parse out the origin of the name of Halloween, it means the evening before All Hallows' Day, which is what they called All Saints' Day in older times.

All Saints' Day goes back to the eighth century or thereabouts, when the Christian Church acknowledged that there were more saints than days and decided to establish one day for the veneration of them all. Several of the sources I checked mentioned that the day coincides with the old Celtic festival of Samhain, which was a harvest celebration for Druids and others. The early Christians seemed to schedule holidays around the same days as their predecessors—to ease transition, I suppose. Thus, the fertility festivals in the early spring became the more Christian Saint Valentine's Day, the day of love. I imagine modern folks would note the difference between love and fertility, but people in the depths of the Dark Ages had a much simpler view of life.

All Saints' Day is recognized and celebrated by many religions, even those that have some doubts about sainthood. The

Catholic Church follows All Saints' Day with All Souls' Day on November 2. On that day, all the dead are recognized and remembered. Not so for Lutherans, Methodists, and some other Protestant denominations, where All Saints' Day is the day for remembering all the dead. In Mexico, All Saints' Day is part of *El Día de los Muertos*, the Day of the Dead. This is a multiday festival, with the first—the Day of the Innocents—for remembering those who died as children and the second for everyone who died as adults.

In the United States, All Saints' Day occurs without much recognition, religious or otherwise. Occasionally, there's a passing reference: In *The Sopranos*, Christopher Moltisanti's last name means "many saints," which might coincide with the day.

This sort of thinking is unusual for me; I'm no liturgical scholar. Put me on *Jeopardy!* and make the category "Religious Doctrines," and I might as well play with a cell phone—my hand won't go anywhere near the buzzer until some other category is chosen. My grandfather, who was familiar with both the Old Country and the New, said that there are two kinds of homeboys: drinking ones and churchgoing ones. He personally had selected the former—and was quite happy with the choice—though he was not all that much of a drinker. We Bridgeports tend to see our relationship with God as a personal one, with communal doctrines of any sort ill-fitting for that relationship. I have more or less continued that tradition.

But early one evening, the faithful dog Stink and I wandered around the neighborhood. The neighborhood routinely dresses for Halloween, and only Christmas gets dressier. True to form, we passed by regiments of pumpkins, several pop-up graveyards, and ghosts, witches, and the undead of every description. Before I moved here, I lived in places where decorating for Halloween was practically nonexistent; but here, people go all out.

This year, one of my neighbors acquired a small herd of dragons. They are inflatable and at least fifteen feet tall—pretty impressive in the company of other Halloween furnishings. He shines a blue light on them in the evenings, which gives the whole display an even eerier effect. During the day, they are simple piles of uninflated polyester. That's a good call, given the high-spiritedness and sense of humor of some of the local adolescents. But at night, it's a really nice spectacle.

At first, I was hesitant to go near the dragons with the faithful dog Stink, but he ignored them, as he does with most decorations. In the other direction, neighbors have an oversized inflatable cat and a spider. These possess a gimmick that moves their heads every so often. Stink's okay with them, too—until the heads move. Then stuff becomes real. First, he retreats. Next, he attempts to attack half-heartedly. Finally, he decides that prudence demands he stand his ground and bark at the monstrosities for as long as I will let him.

Halloween is the time when the saints—or everybody, depending on your tradition—arise from the grave to receive the veneration, I guess. Tradition doesn't explain why. For many of the rising dead, it's going to be a rather confusing trip. They have a day to catch up with everything that's happened over the past year, and that's going to be difficult.

I'm also curious about the logistics of the arising. The number of people who are no longer here is pretty substantial. Who does crowd control, and who does transportation? We have another tradition that has the departed floating out of their graves, but once out, do they file flight plans and with whom? And how do they know where they want to go? They've been stuck in oblivion for a year, and it must take some time to reorient. And what about the ones who are not entombed?

The whole matter of desiring to return takes some thought. If you are already dead, who would pitchfork you out of your grave if you didn't want to go?

The holiday has simply outgrown its roots, and that's perfectly fine. I'm impressed with the displays, which often have outgrown themselves. People are putting a lot of time and effort into them. I hope the children for whom they are meant are impressed as well.

But a day for remembrance of the dead seems like a fitting tribute, too. Without the dead, we would not have plastic or psychotherapy or Elizabethan poetry. We wouldn't even have us, if you think about it.

The deceased are responsible for just about everything we see today, and our lives revolve around their contributions. A day to understand and appreciate that might be a holiday worth having. And All Saints' Day would seem to fit the bill.

I wish we could observe it with something other than left-over candy corn.

A Small Thing

Look, we don't need to get all bent out of shape about this, right?

It wasn't that big of a deal. Here's what happened. An author gave a talk at a university campus in Statesboro and challenged the students on the perks of being Caucasian. Some of the students took offense. They conveyed a few copies of her book outside, where there are those standing grills you usually find in state parks, they ripped the books apart, and they torched them.

I mean, there weren't that many students, right? And from the video footage I saw, that grill couldn't hold that many books. It was such a small thing. Besides, these were students, likely mostly still teenagers, right? You know how teenagers are. They think they know everything when they haven't been any farther from home than Macon.

But, of course, the press got hold of it and made it into a big thing. There was Statesboro, right on the front page in New York and Washington and everywhere else. Now, Statesboro is a nice little town with a pretty campus, and the only time the outside world notices it is when some dopey undergraduates char up a few books. And, of course, the first thing the

newspapers did was interview the author; the second thing they did was interview the students who thought the burning was terrible. So now Statesboro, maybe even Georgia, probably has a bad reputation.

Sure, burning the books wasn't the right reaction, but it wasn't a riot like the one in Charlottesville or a massacre like those in El Paso and Pittsburgh or many other places I could name. This was just a few books.

Well, the university had to say something, and this is what was said: "We regret that Crucet's [that's the author] experience in Statesboro ended as it did. We call on students to remain civil in disagreement, even on difficult issues, and make Georgia Southern University a place we can all feel proud to represent."

There's a stinging rebuke, and those students are probably ashamed to show their faces on campus.

Of course, the people sympathetic to uncivilized discourse were quick to point out that book burning is protected by the First Amendment of the U.S. Constitution. Everyone should carry around a good lighter in case they run into a piece of paper with which they disagree, according to those worthies.

So let's put it in context.

Over the past four years, we've seen mass murders in synagogues, churches, shopping malls, and schools. We've seen rioting by bullies and lunatics. Our leadership seems intent on ignoring all of this and at times has almost seemed to encourage it.

I was being sarcastic in my opening statements, but put this event in context and it was a small thing. However, I really, really don't like the context. Is that who we are now?

Let me try that question again. Is that who we want to be?

I just had the occasion to review some of William Butler Yeats' works, and while there was an objective to the exercise, I completed it with pleasure. This wasn't work, not really. I get something new out of each reading, and sometimes I get to ponder his words again.

In his poem "The Second Coming," there's a particularly acute phrase. The poem was written in 1919, as Yeats contemplated the wreckage of Europe after the First World War. In the poem, he asks "what rough beast, its hour come round at last, / Slouches toward Bethlehem to be born?" Yeats died in early 1939; by then, the beast had been identified and was about to spring into action, starting with Poland.

But that's not the phrase I mean. Earlier in the poem, he mentions that "[m]ere anarchy is loosed upon the world." That right there: mere anarchy.

Maybe what he meant by mere anarchy is ignoring the rule of law, built up painfully over the centuries, in favor of local rule—ultra-local rule as in "I'm bigger than you are, so I get to tell you what to do." Rule based on strong-arm tactics and mob mentality. Anarchy happens when the governing are unable or unwilling to correct the impression that such behavior is appropriate—until the strong-armers take charge. You can bet there will not be any anarchy then.

Earlier in the program, I played some music from *Game of Thrones*. *Game of Thrones* is anarchy with a few dragons and icemen thrown in. The series concentrates on the handful of strong-armers battling for the throne, but that's predictable for fiction. Fiction is full of unnamed characters who are merely part of the background. In *Game of Thrones*, this includes most of the plebeians immolated by the dragons, the foot soldiers in the frequent battles, the watchman who happened to be on duty when winter showed up with a knife.

Reality is when those people aren't plot devices. They have lives and spouses and children. They aren't bent on revenge or plunder or rape—they're just trying to get through the day. When their rulers are bent on some great mission to get rid of somebody else, the collateral damage is sickening. That part of the equation rarely makes it into adventure fiction stories.

So anarchy is the leaders of society not standing up when individuals or even mobs abuse the rest. It's not a big thing; it's small things all grouped together. Once you let an incident go, you are in danger of shining on any incident like it, because that's only fair, right?

Fair it may be, but civilized it is not. It's anarchy, mere anarchy.

It's a small thing.

Football

Just after noon last Saturday, it was fifty-six degrees in Columbus, Ohio. Furthermore, it was raining. A lot of people in that Midwest locale had anoraks on, the ones with a water-re-pellant shell and some sort of warm lining. And there were a lot of people out, because Ohio State University—which has a pretty good football team this year—was playing Wisconsin, which also has a good team. Two hundred and twenty-eight student musicians splashed onto the field to spell out Ohio in script. Imagine how many it would take for the Massachusetts Institute of Technology to duplicate that feat.

The cheerleaders wore tracksuits, puddles of water gathered on the sidelines, and while the rain occasionally backed off to a drizzle, there were heavier downpours, too. Anoraks are good clothing items if you happen to be in Columbus, Ohio, but the rain they shed has a nasty habit of traveling downward. So once it leaves the anorak, it drips onto the jeans you are wearing. Jeans are generally cotton blends and have no hesitation about soaking up rain. If you enjoy wet jeans in fifty-degree weather, Columbus was the place to be.

In contrast, it was somewhere around eighty degrees at the North Beach Bar and Grill on Tybee Island. The sun shone brightly, the salad was fresh and tasty, and the bartender was watchful and considerate. That is where I watched the events in Columbus unfold—or at least the ones that unfolded in the opening stages of the first quarter.

In 2007, the Coen brothers adapted Cormac McCarthy's novel *No Country for Old Men.* I haven't seen the film yet, though it's on my list. I think it takes place somewhere in the Southwest. Based on the Ohio football game, I can't rule out Columbus. But I know it wasn't set on Tybee Island—last Saturday, Tybee was a superb place for old men.

If you have not been to North Beach lately, the construction of the new marine science center is proceeding apace. I can't wait for it to open. Mainly, I can't wait because the construction is blocking my favorite path to the beach that leads to where the river meets the sea. There's a stone jetty there, which I guess is supposed to keep the river and the sea from meeting too abruptly. It's like a chaperoned cotillion for water. But you can look up the river and then out to sea by just turning your head. Pelicans and cormorants fish there, other sea birds breed a bit farther up, and it gives the feeling of being well and truly seaside.

For the past year, the country has been short on "Vember," and as of yesterday, we have No Vember.

While this typically means a change of season for other folks, the Low Country has resolutely stayed with daily highs in the upper seventies and low eighties. This is old-man weather. Age bestows some of the characteristics of turtles on humans: Sitting in the sun is nearly impossible in summer, but it feels good now in short doses.

But no blessing comes unmixed.

The weather for airing out the old men is also ideal for breeding mosquitoes. They, too, have enjoyed the respite from cool temperatures and are out in numbers. Getting three or four with one slap and doing it consistently is heavy bug weather even for Savannah. The noble dog and I have deferred woodland trips for the time being; we circumnavigate golf courses and soccer fields instead.

So we have passed Halloween, and people are switching their displays from black and orange to red and green.

For October 31, the Bridgeports bought candy in quantity and did little else. We were too long in the North in younger days; experiencing pumpkin purchases without wearing coats seem unnatural somehow. Watching neighbors sweat while erecting Santas does, too.

Of course, many Santas these days are inflatable. I wonder if they are victimized by overoptimistic mosquitoes.

But sometime in November, the weather will notice the calendar, and the temperature will drop ten degrees. Old men will abandon short sleeves on both their arms and legs in favor of longer and thicker garments. Rain, when it falls, will approximate the temperature of last Saturday's Columbus precipitation. With a little assistance from the county's aircraft distributing spray, the woods may become walkable again. At least longer sleeves will provide better protection.

In November, we seem less the Low Country and more the Coastal Empire, though I am not sure what that means.

The coastal part is easy enough, but the empire confuses me. The concept of an empire seems vaguely un-American. But Savannah events in the autumn tend to move with a sense of purpose, which I suppose empires do, even when nobody is sure what the purpose really is.

With the commencement of November, we also gird our loins—if our loins require that—for the holiday season. The grim search for the perfect frozen turkey begins in short order. Rainstorms sweep in from the north. Barbecuing seems a less attractive option. Voting is just around the corner.

We are starting to move in earnest... or as earnest as Savannah gets.

But when I think back on the year, it's not my accomplishments of November that will come to mind. Instead, I will remember the Ohio State–Wisconsin game played in a moderate fifty-degree rain. I'll remember watching it from the bar on North Beach and shifting my position every so often to keep my legs from getting too much sun in the alluring eighty degrees.

For me, that's a good football game.

Bert (No Soapbox This Week)

Normally, I'd use this time to share observations from my week. I don't feel like doing that this time.

Last night, a buddy of more than a half century passed away. We developed a fast friendship, and though our lives took us hundreds and sometimes thousands of miles from each other, we reunited every so often and each time added ornaments to the relationship.

Oh, I'm not going to do a funeral oration, but I know that he used his talents and intelligence fully and generously in his life, mostly in the service of others. Scientific studies suggest that we are all stinkers at the core. Occasionally, you run into an exception to the rule, and he was one of them. So let's just listen to some music.

Samuel Barber's "Adagio for Strings" seems the right tenor.

Dreams

I've been thinking about dreams the past week. Dreams come in two varieties. The first variety appears when you go to bed and turn out the lights. The next thing you know, you're driving down the Truman Parkway in a golf cart. Golf carts can't go the posted minimum on the Truman, much less the speed people actually drive, so the cars are honking and flashing their lights at you and of course you are in the left-hand lane. Somewhere just after the DeLesseps exit, a hand from a car driving next to you reaches out and snatches your wood driver from your golf bag. In real life, you don't play golf, but in the dream, that's your favorite club.

About halfway between DeLesseps and Derenne, traffic backs up, so people stop honking in your direction. There's a police roadblock just short of Derenne—they've had a report that somebody is driving naked down the parkway. You wait in line, and a kid in the back of the SUV ahead of you starts to laugh and point in your direction. You look down and discover that you are, in fact, without a stitch of clothing. You fumble around in the bag, looking for your towel, but it isn't there. A patrolman waves the SUV forward. He looks at you, and his eyes narrow. Then you wake up.

Fortunately for all of us, that's not the sort of dream I want to talk about.

The other kind of dream occurs when you are awake and project yourself into another environment that seems nicer than your current situation. We all do it, even children, and maybe especially children. If a child tells you that he or she wants to be a fireman and an astronaut and a football player, you've just received a catalog of the latest dreams. Sometimes those dreams hang on because some children do indeed go on to be astronauts. And sometimes people just remember their dreams. I remember a childhood dream that I was sitting on the bank of a river, under a low-hanging tree, with rushes along the banks of the slow-moving water. It was cool and peaceful.

At the time, I was sitting on a curb, with my back against a fire hydrant on 243rd Street.

But adult dreams don't have the same scope as those of children: Fifty-year-olds don't dream of becoming firemen and astronauts and football players all at the same time, because fifty-year-olds have more information on the subject. For instance, two people I know are right on the edge of not being young anymore. From age three, one wanted to be a doctor; the other wanted to work with animals. Both are now doing what they wanted to do, and both now know the details and difficulties of following their dreams. They gave up other dreams for those they achieved. Having a dream and fulfilling it are just not the same. That's the first thing about projection dreams—they are limited by how much you know about the subject. I can actually live my 243rd Street dream right now, but I'll be living it in a reality that involves insects and mud and glare from the southern sun that I did not know about when I lived close to 243rd Street.

Sometimes dreams are thrust upon us. We have a set of experiences that blows our minds, probably unexpectedly, and we want to go back and have the experiences again, especially if our usual life is very different. Remember how Joni Mitchell sang of just such a situation in "Free Man in Paris"? Sometimes we actually get a return visit, and usually it's not quite the same: Somebody's built a shopping center on the pristine lower slopes of the mountain; a front comes through while you are fishing in the waters of the Gulf Stream and the trip to shore resembles a roller-coaster ride; it rains all week in Disney World, rains nasty. Or simply, those memories have been sharpened and colored by time, and no reality could match them.

Despite realities creeping in, we still have our projection dreams. A few years ago, I wanted to hop a freighter, any freighter, and go wherever it was headed. The destination wasn't important; the journey was. I would watch the changing beauty of the deep sea, sit in my guest cabin, and finish writing my novel. I would contemplate the basic elements of my life and reach conclusions that would serve as a road map for the rest of it. And maybe, just maybe, the trip would end in some port I actually wanted to visit—Singapore, maybe, or Anchorage or Rio. I wanted to be on a freighter, not on a cruise where I might overeat and buy things I don't need to prop up the local economy. Cruises are for the gregarious, and I am not.

I held onto that dream long enough to research it. Freighter travel is no longer the bargain it once was. Crews generally come from other cultures, speaking other languages, and the ship cook attempts to accommodate those cultures, usually with more imagination than skill because ships at sea run out of food fast. Far from overeating, avoiding under-eating might become a problem.

So the dream withered away, and that's all right. Projection dreams are simply a temporary escape from present responsibilities and commitments. That makes them both unrealistic and forgivable.

Sometimes others' dreams are projected onto your reality. A visitor once looked around my backyard and told me I was living the dream. Bless you, my friend, do you not see the smilax twining through the azaleas? The patch where the sun has not only baked off the grass but turned the ground underneath into construction-grade adobe? Bless you, for you are simply comparing my situation with yours, without knowing the details. When you have lived the extra years that I have, maybe you will understand more. I will not tread on your projections with particulars.

And that is the second thing about projection dreams: They are as much an escape from current reality, responsibilities, and commitments as they are lacking in specifics. They are a form of vacation, and we are all due a vacation at some point or another, even in the recesses of our minds.

I've said this before, but every life is a work in progress, and dreams are a product of how far we've progressed and in what direction. But sometimes I go and sit on the cool banks of that river I conjured up while I sat on 243rd Street. The tree over my head provides shade but not chill. Rushes sway on both sides of me, and swans with their young paddle lazily upstream. Bugs are absent, save for the humming of a distant honeybee. Maybe after I finish this, I will close my eyes and go there. I sure hope I don't wind up on the Truman Parkway.

Winter 2019 ~ 2020

Recipes

Name a holiday—any holiday—and people will tell you how it looks. Christmas has trees and lights and presents. The Fourth of July has flags and fireworks. Easter has bunnies and colored eggs. You get the idea. But there is an exception, and that is the one we just passed. For this holiday, there is a sight on the table as the meal is served, but Thanksgiving isn't about sight. It's about smell.

On Thanksgiving, I arose early, as usual. (I would wake up later, sometime after rising, but that's standard on a normal day.) As best I could, I reviewed the day ahead. Oh yeah, it's Thanksgiving. Got to cook the turkey. When you are half-awake, this is not a cheering prospect.

I moved through the early hours reluctantly, thinking of everything that must be done and everything that might go wrong. Then I took the frying pan out of the cupboard and started the sausage. As the pan heated, the sausage began to sizzle, and the smell of sage and spiced pork hit my nostrils. I was transported back to when I was five. That's the smell of Thanksgiving. The adrenaline hit, and then I was ready to do this thing. I was going to cook this turkey and everything that goes with it.

I use my mother's recipe for stuffing. It has been passed down for precisely one generation. We don't have old family recipes.

On my father's side, my grandmother was a cook from the Old Country, and it was a country not known for cuisine. Aside from baked goods, the authentic meals are based on stock-fish—usually preserved in some manner—and root vegetables. Any secret recipes she had went with her to the grave, and perhaps that is just as well. After she passed away, my grandfather lived with us. His delight with canned corned beef hash makes me suspicious.

On my mother's side, she was the daughter of a basketball player in an era that paid them about as well as journeyman plumbers. He died when she was very young, and my grandmother was too busy earning a living to fuss about food.

So any Bridgeport specialties originated with my mother, and I believe she developed most of them on the fly, after marriage. She had an additional problem. My father had spent some months at the end of World War II being fed by the Wehrmacht—as a result of being thrown into the Battle of the Bulge too early and finding his unit overwhelmed. At that point in the war, Wehrmacht food was scarce and not especially well prepared, when it existed at all. He came home with a raging hatred of many of the things that sustained him during that time, with special loathing for onions and other root vegetables. Anything my mother prepared had to steer clear of things other cooks employed with joyous abandon.

She rose to the challenge. Hers was a generation that did that, and she was no exception. Her cooking was not uniformly wonderful, probably owing to my father's taboos. But there were standout dishes and not just a few of them. While we saw meatloaf far more often than a leg of lamb, the lamb was not only delicious, it stayed delicious as leftovers. The few times I've tried to cook lamb, the leftovers have the consistency of fatty loofah, if with slightly more flavor. Her spaghetti sauce, which did not come from a jar and required several hours to assemble, also sang. I don't know how you do that without onions, and I can't replicate it even with them.

I mentioned sausage before. That wasn't for breakfast. My mother did not cook breakfast, not with three children, a household to run, and a huge dinner to prepare. She'd put the box of cereal on the table and a container of milk. The rest was up to us. She fed us with love, no doubt, but the love was encased in the realism, skill, and determination of a pro.

The sausage was for the stuffing. Some people think that's an odd idea, but large meals in her era had to feed us for days. The turkey would last until every shred was gone, and the last few meals would be light on turkey and heavy on the other remains. Sausage not only keeps the stuffing moist, it packs the required nutritional punch for those future meals.

Unrestricted by my father's experiences, I use onions in my dressing along with mushrooms and few other things that were beyond my mom's charter. They improve the taste, but only slightly. The basic flavors of my childhood are there, just as I remember them. It's one of the few things left that is just as I remember it.

That's only the start. When it comes to Thanksgiving aromas, the oven transmits that roasting turkey smell throughout the house. I roast mine, thank you. The whipped yams add a touch of cinnamon and port wine. I use these ingredients instead of blatantly sugary things. No marshmallows are harmed during the preparation of my dinner.

Over the years, one of the few Thanksgiving debates at Casa Bridgeport has been about the cranberry. At other places, I have had cranberries marinated in and mixed with any number of different things. I've even tried a few variations myself. But in the end, cranberry is a garnish. As I underscored last year, I like mine jellied and can-shaped. I even like the *splort* you hear when it comes out of its cylinder. It is one less thing requiring preparation time, and it's a perfectly fine garnish.

That's just my dinner. Everyone has a set of smells—pumpkin or apple pie maybe, glazed carrots, whatever. But Thanksgiving is a smell holiday, not a sight one. Those smells as the dinner is cooking sharpen the anticipation. By the time it all hits the table, nobody cares about the sight anymore—they just want to dig in.

As a meal, Thanksgiving is a task involving multiple dishes and multiple hours of preparation. It involves coordination, skill, and effort. When you contemplate it as a cook, it can be daunting. But then the smells start, and you remember why you are doing it in the first place.

For me, it starts with the scent of sizzling sausage.

Taking Stock

The week after Thanksgiving is stocktaking week in Bridgeport World. It is the interval between the feast of Thanksgiving and the many considerations and activities of Christmas. Like every year, I think we have too much stock, and we ought to take it to the dump. The Board of Directors disagrees, so I'm not even going to bring up that idea.

Thus, the stocktaking begins.

The driveway has achieved an unburnt sienna tone, that mustardy brown that you find on serious work clothes. Oak leaves and pine needles play their part in this, but unlike maples and those other trees farther north, the live oaks and longleaf pines don't just shed in winter. They drop reminders all year. If I were to decide to rake in the middle of August, there would be plenty to do. But many of the live oaks do have acorns, and the colder weather sets them free. A remarkable percentage plunge onto the driveway. They are small, these live oak acorns, from about the size of a pea to half the size of the usual variety. When you drive over them, which is my favorite method for their disposal, they crackle like broken glass rather than popping. Drive over them enough, and the brisk winds carry the grounds elsewhere, at least in theory. Theory hasn't held up this year, and I'll probably have to actually do something about them.

Aside from half a bowl of gravy, the Thanksgiving feast has been digested. All plates and platters have been returned to their usual resting places. They will come out again in a month or so, but for now, they sit silently. Whenever a turkey is roasted, the last portion is a thing of shreds and patches, well-aged, that nobody wanted in the first place. That last meal can be a grim affair, but not for us. The dog belches gratefully. Go figure.

And so we consider the coming holiday. For us, Christmas preparations stay relatively the same from year to year. The children are grown and remote. This gives us a certain amount of time to reflect on the prior twelve months. It's like selling Christmas trees before Thanksgiving; best to beat the rush at the end of the year.

We took hits this year. Some involved health, some involved dear friends who lost their health—as in completely. That also promotes a certain amount of reflection. I would like to report that after mature consideration, we have revised the roadmap for the rest of our lives and plan to implement the changes that will ensure a bright tomorrow. But that would be a lie. It would also be silly, even if we had. Especially if we had.

Instead, the mature consideration, what we've done of it, indicates that we don't have control over our destiny because nobody does. Any road maps, however detailed, are subject to circumstances beyond the writer's control. Since we are right on the edge of being excessively mature, if not neck-deep in it, those circumstances occur more and more. Back in the early days of automobile GPS, your machine would scream "turn here" as you went past a five-car pileup blocking the exit. It's like that.

You can, of course, switch from the assumption that every-thing is going to be okay to the suspicion that something awful is going to happen six breaths from now. But that's immature consideration, well-beloved by fourteen-year-olds. It doesn't work for them, and it won't work for you. As a matter of fact, it travels in exactly the wrong direction: If you are primed to see everything as a potential disaster, it will be.

Nature doesn't do value judgments. Stuff happens, and that's as far as nature goes. Whether it's terrible or not is up to the viewers, and in anything other than an outright disas-ter, there's a wide variety of opinions. When stuff happens, it becomes what you make of it. The value judgments are all yours. That's the part that often escapes the fourteen-year-olds.

And so we begin the run-up to Christmas. My favorite Christmas carol is "Silent Night," if I'm pressed, though "God Rest Ye Merry, Gentlemen" will always be close. But that's for the holiday. My favorite one for the days before the holiday is the "Carol of the Bells," as it captures some of the sense of Christmas preparation.

Earlier on, perhaps it's the Pentatonix version—artful and interesting with a kinder, gentler crescendo of dinging and donging that signals that the process has started. Will we send cards this year? Who wants what, and does it need to be mailed? Are we decorating outside and how much, and which strings of bulbs have to be committed to the ages? There are trees and meals to be considered and all sorts of work required for a time of respite and reflection. The song portrays planning and scheduling, with all the usual non-holiday activities firmly in place. The actual holiday is almost background.

Closer to Christmas, the dinging and donging gets louder and more persistent, like the Trans-Siberian Orchestra's version of the carol. For good or ill, most of the plans are implemented, but there are always problems and some harder things to solve. Does anybody sell "Baby Yoda" anything yet? Ding-dong, ding-dong. What do you mean it has to be assembled? If I have to bake ten loaves of bread and each loaf takes three hours and twenty-two minutes, I'll be up until...

Ding-dong, ding-dong.

Somehow, it all comes together each year. Not the way we planned, but at least the general outlines are there. If you've ever been involved in wedding planning, you understand the concept. At some point, it gets going under its own steam, and then the best you can do is nudge it a little in one direction or another.

Maybe that's true for entire lives. Lennon (John, of course, not Vladimir Ilyich Ulyanov Lenin) once said that life is what happens while you are making other plans. The dinging and donging are there to remind you that there's a deadline. What you do after the planning determines what actually goes down and becomes more important as the deadline looms.

Maybe that's true for entire lives, too.

The Cornerstone Speech

For somebody who has a thing for history, I know very little about Savannah's, even though I have always tried to visualize places as they were when momentous events happened.

Once I lived in New England in a small town that seemed surrounded with momentous events. I dug deep into its history and found, well, not that much.

The town was established after the Revolution, which is sort of a downer in a region proud of such founding roots. Later, it sent a fair number of men to the Civil War. There are about thirty-five names on the monument on the town green, of battle casualties and victims of Andersonville. Aside from that, townspeople had raised cows and crops from the first settlers to the time we lived there.

Here in Savannah, I spend a good deal of time in Chippewa Square, which is also a good place to begin a little history of the Hostess City of the South. Forrest Gump was there, of course, but what else? Digging a little more, the Savannah Theatre

caught my attention. It's always described as historic. What do they mean by that? Quite a bit, as it turns out.

The Savannah Theatre opened its doors in 1818 and has been open ever since, aside from the times when fires or storms closed it. Any number of famous actors appeared there in the nineteenth century. In the 1850s and 1860s, it was known as the Athenaeum. An athenaeum is a place for literary and scientific study. I don't know if the Athenaeum stopped showing plays during this period, but it certainly held speeches. One of the most famous (or infamous) is Alexander Stephens' Cornerstone Speech.

This takes a little explanation. After serving in the Georgia state legislature, Alexander Stephens was a congressman, a member of the U.S. House of Representatives from 1843 to 1859. He gave his speech in March of 1861. He had just returned from the first meeting of the Montgomery convention, which was attended by delegates from South Carolina, Alabama, Mississippi, Louisiana, Florida, Georgia, and eventually Texas and set up the basis for the Confederacy. Several future Confederate states such as Virginia, Tennessee, and North Carolina did not send delegates. Robert Barnwell Rhett, however, a delegate from South Carolina, wrote that it was better that way: He was afraid those states would dilute the convention's attachment to slavery. He needn't have worried.

The convention was a fractious affair, and several histories credit Stephens with holding it together. He had mastered both parliamentary procedure and political maneuvering in Congress and deflected anything that would derail the convention's purpose. Named vice president of the provisional government, the following month he spoke at the Athenaeum in Savannah.

The speech was, for the time, a short one. The report of the address consumes thirteen pages in a book with generously sized type, and the text—as far as the reporter could manage—is a series of direct quotes. While Stephens did not script the speech, he later endorsed the report as an accurate account of what he said.

What he said, fresh from the Montgomery convention, was a plainspoken digest of Confederate philosophy and goals. He said that Jefferson and the other founders were blinded by the temporarily fashionable idea that all men are created equal and that this had proven illusory and unrealistic. He added that the Confederate government was the first to be realistic, assigning anyone not white to a subordinate role and, in the case of blacks, to a permanent state of slavery.

Here's his solution: "Our new government is founded upon exactly the opposite idea; its foundations are laid, its corner-stone rests, upon the great truth, that the negro is not equal to the white man; that slavery—subordination to the superior race—is his natural and normal condition."

That's why it's called the Cornerstone Speech. He also stated that any federal fiscal activity, either in the collection of revenue or the dispensing of it, aside from the cost of governing, is a violation of natural rights and would be forbidden by the new government. The states would handle all financial matters.

Right there, in those simple principles, he guaranteed the failure of the Confederacy. The first statements made it abhorrent, and the second made it unworkable. Those brave men who fought for the Confederacy did so badly clothed and sporadically fed. The Confederate government was hamstrung by a lack of funds. Jefferson Davis wrote several letters that varied from blistering to despairing about his attempts to wrest proper funding from the states.

Okay, so what? That's just history. Well, maybe not.

On December 6, that's of this year, in an interview with Glenn Beck the former governor of South Carolina recollected removing the Confederate flag from the grounds of the state's capitol. The removal happened in the wake of nine murders in a Charleston church in 2015, murders committed simply because the victims weren't white.

She described the murderer, Dylann Roof:

> [H]ere is this guy that comes out with his manifesto, holding the Confederate flag, and had just hijacked *everything* that people thought of. And we don't have hateful people in South Carolina. There's always the small minority that's always going to be there, but, you know, people saw [the flag] as

service and sacrifice and heritage....But once he
did that, there, there was no way to overcome it.

This was not a hijacking of Confederate values. This was a
ride-along. Mr. Roof and his ideas integrate perfectly with those
of Alexander Stephens. Mr. Roof's ability to adopt 150-year-old
ideals—ideals that were proven both immoral and inept—is
somewhat astounding, but that's what he did.

I can see where there is service, sacrifice, and heritage in
the Confederate cause, but these values supported a horrible
philosophy and a flawed governing system. Ignoring that is
bad history, and bad history makes bad politics. If history is
to teach us anything, it must be presented as it happened, not
spun into cotton candy.

A Moment of Wonder

Mornings are early at Rancho Bridgeport.

Aged muscles cramp when left in the same position for very
long, and old bladders don't seem to have the capacity of young
ones. Curiously, old brains appear to need the same amount
of rest, if not more. So while the vehicle might be in motion,
avionics and navigation are still booting up. I get up well before
I wake up.

This morning, I wandered outside to pick up the paper. It was
still dark. It was also cold. Daylight hours in Savannah may
resolve into the mildest of climates this time of year, but pre-
dawn is reliably chilly and damp. Here and there, holiday lights
shone in the morning gloom. The paper had landed safely clear
of both our outside holiday decorations and the puddle in the
driveway—perhaps that's the sign of a good day. It was quiet.

And yet, I sensed a signal. I can't say something was calling
me; it more resembled a blip on a radar screen. It was inaudible
and transparent, but there was something there.

Like the unsoiled paper, that, too, was unusual. The psychic
and metaphysical usually choose someone else to accost. I am

generally far too engaged with the audible and visible to trouble about other things. Maybe the rattle and clatter of fully booted avionics and navigation drown them out, I don't know. But the signal was there.

It wasn't that I didn't have other things to do. I have the full burden of things left undone that most people do around this time of year. But I decided to follow the feeling. It seemed remote, so I got into the truck. Add putting the truck through the car wash to the list of things left undone.

The truck took me to a road that runs across a small finger of the marsh. I parked alongside the bridge and sat on one of the abutments. I pulled my jacket closer around me. To the east, a bank of clouds muted the light of the still-unrisen sun. I faced west. The morning stars twinkled overhead. The morning fog oozed among thick canopies of trees on either side of the wetland, graying the foliage out in places. A sea of marsh grass stood before me, the tips bending in a slight breeze. No living thing intruded, apart from the slightly sour smell of the winter marsh.

I sat transfixed until the rising sun erased the stars and traffic started to crowd the road that winds its way to a convenience store where people procure their morning coffee. But before that, it was a moment of wonder.

All right, I sat beside a muddy marsh in the early morning hours and had a moment of wonder. What does it mean to you?

For all of us, moments of wonder are rare. As children, we have more of them, probably because as children we lack the experience and information to call them anything else. As we acquire those things, we learn to distinguish moments of wonder from spectacle, glittering displays of light and sound that are pretty enough but don't really reach into our core. And the gaudier the spectacle, the less it seems to mean. Think about Super Bowl halftime shows. We manufacture spectacles at will, and sometimes they overwhelm the very reason for the spectacle. Is Christmas really about lights and Santa, Easter about bunnies and eggs, Thanksgiving about elaborate meals, or the Fourth of July about fireworks? Not really, but we can manufacture those things, and we can't manufacture moments of wonder. And if you wonder about the reverse relationship between spectacle and wonder, ask a twelve-year-old about Santa.

Too bad. Moments of wonder are good for us. They give us perspective on ourselves, reducing our activities and beings to the size the universe has really given them. Context is everything. Darwin said survival depends on how well you adapt to your environment, and that's just another way to say context. We live in a complex society that requires our constant attention. Mostly we do so in boxes that shield us from larger issues—sun, moon, rain, temperature. We last longer that way, but we also focus on things that may have limited meaning.

You cannot watch the stars, sit beside the ocean waves, or observe the fog seep around woods surrounding acres of marsh grass and be very impressed with your own accomplishments. Above and beyond all the connections that human society demands, we are part of a greater whole. And in the end, that greater whole is far more important and meaningful than the things we do. It is in the marsh grass, but it is elsewhere, too. A friend of mine glows when she speaks of her home desert and another of his mountains. I have had other moments of wonder—beside a winter brook in a Connecticut valley, watching water rush out of the Vermont hills on a steep incline, seeing the turns and folds of the Pennsylvania highlands from a plane. Beside those, the works of Bridgeport are negligible.

Having a moment of wonder at this time of year makes it more special. I can look at my own spectacles—the lights, the tree, and so forth—and understand their symbology a bit better. They don't seem like spectacles as much as symbols of something with a connection to that greater whole. I am a notorious skeptic of the paranormal and metaphysical, but there's a universe of things out there that has nothing to do with us. We don't even understand it very well. Just like the cave persons, we symbolize it to the best of our ability.

And so the symbols develop their own meaning. What and how much they mean depend on how each of us regards them. But the really important ones still have their basis in some moment of wonder.

For each of you, I wish you your own moment of wonder, from whatever source you derive it and whenever it appears. It will engage both your emotion and your intellect. I think it's the finest gift you could receive, and it's not even from me.

Be of good cheer.

The Old Songs

This point in the calendar is the trough between Christmas and the New Year, and it is a time for reflection. During World War I, American soldiers sang "We Don't Know Where We're Going, But We're on Our Way." About the same time, British soldiers were singing "We're Here Because We're Here" to the tune of "Auld Lang Syne." Both seem to resonate in the week between December 25 and January 1.

Perhaps it's best not to overthink the issue. The Dutch have a saying: "One should not think about it too much when marrying or taking pills." That might be true for entering a New Year, too.

Conceptually, we start the year the same way we start other years—enduring a skyrocket fusillade, writing a number of checks with errors in the dateline, and hoping that February's weather will be better than the month before. There's the illusion that what we resolve to do in January will still seem relevant on the other end of March. Resolutions are triumphs of the will, the determination to do something no matter what. When the "matters what" appear, the resolutions become undoable, silly, or irrelevant. We have forsworn resolutions in the Bridgeport domain. The Bridgeports ride the tide, going with the flow, as the great philosophers James Taylor and Carly Simon once recommended.

Maybe part of the problem is that we have too much time now. We go from Christmas, when many things must be accomplished by a certain near-term deadline, to trying to think about where we want to be in twelve months' time. And we try to do it just as the fatigue of completing the Christmas exercise sets in.

The holidays make those World War I sing-alongs seem pretty relevant. We do not in fact know where we are going, and we are in fact on our way. And we are past worrying about our place in the universe. We are here because we're here. No further justification seems necessary. My existence was ordained without any opinion from me; my thoughts wouldn't have mattered anyway, even if I had developed any.

The world is richer and more variable than one's ability to plan. You will collide with it in unexpected ways. Back in the days of the Franklin Planner, the trainers told us to plan half our time, because the other half would be taken up by things we never dreamed about. And so it turned out to be, and that was on a good day. That's the great secret: The essence of life is unforeseen consequences.

Here's how it works.

The palatial Bridgeport residential compound consists of the main house and guest quarters we refer to as the toolshed. The main house provides shelter for us; the toolshed is a hostel for some of the random and occasionally obnoxious wildlife that travels through our domain at night.

The main house has a sunroom that overlooks the toolshed. Sun only enters the room erratically, so there's less emphasis on "sun," but the room is glassed in, so it's not a porch. Now, the glazing is double-paned and old enough to vote. That means the seals gave up the fight long ago and moisture and crud have crept between the panes. That, in turn, means the out-of-doors always looks smoggy from the inside—kind of an industrial, nasty smog at that—no matter what the weather is.

Until they develop a washer fluid that penetrates the glass and cleans the other side of the double panes, this is an issue. For many years, we followed the "Serenity Prayer" and accepted it as something we could not change. The wheel turns slowly, but it does turn. We ordered new glass this year about the same time that I started to shop for frozen turkeys, and the new panes are in. Our backyard now looks like Savannah, not London in a fog of coal dust. Mission accomplished.

Except . . . now that I can see the backyard in detail, I can see all the garden maintenance I didn't get to in better weather. The glass task is over, but the yard work has just begun, and that was completely unforeseen. And then there's Stink. Previously, we let the dog out at night to discourage toolshed dwelling by uninvited creatures. He stayed out for long periods of time shooing off possums and worse, so we thought. It's dark out there, but with the increased visibility, I could swear I saw him playing pinochle and popping brews with whatever else sauntered by. I can't be sure, but I have my suspicions.

Unforeseen consequences . . . I know people who grumble at every political initiative because they are afraid of unforeseen consequences. And they are right, because anything we do will have consequences, foreseen and otherwise, even swapping out glass panes. There's worse news for all of us: Even doing nothing begets unforeseen consequences.

We have two choices. I can pull up my big boy pants and deal with what I did not foresee, or I can start chanting the "Serenity Prayer" or some other invocation. For issues that involve more people than just me, the "Serenity Prayer" option isn't really available.

That's it right there. Unforeseen consequences make the world go round, and we spend much time dealing with them. The fixes for the unseen will result in further unseen—and on and on. Because we are clever sorts, after we deal with something for a while, much of what happens becomes more foreseen. We currently live lives that the doughboys and Tommies of World War I could not have imagined, and much of that is positive.

But the songs they sang in the war are still true: "We're here because we're here because we're here," and "[w]e don't know where we're going, but we're on our way." We still do not have a firm grasp on direction, and our location is simply where we are now. The business of dealing with situations is most of what we do, because that's as far as our visions extend. Do that well, and we don't need to know where we are going.

It's a New Year, not a new life. We will build on the solid foundation of what we have previously accomplished. We will have successes and setbacks, fight the good fight, and win often enough, if not predictably. When we wed or create a child or do anything else worthwhile, life rarely turns out the way we planned. But an awful lot of the time, it turns out okay. And that's a big advantage the doughboys and Tommies didn't have.

Enjoy your year as long as you have the opportunity. I'm looking forward to mine.

The New Slate

My noble companion Stink and I toured the neighborhood on New Year's Eve, just after the sun left the horizon. The sky was clear, and the moon was waxing in its first quarter. It seemed more distant, and the evening star, which I believe is Venus, shone almost as brightly. Soon we would witness the rocket's red glare, but that wasn't what we were out for. The holiday lights were still up, and the neighborhood was quiet. That was our aim.

The outdoor lighting on this particular night appeared especially attractive. Perhaps my neighbors outdid themselves this year, or maybe I was just in the mood. I looked at my own decorations as we wound our way home. The lights on the doe's head were gone, and some of the bulbs on the azalea bush were only half lit. And something had collided with one of the little lighted trees, snapping it in half so that it looked as if the doe were chewing on the remains. Next year will bring some replacement and renewal. But these will serve for what's left of this year's display.

As we sail into 2020, we will leave behind the lights of 2019. Since we are traveling in time and not distance, the lights will go out; people will take them down and put them in boxes until the next holiday season. But there were some really nice displays this year, and when the time returns in 2020, they will be a welcome sight.

And welcome to the New Year, which will be "full of things that have never been," according to the poet Rilke.

For right now, it's full of things that have been around for some time. That said, changes may happen suddenly, and we will spend a lot of time adjusting to them. That's called punctuated equilibrium in evolutionary thought, and it applies to home heating and traffic issues as well as the evolutionary process. At odd moments, for instance, I will be delayed en route in my life when boxcars are rearranged in the rail yards, blocking traffic on President Street. This adds time to trips and, sometimes, panic. I don't think the President Street rail yards play much part in evolutionary thought, but the principle is the same.

As of the first of January, we also have a new mayor in Savannah. Much of the city council is new as well. I know some of these people to some degree, and they seem to be good folks. I especially like the ideas I've seen about transparency in government. It may make the jobs of elected officials and city employees more difficult in certain ways, but in the end, the results will probably be more satisfying to residents and constituents.

As it happens, I also slightly knew some people on the former city council, and I've spoken with the former mayor a few times. They, too, seem to be good folks. I think they probably are.

But as a country, we've fallen into the habit of supposing that our governing bodies are run by either scoundrels or miracle workers, and that doesn't create a healthy atmosphere within a community.

The new administration will take some time to find its feet. No surprise there; the former one did, too. And some of the things they have to deal with are things that have never been, just like Rilke predicted. But the more important ones are the ones that have been around for a while. It's not the former administration's fault. It's the nature of this human life.

Every collection of dwellings has its problems. Savannah is no exception. Some of Savannah's problems are of long standing and involve thorny disputes that reach into the culture, the geography, and the economy. They will not magically disappear because we have new faces representing the city.

The new mayor will still act within the legal limits and context of his position. He does not possess superpowers and would be legally limited on what he could do even if he did. Ditto the new alderpersons. There is great complexity in how we are governed, and no one person can wave a wand and make things happen.

Electioneering hypes us into thinking that those whom we favor are shining exemplars and those we do not are scurvy, cursed beings. That is very rarely true.

I don't know why, but lots of people treat politics like sporting events. But there's a difference. When the Dawgs play Alabama, once the game is over, that's it until next year. There's no further contact. When an election is over, we're all still here. We must still deal with each other. If we treat one other like enemies, that's another thing that doesn't create a healthy community atmosphere.

In business, one of the great tricks is to manage the expectations of your clients. In elected office, that's awfully difficult to do. Constituents must develop some idea of what it takes to do the things they want done. Business has a piece of advice:

Manage your expectations, or your expectations will manage you.

So maybe in this New Year it will be possible for us to believe that an elected official is mistaken or badly informed without thinking that the person's entire life is motivated by corruption and fanaticism. In my opinion, the former council and mayor did the best they could, given the circumstances they encountered and the beliefs they held. They were not bad people. I expect that the new council and mayor will do the same. None of them has proven to be a scoundrel, and none of them should be treated like one.

That's really important, because there are scoundrels out there—and not just locally. Every once in a while, we elect someone who is a scoundrel. When we do, the scoundrel is able to deflect all the merited charges as politics, and as long as he remains the slightest bit credible, the people on his side will support him. Do I have anyone in mind? Why yes, I do.

Our ability to call out scoundrels and make the charge stick depends on our not demonizing everyone who thinks differently. It's the old story about the boy who calls wolf: If you say they are all wolves, people less passionate than you will decide that none of them is a wolf.

Adjust your seat belt and return your tray table to its upright position: 2020 is going to be an eventful year.

Winters Elsewhere

The Savannah winter so far has been mild enough and wet enough that the clover and some of the grass are exiting hibernation. In full sun areas, both grow with that really brilliant green we normally associate with spring. That lifts my spirits. I spent many a winter in places watching snow turn to ice when the temperature warmed and waiting until March for the whole mess to disappear.

Therefore, I was surprised when I checked in with my old hometown newspaper and found an article that stated "you can

My last winter in Virginia

learn to love snow, short days and subzero temperatures." Oh, really? I also noticed that the column appeared in the business section, a rather strange choice for that sort of thing. Maybe things that are counterintuitive go in that section—I don't know.

I read on.

The author lives in the Red River Valley of Minnesota. I looked that up: It is about fifty miles due north of Fargo, North Dakota, and almost halfway between Fargo and Winnipeg, which is the provincial capital of Manitoba, Canada. So the author's experience with winter woes is firsthand and reliable. Furthermore, he quotes Arctic explorer Fridtjof Nansen, a Norwegian who was iced in on his ship for six months. These are people who have extensive and unimpeachable experience with the winter season.

The thesis of the article is that people go about winter in the wrong way, and that if you fix that, it's a perfectly serviceable season. So let's look at the right way to go about winter, according to Mr. Red River.

The first tip is to dress warmly. The author thinks that we're being too stylish in our ambitions and that proper winter clothing is thick, bulky, and baggy. Well okay, you do have to dress for the weather outside. I have an advantage that most people don't—I am thick, bulky, and baggy all by myself, so my clothes are, too. And when I lived up North, I certainly dressed for the weather: I took an impressive mound of winter clothes to Goodwill after arriving in Savannah.

But—there's always a "but," isn't there?—you are going to be cold anyway. Unless you wear a ski mask, your face will be exposed to the open air, and if the temperature gets only a little below freezing, you'll no longer be able to feel your face. If you do wear a ski mask, you're liable to be stopped by a series of law enforcement officials who are certain you are on your way to rob a convenience store, and if you venture into any commercial establishment, the clerk will have a finger on the panic button before you draw your first breath of warm air. Don't even think about going to the bank.

Outside, winter air is supercooled, so as you breathe condensation forms around your nostrils and either drips or freezes. Whatever you do to fix that condition will be unpleasant, but leaving your nose dripping or frozen will be equally so. Your fingers and toes will never be sufficiently warm. I once had a pair of gloves made for winter skateboarders; they were thickly insulated against both weather and unfortunate landings. They came closest to keeping my hands warm and added a whole new thrill to winter driving, which can be a thrill in itself. Thickly insulated fingers do not grip well, and don't even mention mittens. Now, feet are a different story. When your feet are clad for the outdoors, the first thing they do is sweat. Then the winter temperatures reach the wetness and transmit the cold faithfully to the toes. It really doesn't matter what the outer layer is, those toes are going to be uncomfortable.

So now you are cold, regardless of how you're dressed. Let's go on to the other items on the list.

The second tip is to find something to look forward to. By that the author means outdoor activities. Cabin fever can be a problem in winter; spending too much time in the same closed environment can be unhealthy. I get that. But romping around in the winter woods has a limited charm—because you are cold. Remember what I said about condensation? A romp in the woods will provide you with just about every variation on that problem. And you will be cold.

Third, embrace the darkness. Well, there's no need, really, because the darkness will embrace you. And it's almost universally true that darkness is no warmer than light. So you will still be cold. Among other in-the-dark activities, the article recommends cycling, stargazing, and skiing. Feeling the rush of cold air as you negotiate an icy street or tree-studded slope in limited light has some appeal to him, I guess.

Next, get a dog. Why? Because misery loves company? We had dogs in winter climates. One winter, a snowfall dropped more than a foot, then gave us a day's rest, and then another fifteen inches. The power went off because that's what power does in snowstorms. The dog and I sat by the fireplace and practiced being Zen. But after a while, I decided to explore the catastrophe and took the dog with me. The dog was assembled along basset hound lines. When we were five steps outside, he turned and gave me a look. I'm no animal expert, but dogs can express disgust. Mr. Red River also recommends urban mushing, where you put yourself on some runners or wheels and let the dog pull you around. The radiant Ms. Hamden once tried that using Rollerblades. Even though much hilarity ensued, it did not end well—for her or the dog.

Last tip: Think of your grandchildren. His thesis is that they won't have any winter because of global warming and so forth, and you'll have to describe it for them. Thanks, I believe I just have.

I do the same things here in the winter. I wear socks almost every day, and I throw a warm shirt over the tee. I look forward to the days when I won't need socks—because of the change of months, not global warming. The dog and I walk outdoors, being careful to do so when the sun's at its most radiant and the clover is in bloom. I don't have to learn to love Savannah winters. I already do.

The Trade-Off

Recently, I was certified by several well-paid and skilled medical professionals as being ready for the rough and tumble of daily life. I did have a problem, but those very same medical professionals used their skills to relieve me of it. The experience was far less unpleasant than it could have been, and I am grateful. But whenever you are hooked up to an IV drip and somebody tells you they are giving you something to relax, whatever happens after that is going to require some recovery.

Now back at home, life butts up against recovery. My noble companion Stink likes to snooze under my desk. If it is possible to snooze disconsolately, that's what he does. The rough and tumble for which I am now ready does not include long walks with the dog—not just yet. I hired a proxy for the morning walk, and in the afternoon, we have replaced rambles in the woods with totters around the block. They will come back, those rambles, but not just yet. He's puzzled by the change and not entirely happy about it.

Stink is a yellow dog or, if you prefer, an American dingo or Carolina dog. Neither one of us knows if he is pure yellow dog; in fact, there's no way to tell. Yellow dogs don't have a set of genetic markers to determine that. Fortunately, neither of us cares. Our relationship is better than that.

Unlike most dogs, yellow dogs supposedly came across the Asian land bridge with the first immigrants, well before the first cockapoo hit our shores. They are extremely functional dogs with a full set of equipment for living in the wild. Some still do. They will breed with anything that will breed with them, which is a problem if you are looking for tidy genetic markers.

Stink and I have a social contract. The social contract removes some of the doggishness from him and some of the humanness from me, in favor of our relationship. For example, a more doggish dog would not stand by the back door when he needed to pee. He'd just let go. He'd gnaw on roadkill, teach the amber cat that lives up the street a thing or two, and become a contributing member of a pack. As it is now, I am his pack, and he is mine. I like that, and he seems to as well. When I am not recuperating, I walk extended distances twice a day. I warn guests who want to sit on his end of the sofa, and I fret about leaving him alone for too long. He is not reaching his full potential as a dog nor am I as a human. That's okay. We're happy.

On January 30, the founder of PETA wrote a letter to the people of Punxsutawney, Pennsylvania. She demanded they replace Punxsutawney Phil, the groundhog who predicts the end of winter, with an animatronic version. The letter portrayed a maltreated wild animal being ripped from his burrow in the name of having a good party.

There's more than one way to look at the situation, and many of those ways have already been splattered across the Internet. The Phil keepers contend that he is well fed and looked after. The Pennsylvania Department of Agriculture inspects his burrow, and he is joined by his groundhog mate, Phyllis. Aside from being pulled from his burrow one day a year, Phil isn't doing badly. A groundhog that lasts six years in the wild is working above average; Phil is in that above-average group. He cannot reach his full potential as a groundhog probably, but I'm not sure what potentials groundhogs have. Many of them fall prey to other more predatory beasts.

From a purely functional point of view, an animatronic Phil might be a step up. I once lived in New England, where people pay attention to any indicator of the end of winter. Phil, quite frankly, does a terrible job. Maybe his predictions are better for the greater Altoona area, but they don't apply to the rest of the country. In that same region, we had *The Old Farmer's Almanac*, started by farmers in Nashua, New Hampshire. I don't see either replacing the National Weather Service anytime soon.

However, that isn't the point. This year, about thirty-five thousand people swept into Punxsutawney for the ceremony, including every TV station that can afford a car big enough to carry a camera and cameraperson. Will they do that for Phil2-D2? I am not optimistic.

The PETA letter refers to groundhogs as a prey species, which they certainly are. They are a food source for bobcats, badgers, hawks, foxes, and coyotes in the wild. They are also frequently terminated by dogs and by traffic. They are not suitable for animal parks and such, since they are extraordinarily aggressive to other groundhogs and anything else that gets in the way. That is the testimony of a keeper at the Staten Island Zoo, which keeps and raises groundhogs.

The idea behind Groundhog Day didn't originate in Pennsylvania, by the way. It is part of Celtic and early German lore, though the Celts and Germans didn't concentrate on the groundhog. If any hibernating animal came out and saw its shadow, it meant winter would continue.

I wonder if Phil has the same sort of social contract-type relationship with the people of Punxsutawney that I have with Stink. At the very least, Phil will not end his days as badger food or roadkill, and he will likely live more days than he could expect were he in the wild. He has certainly given up his right to be the acme of groundhoggishness. But who is to gauge his potential for that in the first place?

Groundhogs are not an intensely studied species. Punxsutawney says Phil is happy; PETA says he is not. I don't know if either is in the position to gauge the contentment of a groundhog, and I am positive that I am not.

The winds of February are sweeping across more northern parts of the country and keeping people indoors. There they work on their pet theories. I wonder if they shouldn't check for sunshine before they bring those theories out. Who knows which ones might see their shadows?

Failure

I wish I knew more about science, but I don't. It seems that we are on the verge of many scientific breakthroughs that could make our lives much easier and perhaps longer. We are also on the verge of breakthroughs that could remove us from evolution's catalog or leave the globe a charred ruin.

Science never really penetrated my awareness in the years when it was supposed to. Now I peer into magazines that I have no business even opening. Occasionally, I open and read an edition of *Nature.*

Nature is one of the prestige publications. Several really important scientific breakthroughs were first made public through *Nature.* It publishes papers in just about any branch of science, but not just any paper. It accepts approximately 8 percent of the papers it receives, and unless you write a paper that follows sterling academic practices, don't even bother sending it to the editors.

So I was fascinated when I picked up an old copy and found this article: "Quantifying the Dynamics of Failure Across Science, Startups and Security." It seems that a group of mathematicians has developed an algorithm for failure.

I didn't know we needed an algorithm for failure. Most people fail without needing a set of instructions. I know I do. I can fail even with a set of instructions—some of my furniture exhibits unique features because I assembled it per the instructions. I have become pretty familiar with failure over the years, but I never came up with an algorithm for it.

So I read on.

The mathematicians didn't develop an algorithm for failure either. They produced an algorithm to predict failure. Aha, that's better.

They call it the *k* model.

I dug deeper. The first thing I noticed was the size of the sample. One persistent problem with studies based on samples is the sample is too small. A surprising number of people will reach and publish conclusions based on a sample consisting of their Uncle Horace, the UPS guy, and the lady with the yappy dog who lives down the block. An unsurprising number of their conclusions will be flawed.

Sample size was not a problem for the failure-study mathematicians. Their sample came from more than a million cases. Though, if you think about it, a million failures is a pretty small number when you consider the number of failures in any day. I don't know how many submissions *Nature* receives, but 92 percent of them wind up in the sad-face box. That's a lot right there.

Next: methodology. The mathematicians first picked cases from three different activities within a specified time frame. They looked at applications for National Institutes of Health grants (776,221 applications from 139,091 investigators), filings for business start-ups (58,111 by 253,597 individuals), and events included in the Global Terrorism Database (170,350 incidents by 3,178 terrorist organizations—by the way, "success" here was having killed at least one person). So these are serious endeavors. Failures here don't include leaving the cap off the toothpaste.

The mathematicians then put all these cases through rigorous analysis. That's where they lost me. For example, they found that failure streaks follow a Weibull distribution. I don't know what that means, so I don't know the implications. They also used Welch's t-test, which is more robust than the Student's t-test. All righty.

If you understand these things, I suggest you look up the paper—I can't really help you. But there were some conclusions that I did understand.

First, groups that learned from their failures succeeded more often than groups that just thrashed around. Groups who learned from their failures attained success faster. That could mean that what works well is retained and what doesn't work well is revised or discarded.

Second, once an endeavor reached a certain level of competence, it underwent a phase transition—that is, it was more likely to succeed than to fail and do so faster. Using the researchers' k model, you have a better idea which ones will eventually succeed.

Third, all the cases had a fat tail statistically—they continued to fail longer than predicted before they succeeded.

The authors warn that this model is incomplete and needs other factors to be plugged in before it is a reliable tool.

I wonder if those other factors can ever be determined. Without recourse to mathematics, I can tell you that failure is as rich and varied as any other human activity. It derives from unachievable goals, flawed analogies, inattention, a lazy learning curve, shifting priorities, and what I'll label Kismet—circumstances change.

Sometimes it's even difficult to distinguish success from failure. In medieval days, any number of alchemists tried to turn other substances into gold. They all failed, but their experimentation provided groundwork for our understanding of the substances and their properties. Failures may provide knowledge useful in some other endeavor or maybe at a later time. Failure and success are sometimes more nuanced than words, much less mathematics, can portray.

The universe is an untidy place, as we are finding out. It is fashioned from submicroscopic pieces arrayed in clumps that somehow create vast galaxies. At every level of construction, things act in somewhat predictable patterns, with emphasis on the word "somewhat." Changes in environment and the peculiarity of particles and their assemblies, up to the galaxy level, lead to unpredictable results.

Our unique talent for analogies has helped us deal with that untidy universe. Mathematics helps us recognize patterns, but not exceptions. How many times have you seen a human triumph over rigid "robots" in a movie or on television?

I'm not goofing on the paper—it seems impeccable mathematically and confirms observations we've made elsewhere on failure and success. There are some interesting conclusions contained therein. But I also think we are pushing the limits of mathematics. We can use the k model, or some other of its kin, with complete confidence once we have complete data on failure. I just don't think we'll ever have that. Failure is too rich and variable to characterize with an algorithm.

I do want to check the cap of the toothpaste tube when I get home.

Comprehension

When I was in college, I marked up my textbooks. I drained packages of yellow highlighters, annotated margins with blue ink, and stuffed bits of paper between pages that I thought had important ideas. This week, I opened one of those books in search of something I remembered in the text, and it was a trip down the rabbit hole. Rather than finding what I was looking for, I started to read my annotations. They were misguided, somewhat callow, and missed some of the main points of the book. I had not reached my full range of perception as a college sophomore; I now wonder why I've lasted this long. After I wasted time wandering through the text, a quick flip back to the index located the passage I was looking for.

Some serious, analytical people mark up texts today. It helps them understand a book better, and since they usually don't wait decades to open the book again, the annotations are probably useful, unlike mine.

It's harder to do markups today because owning a book has become a major investment. I browsed through the textbook area of an Internet book site. Do you want to learn geometrics, the gentle art of surveying? Here's a book that will give you the basics, for $210. Here's another on the basics of being cool, from air-conditioning to refrigeration. That's $133, but wait, you can rent it for $89. Of course, if you rent it, you'd better put away your highlighter and blue pen. Markups may result in extra charges.

Then there's the physical quality of the book. I have run into a few where the paper is so thin that highlighting would show on both sides of the page. I haven't seen any onionskin in some time, but in the age of typewriters it was used for typing notes to yourself, tracing (thanks to its translucence), and holding carbon paper in place. The pages of some of today's books are thinner.

Modern technology has come to the rescue—or at least it's tried. Much of the material required for college courses is now online. Students can read it for free on their desktops, their laptops, their tablets, or even their phones.

But that has limits, too. That book on geometrics weighs seven-and-a-half pounds. I don't know how many pages that is, but it's a lot. Imagine trying to read a book that size on a cell phone, let alone comprehend what it's telling you. Even reading it on a laptop could be a challenge. Actually, reading it anywhere will tax you. Every computer screen is backlit, which takes a toll on the eyes. The solution might be to print it, but that's not going happen from a cell phone and will take forever even from a larger device. Bring a lunch and maybe dinner, too. And forget about free, what with the price of printer ink.

Even with a capable computer, problems remain. Reading anything on-screen sequentially works fairly well. Reading anything nonsequentially takes more time and effort than it does from a book. If you want to compare a passage on one page with a passage from a few pages back, you'd better remember which page that passage is on. If not, you're going to have to flip through digital pages until you find it again. Sure, you can search for it, if you remember a clear phrase and don't want to sort through every occurrence of the term "set theory." Want to follow a passage to a footnote or a reference? It's possible, but if the source isn't hyperlinked correctly, it could take time and effort to jump forward and back. And sometimes the digital layout changes. What was once a page on the right is now on the left, and you haven't altered a setting. As a rule, students do not need to take on added investments in time and effort.

Not surprisingly, studies have found that comprehension tanks when information is presented online. Those studies are by Professor Andrew Dillon in a paper from 1992 and Professors Patricia Alexander and Lauren Singer from another in 2017, among others. You can find both articles online, but I suggest you print them out. I did.

So between the price of hard copy and the limitations of electronics, we have students between a rock and a hard place. And that's before you consider some of the other disadvantages of digital tomes. A printed book can only be changed when a new edition comes out. Online information can be changed at will, for good reasons or bad. Have you ever seen the TV series *Black Mirror*? If you have, you are very aware of the consequences of presenting information online.

Within education today, one of the main topics of conversation, both personal and professional, is the limited attention span of current students (and the public at large). Much of the discussion presumes that students today are more limited than those of the past. Remembering some of the students in the past, including me sometimes, I find that difficult to believe. Some of the debate rests on ornate sociopolitical theories that have to do with motivation. For all I know, at least some of what's discussed is justified.

But at least part of the problem is how the information is presented in the first place. A wad of paper, within book covers or not, can be read in most conditions where there is light and whether there is electricity. It can be marked up and noted upon. It can be pored over and reread with a minimum of difficulty. No one need check how many bars they have or what percentage of battery is left. In short, for those who make the effort, it can be comprehended in a way that online information cannot.

The communication revolution of the last few decades has made greater amounts of information available and cheaper. It's pretty efficient, from a producer's standpoint. But all of this has come at the cost of comprehension, and there are those seditious observers who think comprehension is the point of the exercise.

In history, every successful revolution transitions into a maintenance phase—either you figure out how to run things or you lose the coup. Maybe the same thing is true here. I've seen much effort in making the information delivery even more efficient by producers and very little effort in making the information easier to understand. Storming the Bastille takes one set of skills; running France afterward takes quite another. I'm waiting to see how the maintenance phases work out on this one.

Customer Support

Science, I am told, has no culture. The mathematics, algorithms, and physical certainties of science transcend cultural boundaries and may be understood universally by anyone who uses them. Engineering, which is nothing more than applied science, should work the same way. Someone who understands a system, no matter his or her culture, will be able to solve problems in that system because he or she understands the mathematics, algorithms, and physical certainties of that system.

Let me introduce you to a place you may have already visited. It's called Jerkistan. Jerkistan is a virtual country, not a physical one, so don't look for it on a map. But even if the map doesn't show it, it's real.

Despite the name, Jerkistan is not necessarily central Asian or even Asian at all. The first language of the inhabitants may be Hindi, Spanish, Tagalog, or several other languages I could name. However, every Jerkistani speaks English to some degree. Similarly, the inhabitants of Jerkistan do not share a unified culture. When they are at home, they live in one of several cultures. They only become Jerkistani when they arrive at work.

The vast majority of Jerkistanis work in customer support for large technology corporations. There are two main types. First-level support handles all customer contacts with the corporation. The technicians here are trained to make sure that the problem isn't of the customer's making—a misunderstanding or a rookie mistake. First-level support asks you, in the vein of *The IT Crowd*, if you "have tried turning it off and on again" and other similar things. Their questions are pretty basic, and you may become frustrated because they seem to intimate that basics are all you know. Cool your jets—it's all they know.

If first-level support can't solve your problem, you are passed to second-level support. The folks at second-level support know a bit more about the system, have more tools available, and have access to more information. But they don't have complete access to the system, and if you had cultural problems with first-level support, the same ones will appear with second-level support. First and second levels usually get handled from the same facility.

In many cases, these people represent the Big Ol' Technology (BOT) firm with which you are having a problem, but they are not employed by it. The BOT outsources the job to some intermediary who will do the actual hiring. So the BOT has no real visibility on how well these people handle the problem or if they handle it at all. The BOT may send a questionnaire asking if the representative was polite and so on. Rarely will such surveys ask if the representative solved the problem. The BOT sees that as irrelevant to the evaluation. (It probably goes without saying that I have another viewpoint.) Based on how the organization is structured, are you surprised when customer service can't handle your problem? Would you be more surprised when it can?

If you manage to convince those in second-level support that the problem is beyond them, they will refer you to a special action team (SAT) or some such. These people may actually be employed by the BOT, and some of them may speak English as a first language. You may finally have reached a level where somebody can actually solve your problem—or, at least, diagnose the problem. But be aware: You are still in Jerkistan, you've just reached a more transitional level.

The SAT contains people who understand the system well enough to meet the requirements I stated at the beginning of this commentary. You must just first engage in a pitched battle and convince the two lower levels of customer support that your problem is real before being given the privilege of speaking with SAT.

And that is precisely why the lower levels of customer service are the first points of contact. They are snares to make sure you don't bother the knowledgeable employees with a trivial problem. Because there are cultural and linguistic differences in Jerkistan, the chances of becoming ensnared at the lower levels escalate. If you get frustrated and give up, it's a victory for them. They don't have to deal with your issue.

Chances are, this isn't the first time you've heard this complaint. It's been around for years. It's an industry standard that hasn't been solved, though it's existed since the first customer service director created a Jerkistan. The reason I mention it now is that, after all these years, it hasn't gotten any better. It works well for the organization regardless of how well it works for you. The only way it will change is if customers refuse to accept running through the maze.

Unless this is the first time customers have dealt with customer service, they know what they are in for—emphasis neither on "customer" nor on "service." To survive the interaction, customers will attempt to become immune to the repetitive questions, the cultural differences, and the general lack of understanding. Generally, they focus their frustration and anger on the representative. Sometimes that's merited, often it is not.

I mentioned that *most* Jerkistanis work in customer support and most speak English as second languages.

But that's most, not all.

These people are the peons of Jerkistan—the sharecroppers, harvesters, and plowers of technology. They don't run the show. Like any other nation, Jerkistan is led by managers, individuals who direct the customer service segment of the Big Ol' Technology firm, on up to the CEO who allows it.

By and large, the managers don't have many cultural differences from you and me. They speak cultured English, and they are aware of the nuances and difficulties that come with dealing with their employees. They may even live near you. The owner of the Mercedes who cut you off on the parkway—the one with the boat that takes up three slips—might be one of the managers. They know about Jerkistan and the problems you're having.

They just don't care.

Jerkistan, like any other country, virtual or territorial, is not run by the peasants who make peanuts for doing some of the most difficult jobs. The managers are in charge and are fully aware of what they are doing. And like any other country, what they do or don't do at their organizational level determines your perception of their domain.

And that kind of management is why I call their domain Jerkistan. It's not the fault of the peasants trying to help you out and be as nice as they can within the confines of the BOT doing it. It's the managers who design, direct, and dominate it.

Corona

We have this arrangement, Mother Nature and I. When the weather warms and the plants release their pollen to propagate their verdant existence, I sneeze. I don't want to, but the excess pollen always seems to find its way into my nasal passages. Since my nose contains neither pistil nor stamen, it expels that pollen, the better to find a more promising landing spot.

I am not alone. We pollen-expellers fund a significant portion of the drug industry. Most of us have learned to duck and cover when we sneeze, and we do. But this is not the year to sneeze.

We are the edge of a novel coronavirus pandemic. From all accounts, this coronavirus infection can be anywhere from uncomfortable to fatal. Like SARS and swine flu before it, it represents a threat to the nation's health and the world's health. It also represents a threat to the economy. The stock market took a nosedive this week because of the coronavirus. Apparently.

I've always wondered how these stock market analysts determine what causes stocks to rise and fall. I've seen it rise and fall for excessive rain in Bengal, uncertainty over Poland's membership in NATO, and various other advertised reasons that don't seem to merit any market reaction, much less an excessive one. Uncle Fred just ditched his telecom stocks because of Bengal's rainfall? I don't think so. I suspect the analysts read the front page of the paper and try to connect it to whatever the market has just done. Did "Baby Yoda" find some chicky nuggies? That's worth a few hundred points right there.

This is part of what I perceive as an overreaction to the problem of the coronavirus. I have seen articles proclaiming the end of China as a manufacturing hub because of it. Well, maybe, but I kind of doubt it. I have also seen people tapping feet rather than shaking hands. I'm not sure that will catch on.

Which brings us back to sneezing. Sneeze in a public place nowadays, and you are fixed with raised eyebrows or steely glares, even if you throw your jacket over your head before you do so. You'd create less of a fuss if you pulled out a pistol. Allergy season is bad enough without social pressure.

It would be easy to call all this an overreaction, but it's a serious one if the stocks tumble and the Fed gets involved (let alone people becoming ill or dying). Is it time to restock the fallout shelter, like we did for Y2K? Maybe that's a good analogy, and maybe it isn't.

Here's Newton's third law, updated for modern times: For every overreaction, there's an equally stupid underreaction. The people who burn incense at the altar of the stock market ticker fear a catastrophe and so seriously minimize the effect of the virus. That includes some who have responsibility for public health. I have noticed that many of them spell it with an *a* rather than an *o*, as in "caronavirus." Aside from that, they deflect any information that might indicate there might be a problem. That, too, is unhelpful.

This virus is a problem without an easy right answer, but the risk and the likelihood are too distinct to ignore it. Nor is it the end of the world. Like most persistent problems, it has to be managed. If I don't see its potentially vast impact on the human race, then I don't see proper management of it either. Without capable management, the effects of the coronavirus might get worse.

That's the good news.

The bad news is that this is part of a pattern.

There are, as of this writing, nearly eight billion of us on the earth and counting. With that many humans in residence, viruses more at home with other life-forms will continue to adapt and mutate and jump on over to us—what scientists call zoonosis. In many places, people live on top of one another and have engineered animal husbandry so that animals live on top of one another, too. Like swine and chickens, for example. Swine flu and avian flu are real now because new viruses love condensed populations: They have more places to go and less distance to travel. Sometimes, animals live on top of one another in the wild—bats, for example. Bats supposedly are the original carrier for this particular virus. Dense populations breed more disease, and the disease may jump from one sort of host to another.

Viruses are one of the most adaptable organisms, even better than humans. We will continue to see similar outbreaks, and there's no guarantee that we'll be able to medically respond to all of them. One of them could be the big one that many people fear.

David Quammen wrote an informative book on the subject, titled *Spillover: Animal Infections and the Next Human Pandemic.* It came out in 2012. It takes readers through some of the realities and many of the myths of pandemics. Flu viruses are bad enough (think 1918), but there are other viruses waiting out there, too. There may come a time when sneezing is as bad as pulling a pistol.

This is a legitimate problem that no magic wand will solve. It will require vigilance and management. It will not abate through tapping feet in greeting, and we need to protect ourselves against pleas to "bring out your dead." Nor will it respond to turning a blind eye and probably not to prayer, however heartfelt. We have the tools to manage it—we just need to use them.

Whatever coronavirus does, the pollen will continue to waft thickly in the breeze. The usual bacteria and viruses will circulate, too, and a certain portion of us will wheeze, sniffle, cough, and sneeze. That slice of the population will include me, if the record of the last decade holds true.

If I get sick or am a victim of pollen-inspired allergies, I will manage my bronchial resonance to the best of my ability, with special attention to the sneezing. Most of my fellow sufferers will as well. We're used to doing that since wheezes, sniffles, coughs, and sneezes—not to mention general annoyance as our eyes water through the achoos—are part of our normal spring. Adding rancor to our miseries helps no one.

Faith Healing

One fine spring weekend, while I was in college, I went on a camping trip with a fairly large group. I was living in Washington, D.C., at the time, and the trip took us to the Appalachian Trail, close to Harpers Ferry and a good drive from our usual haunts. This was in a day when going camping in that area cut you off from all forms of communication.

The trip went well enough, but the organizers ended it a day early. That was okay with us—we were tired and hungry for non-canned food. The bunch I was a part of climbed into the car, and sometime before we hit Leesburg, we turned on the radio. That's how we found out that, while we were stumbling around the woods, Martin Luther King Jr. was assassinated and people had taken to the streets. We left the radio on as we drove, and as we neared the city, it became obvious that this wasn't a demonstration. It was a riot.

Our university campus was in a part of the city away from the rioting, but it had changed utterly in the eighty or so hours since we had left. It was quiet and tense. Some people had fled, and we all had to process both the death of King and the whiff of personal danger.

We remained unharmed, but I stayed in that area for decades after graduation. In the immediate aftermath and those decades, I traveled through some of the areas that were affected. The charred ruins of 7th Street and North Capitol Street and Columbia Heights stayed there for years. North Capitol Street was an especially powerful image. Right in the shadow of the U.S. Capitol, streets were vacant, burnt, and full of rubble, looking like a bombed city during World War II. Lives were lost and so were businesses. Some communities became unlivable.

Washington was blessed with a booming economy in the years that followed, and new construction eventually replaced the hulks. New communities replaced the old. But today, more than fifty years after those riots, there are still places where you can't find a grocery store or much of any other commercial life. The people returned, but the businesses didn't, and those places remain impoverished. In cities where the economy was not as robust, the situation was worse and stayed worse for a longer time. There may be some stark reminders of that time yet in some places.

The death of Dr. King was an outrage, but the rioting took it to a new level, and incidents occurred for months afterward. Sometimes they were based on fact, sometimes on mere rumor. Whatever the immediate cause, there was one overall reason they continued. The people had lost faith in the ability of officials to govern. With the advent of the Vietnam war, the lack of confidence continued.

And when it was restored, it wasn't restored by militancy among the peace officers, whether they were police or National Guard or anyone else. That only made the situation worse. Remember Kent State?

It was restored by people, at all levels, who listened. Some of them were peace officers, some of them were city officials, and some of them held higher office. When citizens decide to destroy their own communities, leaders need to listen. This was a hard lesson then. It would be several years before any portion of that faith in government was repaired, and it was a close run. It required the resignation of a disgraced president and the cessation of a bloody conflict before the healing began.

The effectiveness of any government begins with the idea that the people have some stake in its functioning. If they don't, they either confront or ignore the governance. There are several European countries where doing personal business—such as buying or selling a house—entails such a thicket of regulation that people ignore it. What we saw in the days of Dr. King's murder was too large to ignore, and people confronted it. And when they did, they didn't encounter those who truly deserved their ire. A number of people I knew went into the National Guard as a better alternative than the horrible and morally deadening war in Vietnam. They were the ones confronted, and they were as afraid and heartsick and uncertain as anyone they faced.

One of the dubious privileges of age is to watch situations repeat themselves. I didn't choose to dredge up fifty-two-year-old memories on a whim. And there are all too many people ready to believe that this situation is different somehow, and that shows of force are the correct response. That may be true, but I don't think so, because that loss of faith in the ability to govern is still the reason that communities tear themselves apart.

One of the dubious privileges of living today is that you can witness incidents for yourself. We all understand that when people describe situations, the reality of the event gets distorted. When you can see it for yourself, the image is closer to real. And if you have no faith in that ability to govern, it is all too easy today to imagine the outrage happening in many places, maybe in your own city, your own community. Maybe even to you.

The response to that desperation is usually overwhelming force. It's the way they deal with it in, oh, Myanmar, El Salvador, Egypt, and too many other places to name. We even see it in China. Sometimes it works temporarily, but the causes of the unrest remain and fester, creating the potential for a more violent reaction later on. Sometimes officials use the time between events to confront the problems rather than the people, and in those cases, they can defuse the problem. Sometimes they just go back to business as usual, and the problem worsens.

The solution to the problem is not to send more uncertain and heartsick armed people, however uniformed, to the streets. The solution is to restore faith in the ability to govern in places where that has been lost.

The government that cannot do that must resort to those authoritarian tactics, and even with those, it will eventually fail. The response of our government in the near future will say much about how we will be governed. Sometimes it's hard to be optimistic, especially for people with fifty-two-year-old memories.

Spring 2020

Staying Put

Restricted travel. Shelter in place. We are staying put these days, in ways we never have before. It's not fun, but it's necessary. Our basic nature, developed back before civilization, is to roam around a bit. The earliest humans did that, if only to stay fitfully fed. They would probably tell you that it's not fun, but it's necessary.

I grew up on cowboy movies, and the heroes of cowboy movies were roamers—coming from some unspecified place and heading somewhere else. They rode into town, cleaned up bad situations with their six-guns and innate goodness, and then went away again. They lived outside the bounds of civilization. How manly! How romantic! By and large, our fiction is kind to roamers, from Ivanhoe to Shane.

As usual, reality varies from fiction. Egyptian civilization goes back further than the cowboys, and our first hints of civilization in Egypt are about five thousand years old, beginning with Narmer, the first recognized pharaoh. The ancients stopped wandering around and started farming the Nile Valley. The more reliable food supply allowed them to develop their society into a civilization, for good or ill.

The renowned art historian Sir Kenneth Clark recognized the value of immobility in his landmark TV series *Civilisation* (with an *ess*, as he was British) many moons ago. On the one hand, he pointed out that art may come from more mobile societies—think African fetish masks and Viking ship prows. They are good art, but they are not good civilization. The Winged Victory of Samothrace, on the other, may not be as good of a piece of art, but it is the product of great civilization. It's also so massive that it can't be moved easily. Civilization (with a *zed*, as I am an uncouth American) depends on staying put.

Since I've already dallied with the ancient Egyptians and ancient Greeks, among others, I am spending some of my current staying-put time exploring the Jōmon culture. For those of you with better things to do, the Jōmon were the first people in Japan. Some Jōmon potsherds have been dated to sixteen thousand years ago. Like anyone else at that time, the Jōmon were hunter-gatherers. They've always been an archeological curiosity. Whoever heard of hunter-gatherers who had the time to sit in one place and fire up a kiln for making pots?

As usual, the answer is more complicated than that. Early on, they probably did roam around randomly, fulfilling the textbook definition of hunter-gatherer. But roaming around is a tough life, and they stopped as soon as they were able. Some cut it down to two or three residences a year, depending on where the best food was. They became foragers, with more or less fixed residences. Some became collectors, having found areas where they could do that and still remain in one place. Ancient peoples had this irritating habit of living without reference to handy academic categories.

The earliest Jōmon depended on nuts for much of their nutrition, especially in central Japan. Many of the nuts off the tree were either distasteful or downright toxic—containing too much tannin or other unhealthful chemicals. But the Jōmon discovered that, if you submerge those nuts in water, the excess tannin leaches out. They became adept at the process, and that led to the development of pots.

Some anthropologists think that the Jōmon created the first pots, and some think that they borrowed the idea from trade with the mainland. But so far, Jōmon pots are the oldest pots found in Asia. Their early pots were spare and functional, with decorations created by pressing beans or rope into the clay. Later ones became more ornate and elegant. I think the earlier ones are really better looking.

The Jōmon had a common culture, more or less, but they did not spring from a common source. Jōmon bones found and tested reveal genetic similarities with mainland groups from both the south and the north. This seemed to flow primarily in one direction: The Jōmon didn't pass on much of their DNA. Modern Japanese possess about the same proportion of Jōmon DNA as Europeans do from Neanderthals. The Ainu, an aboriginal people of northern Japan, have the most.

So what happened? Around 1000 BCE, new settlers started to move in from the mainland. They were wet-crop farmers, mostly meaning rice, and they had iron and bronze. As far as we know, there were no major conflicts—the two cultures lived side by side for about a thousand years, or at least we find artifacts from both cultures for that period. Since rice farming demands the farmer stay in one place, the new group, called the Yayoi culture, were stay-at-homes who might have done a little collecting and perhaps much more trade.

Some theorists of humanity have said that hunter-gatherers, like the Jōmon, lived a healthier life than farmers. That may be true in times when foraging is productive, but not when it isn't. Staying in one place allowed the old to live on and the young to grow up with less risk. And the Jōmon diet included several things that we put herbicide on today or call the shore patrol to haul off the beach. Rice, whatever you think of it, is tastier than burdock and more nutritious as well. Staying in one place also allowed the Yayoi to develop an intricate society, the basis of what we see in Japan today. The Jōmon were a fascinating people and clever for their time, but they didn't last.

Staying put, at least at the level we now practice it, is a nuisance. But being forced to move around, spurred by hunger or hostility, is much more than a nuisance. I doubt I would be possible, in my present form, under those conditions. And burdock makes me itch. Given the opportunity, I will stay in one place, suitably equipped, until further notice. True, I look sadly at the empty paper products aisle, but then I remember the Jōmon. They didn't have paper products or stressless chairs or online booksellers. I'm good with staying put.

Local

News item: Georgia governor sets epidemic restrictions, forbids localities from adding further ones.

Like most children, I was confronted with idea of choosing a career in my mid-teens. I didn't have the faintest idea, though I know some kids who already had plans mapped out. Today, three are well-functioning adults, and two of them made their choices shortly after they started to toddle. But not me.

After as much consideration as teenagers give to any endeavor, I decided I wanted to be the "Man on the Spot." I would be a professional diplomat, sending vital information back to the homeland for policymakers who must make decisions based on those communications. It was an odd choice for someone who has no facility for social gatherings or other languages, but that didn't occur to me then. I intended to be a serious diplomat, not a social one. I maintained this ambition through college, though life deflected it when I actually entered the workforce. Diplomats are still the men and women on the front lines, but the rise of new and more forms of communication has given policymakers the idea that they know more about any situation than the person on the spot. It would have been an exercise in frustration. Life might have been right about that after all.

There are many jobs that require being the person on the spot: police and other first responders, sales and marketing reps, field engineers, jet pilots, infantrymen, the list goes on. In the field that life eventually chose for me, I was the man on the spot a few times, and I supervised people on the spot, too. It's an odd position and, for people like first responders and service personnel, frequently a risky one.

The person on the spot is usually removed from the usual society—along with the safety nets and amenities that cushion the rest of us. That means more thought and effort are necessary for staying safe and accomplishing whatever it is that person must do. Frequently, the person on the spot is an essential stanchion of the safety net in the first place. ER nurses whose patients start to squirt blood around the room have to stop the flow and make sure that whatever contagion caused the initial illness doesn't get them, too.

I recently read a book by a woman who had become the person on the spot by dint of marriage. She had married a skilled member of the British Foreign Service, and their first posting was in Algeria during that country's civil war. There were many people on both sides who would have happily slit her throat and the throats of her children and dog, to say nothing of her husband. She had to contend with that while graciously hosting callers, participating in diplomatic society, and constructing initiatives to improve Britain's image in a very messy environment. If you don't understand the risk, her husband was murdered by the IRA after he was posted to Ireland.

All people on the spot must deal with policy as well, and that complicates things further. Policies are made by people who imagine they are guiding society in some way. But the society they think they are guiding has many facets. Frequently, policies look silly, inapplicable, or just plain wrong to the person on the spot. Usually, because they are. People on the spot live in environments that policymakers never dreamed of.

That problem has two sides, of course. People on the spot are micro-focused on their own situations. What they decide to do may not be the best idea for society at large. Their recommendations may not have much applicability on the home front. Still, they know their own circumstances best.

When supervising people on the spot, I went with the assumption that they knew more about their situations than I did. That was almost always true. We spent a lot of time talking: I told them about things in the home office that might affect them; they told me about the problems and opportunities those things brought to their positions. I almost always let them make their own decisions.

It worked well.

So it amazes me when policymakers decide that whatever they've come up with applies to all contexts and environments. There are lots of examples at the federal level, but the best ones occur within the states. For example, the government in Kansas has to make gun laws that apply to Topeka, the poorer side of Kansas City, and a soybean field in the central plains where the population is two or three per square mile. I would think that any policy would require local tailoring. But increasingly, states demand that localities conform strictly to state policies. Localities cannot make any laws that supplement the state mandate.

This seems a certain recipe for failure. The vision of governments at higher levels is blurry at best; it's true of any bureaucracy. Industry has coped with that by removing so many layers. Today, organizational charts are flat, with lots of communication between the top and the bottom. Not flat enough, in some cases, but industry has gotten the idea. State governments seem to have ignored it.

The person on the spot knows that spot best, and that's especially important in crises. Ask the soldier in combat if the standard issue of ammunition is enough. Be prepared for either laughter or scorn.

The mandates passed by the State of Georgia for the current pandemic are sensible enough at a policy level. They cover the basics. But the state government has also restricted county and city governments from passing laws that apply to their local situations. That's arbitrary, and it ignores the people on the spot. Savannah isn't Rome, and Tybee Island isn't Dalton. Both Savannah and Tybee protested, so far to no avail.

We're in early beach season now, one of my favorite times of year. It's good for walking, it provides great opportunities for photos, and it nourishes the soul, if done right. I could probably go walk on the beach because Tybee is closer to me than to most people and—technically—it's legal. But I won't. The people on the spot say it's too risky, and I believe them. I've seen the beaches, and I know the situation. Once again, I believe the people on the spot.

I wish that concept extended as far as Atlanta.

Quiet City

Herb Gardner was a fine cartoonist, but he was also a pretty good playwright. He wrote *A Thousand Clowns*, a movie from 1965 that still resonates with life in the new century. I recommend it—Jason Robards stars.

The "City" as a concept, with capital letters, is a major player in the movie. Several scenes contrast the city at rest with the city at full speed. I lived in major cities twice. Both times, it was in quiet neighborhoods. That is to say, quieter neighborhoods; cities are never without noise. The first time, it was a quieter neighbourhood with a rail line behind, which brought freight and commuters back and forth to the city centre. On the other side of the tracks, a parking lot for the racetrack provided additional noise from time to time. Two blocks away, a major north-south connector generated a steady hum in the best of times and more if something untoward happened. When my family and I left the area, I'd wake up in the middle of the night wondering what happened to the three o'clock potato train. I was that used to the rhythm of the region.

Where I live now makes that neighborhood sound like a heavy metal concert. We reside in a very quiet area in a quiet community far away from the city limits. But there's still noise. One recent morning, I tried to get the dog around the neighborhood before an impending storm. We almost succeeded. But before the weather began, a bullfrog sounded off down the street, and a neighbor's rooster started to crow, then thought the better of it. The birds twittered in the trees. A jogger passed us; she was listening to Alicia Keys. I could hear the music, and my sonar is not the best it's ever been. Rain has its own sound, of course, but if you are out in it, you appreciate it less—unless you are in a Gene Kelly movie. Neither the dog nor I elected to start singing in the rain.

We humans are a noisy lot. If it were not for the vacuum of space, we would have aliens banging on the upper atmosphere, telling us to keep it down, for Pete's sake. Humans are mainly about activity, and activity breeds noise. And if you herd many of us together, which is a central characteristic of a city, noise will be heard—constantly and sometimes raucously.

So activity plus a thick atmosphere equals noise, and most mobile beings use that as an indicator. The dog's audio system is far more sophisticated and sensitive than mine. He hears things that I cannot until they get much louder. Dogs were probably the Distant Early Warning Line when people drew buffalo and mastodons on the walls of their stone residences.

Humans, on the other hand, become used to the noise of activity. They tune it out, or they hear it, but subconsciously place it in the realm of the insignificant. Occasionally, we get so accustomed to it that the quiet alerts us to something missing. So when the Bridgeports moved to a rural community, I woke up for not hearing the potato train that, at that point, was hundreds of miles away.

Being alerted by the quiet is happening a lot more lately.

Visually, Savannah is a very pretty city. It probably generates more postcards than two other cities of the same size, and the more you know it, the more you appreciate its scenery. I wander around from time to time, taking photographs, and after many years, I'm still finding things that surprise and delight me.

But right now, something's missing. The streets are still picture-perfect. All the visuals are there, but they are quieter than I've ever heard them. I come to the radio station on Fridays and Saturdays, peak days for people to arrive and explore this Hostess City of the South. But the streets are nearly empty of traffic and almost entirely empty of pedestrians. The bipedal explorers weren't here last week, they aren't here this week, and they probably won't be here next week either. There's a reason for that, of course, the same reason that I don't wander around the streets—though, these days, I could take pictures of landmarks without crowds.

It's a quiet city, quieter than the New York at night that Aaron Copland turned into a tone poem. There is a charm in the quiet. Near the station, the cathedral bells mark the hours, ringing down empty streets. Tourists and students have vanished seemingly overnight. There is generous parking where there was none before. But the vacant city is also disquieting in a way. Parking is simple, elegant, and somehow wrong.

I once toured an extensive movie set, courtesy of a buddy who worked there. It was either before or after the film was being made—I forget which. The buildings had been erected, and cars carefully lined the streets. Otherwise, it was positively deserted. It was a pretty enough place, but it felt spooky. No people.

That was a place I didn't care for or about. It was for a film that, when released, only did medium well. Savannah is an actual city, with things that are a daily delight. That only increases the spookiness, to a degree that those who sell tours of haunted places can't match.

My quiet neighborhood also is a delight. It soothes me when I am at rest, and I enjoy hearing the bullfrogs and roosters without the interference of trains or traffic. But life is not lived at rest, not entirely.

The noise resulting from activity has meaning. It's a connection with others, the idea of moving forward with someplace to go, a validation of our communal instincts. It's part of who we are.

I don't enjoy jousting with tourists or scholars over parking places, any more than I do waiting in a long bank line or navigating through crowds at the Forsyth Farmers' Market or on River Street or Broughton. But in a strange way, I miss it. The crowds and the noise are as much a part of the street as the asphalt.

Their return will be welcome.

Murders

They are two of the most dastardly people who have been made known to me. In the end, I just feel sorry for them.

My personal life doesn't bring me particularly close to dastardly people. A few first-rate con men, sure. There was one guy who had tried to make a living emptying small business cash registers at gunpoint and another who would peddle class A pain medications to most anybody who wanted them. Both of those wound up in orange jumpsuits for extended periods of their lives, and so did some others who committed less flagrant violations.

But I read, and in my reading, I have met dictators, medieval torturers, serial murderers, and any number of people I would not care to encounter personally. Even with that, these two are the most dastardly. Their list of crimes includes kidnapping, extortion, murder, manslaughter (in the sense that if you set off a bomb, you don't much care who dies), robbery, rioting—both incitement and actual participation—and several other things I've forgotten or the book didn't cover.

It's a twentieth-century story, so you may suspect that something else is involved, and you'd be right. They were trying to create an armed revolution. And it's a true story, documented by newspapers, witnesses, and in the end, the participants themselves. One was a man, and the other was a woman.

Both of these people came to their cause at an early age. Their cause was latent in their families and communities—they took it up actively. As it happened, they were gifted at mayhem. The male quickly became the commander of the rebels in his region but never really gave up active thuggery. A normal day, for him, was perhaps a bank robbery, a few hours looking for an opportunity for a drive-by shooting, setting out a few IEDs, followed by a late-night gun battle. That's his own description.

As a commander, his biggest achievement was bomb-setting. In one incident, he detonated twenty-two bombs almost simultaneously in the same city. Nine dead, one hundred and thirty injured, including not a few people in the community he said he was trying to protect. In another, one dead, two hundred and twenty injured.

The woman followed the same pattern, but without command responsibilities. In addition, she was involved in some executions of suspected informers, the sale of forged prescriptions, and various other antisocial behaviors. She participated in the second bombing.

Both of these people were utterly dedicated to their cause. As it happened, they were more dedicated to the violence. Rather than creating armed revolution, their actions created fear, resentment, and exhaustion in their community. Slowly but surely, their leaders and the leaders of the opposition worked out a political compromise. The time for their sort of violence ended and left them behind.

With no call for their skills, the lives of both ended sadly. The man succumbed to regrets and cancer, the woman to alcohol and misadventure with narcotics. In both cases, they felt betrayed by the political solution and regretful about the extremes they had used to further their goals. That's by their own admission, and their stories became pathetic, generating my sadness.

But their effect on the people around them generates even more sadness. Ten dead, three hundred and fifty injured from two bombing incidents alone, and who knows how many others robbed, beaten, or murdered.

Oh yes, it's a twentieth-century story. This century, from which we are not far removed, was filled with noble causes that required people to act in utterly brutal ways. Pick through this time, and you will find warmongering, mass murder, genocides (several of them), deportations, and political imprisonment on a mass scale. Many of those outrages were committed in the name of a higher aim. The violence at lower-than-national levels is unimaginable and largely unreported. If you have a mind for traveling, you can select tourist destinations like Auschwitz, the killing fields of Cambodia, and the memorial at the Katyń Forest massacre. You don't even have to travel that far—there's a memorial to Katyń in Jersey City, and that's on your way to the 9/11 Memorial in Lower Manhattan.

Perhaps the highest cause is not the future but the present. Brutalizing the people living now in the name of some future good is illusory. The future good never seems to appear, and the brutalization seems only to intensify. If a political solution arises, the truest believers get left behind. The man who led the two dastardly people I have described not only renounced political violence, he denied he ever was a leader—though the denial cannot be supported by fact. Several of their contemporaries who chose to support the political solution became comfortable functionaries in the new hybrid regime.

Revolution is a hard road to travel. First, you have to get people to agree it's necessary and worth the loss; then, you have to marshal them to defeat the enemy. If you are successful, next comes the trickiest part—making the revolution permanent. In part, that's because the people who disagree with your ideas are equally trained, armed, and quite used to being violent. The misery of Republican France between the Revolution and the rise of Napoleon is a good case in point.

In the new century, we have become suspicious of noble causes, especially those that require acts of brutality. The nobility washes away quickly, and the cause becomes lost in the death and destruction that result from it. That happens even when the cause is successful, like the Cultural Revolution or the Soviet-created famine in Ukraine.

Perhaps the highest cause is the well-being of your contemporaries. Perhaps there is no "-ism" more worthwhile than that. It's an interesting thesis. I hope we can test it in the twenty-first century. That's neither exciting nor romantic, and the fiction we devour is usually based on excitement or romance or both. Our diversions are very different from our reality. I didn't mention the cause or the people I described earlier because they don't matter. There are parallels and people like that everywhere. And everywhere, there are victims.

We Still Don't Need One

Who doesn't enjoy a good story? Stories have been with us since we could communicate. They are entertaining, inspirational, and instructive. Today, many of our stories revolve around alternate galaxies, times, and creatures, some of whom have superpowers but get tangled up in bad situations anyway. But in the past, stories mostly dealt with Earth, which seems to find enough trouble without seeking it in other places and times.

Good stories started way before Homer, but the earliest ones that still move us come from him, a Greek poet, either real or legendary. The *Iliad* and the *Odyssey* are cracking good stories. Like most good stories, more people ought to read them. Summaries on the 'Net won't give you the power or the language of Homer, and the narratives themselves explore major themes that still perplex us today—man versus man; man versus nature; and men, monsters, and gods getting tangled up in each other's affairs. The Homeric tales were condemned by some ancient Greeks as blasphemous, attributing human failings to the gods. Critics include Xenophanes of Colophon, a philosopher who was born around 570 BCE or so, so these stories are older than that.

The *Iliad* is a tale of men in groups, but the *Odyssey* revolves around one man—Odysseus, who is trying to get back home after the Trojan War. It takes him ten years, in part because he keeps on running into natural disasters, monsters, and fickle gods, but in part because he's not treating it like the evening commute. Odysseus has a taste for adventure, and some of the diversions are makings of his own.

He's the template for heroes. Thrown into strange situations, he survives with a combination of human skills, including some that don't jibe with civilized practice. I can't think of one of the Ten Commandments he doesn't break at one time or another, with many readers cheering his aptitude and craftiness. That's what humans do in strange and threatening circumstances—they use every device available to remain alive. Heroes after Odysseus, whether they are pioneers, cowboys, soldiers, gang members, astronauts, or superpowered beings, tend to use those same skills.

But stories are instructive as well as entertaining. We tell stories to children to teach them lessons. *The Tale of Peter Rabbit* is a tract on disobeying mommy, as is *The Pokey Little Puppy*, a personal favorite in the dawn of my times. I thought Dick and Jane were rather dumb and so was dog Spot, though I thought the cat Puff had unrealized potential.

The problem in later, more sophisticated reading is that entertainment and instruction remain merged. There is philosophy behind the adventures of Macbeth, Yossarian, Billy Pilgrim, Jack Ryan, and most other protagonists who come to mind. Sometimes it's smeared on so thickly it causes asphyxiation. Howard Roark in *The Fountainhead* is one of these.

But in general, the heroes of our favorite stories deal with the unfamiliar and the perilous by employing their full range of talents and abilities, including the rather shady ones. Some people take that to mean that heroism sanctions using those skills in all situations, even those that are more familiar and less dangerous. They take that up as a life philosophy.

It's not new, and it involves not only literature but also philosophy, politics, and most studies of human nature. The eighteenth century conjured up the idea of the noble savage, that people in their primal state are full of virtue and only civilization corrupts them. Jean-Jacques Rousseau is famous for his works on the subject. According to legend, Voltaire invited Rousseau to cross the Atlantic and discuss some of his notions with the Iroquois. I'm with Voltaire on that one, and so is anyone who has witnessed a grade school playground.

The notion appears in political philosophy, too. Anarchists believe in the virtue of the individual over any sort of organization or group; dedicated Communists believe that the state will wither away. Some of them, of both sorts, believe in sacrificing their lives to the sentiment.

I recently leafed through the works of Edward Abbey, somebody who embraced anarchist philosophy. He was brought up into it: His father was a convinced anarchist. In his late teens, Abbey found the Desert Southwest, and it moved him—not just with its beauty but with an environment where he could practice his principles to his heart's content. Being miles from anyone more or less demands a certain amount of anarchism.

But the environment calls the tune. The Cabeza Prieta Wilderness requires a set of skills and attitudes that won't work in Boston or L.A. Abbey was able to build himself an agreeable life in surroundings that suited him and his philosophy. So should we all. We will be content finding an environment where our skills and attitudes make us comfortable.

There are too many of us and we are too interconnected for anarchy. My particular comforts depend on the lawn guy coming, the restaurant with the great barbecue being open, and the grocery store having the proper foods in the proper amounts. I would find existence troublesome, if not impossible, without those things. COVID-19 precautions are a reminder of how heavily each of us relies on our connections with society.

Even without those connections, I doubt my own perfectibility—to say nothing of anyone else's. Those of us who act as heroes, and there are some who do so in our name, seem to assume otherwise. Some say they speak with my voice; they do not.

Life is a mixture of individualism with social integration. In fact, when I see people acting heroically, I start to wonder what they are hiding. I have had a number of opportunities to do that lately, mostly when following politics. What looks like heroism in the mirror may appear to be capering and posturing to other people. It's not how it looks, guys, it's how it works.

Heroes are for fiction, not philosophy. I'm philosophically aligned with Tina Turner on this: We don't need another one.

Cleaning Up After Yourself

When very young, I scraped together enough cash to visit England. Roger Miller had musically informed us that "England Swings (Like a Pendulum Do)," but I wanted to go there even before that. So I bought a ticket, got on an evening jet, and sat in tourist class for about eight hours, while the plane well and faithfully traveled the great-circle route to Heathrow. At this time, tourist class had all the charm of a rural Pakistani bus, just without the goats. Aside from several crying children, everyone tried to get some sleep. I tried and failed. Some of it was excitement, some was the rather narrow seating, and then there were those children.

We arrived at Heathrow, and I boarded the tube for the city centre. I found my guesthouse, was shown to my room, and slept off the trip. Traveling great distances to your east smashes your personal time clock.

I soon found that London was expectedly large and unexpectedly expensive. For those of us who made the trip on the cheap, the part that swung like a pendulum wasn't quite as available. I left London earlier than planned. The next stop was York by train.

The train station in York is south of the river, away from much of the rest of the city. I crossed the river, toting my suitcase, and headed to York proper. I learned that the heart of the city was not only across the river, it was uphill. I had to stop twice, mentally calculating which of my belongings in the suitcase would better serve me deposited in some trash can.

Just before the crest of the hill, the row houses lining the streets opened, and I caught my first glimpse of the cathedral: York Minster. I stopped again and gawked. It was huge, towers soaring skyward, with nothing that surrounded it even half as high. It was breathtaking, mind-blowing. Right there, all the cash-scraping, ocean-crossing, suitcase-toting difficulties fell away. This was going to be a great trip. And so it was.

Ever since, I've had a thing for cathedrals, though none ever struck me as profoundly as York Minster. Before I came to Savannah, I lived in a city that had a really nice one, and we have a dandy here. The good cathedrals impress you from any angle. I mostly see the south side of ours, not the entrance, and even that has several things worthy of appreciation.

People in groups can create amazing things, even the thirteenth-century artisans who built York Minster. Why did humans survive, and Neanderthals didn't? Some anthropologists say it's because humans have a much greater capacity for concerted action. Our capacity for concerted action is obvious, and we have done some astounding things with it. But our social instincts are not hardwired. Bees are champion social creatures, so are termites. We don't reach the same eusocial heights, but our lack of hardwiring actually works in our favor. Put one hundred bees together, and each bee will perform a set of predictable tasks endlessly. Put one hundred humans together, and you get one hundred perspectives and sets of skills. The way these humans perform those tasks will be based on how they judge the product and its quality, and they will frequently make it better by proposing changes in what gets done or how.

One hundred bees gets you a hive. One hundred humans may get you a cathedral.

Of course, that assumes that they commit themselves to the task and expend the effort to make it happen. That kind of goal takes planning and organization, which is another way of saying doing it somebody else's way and concentrating on one task, even if there are other things you can do. That's difficult for some people, a lot of people, and organizations require much time and effort. Keeping everyone aware of the objective alone is a big job. Simple things can become difficult unless everyone understands.

When people work in groups, sometimes they have facilities that support all of them: copiers and other equipment, maybe rooms with furniture, perhaps journals or other sources of information. There are a few simple rules when working with common resources and in organizations:

1. Leave it the way you found it. If you are responsible for it, leave it better.

2. If it won't work at home, it won't work here.

3. Leave other people's things alone. (I swiped that one from the Bangor Police Department's Facebook site.)

Let's focus on that second one for a moment. When you were somewhere between three and five and stuffed things down the toilet, it clogged. When your children were between three and five and repeated the experiment, it still clogged. Do you need an update? If so and you are at home, get a wad of paper towels, throw them into the commode, and flush. Did it clog? Probably. We call that settled science, with results that consistently reproduce.

Don't bother with the experiment. This week, I received an e-mail from somebody who leads a group I belong to, one with common facilities. Someone tried that very same experiment and got those predictable results. Because it was a common facility, the experiment caused alarums and excursions, as Shakespeare might say. So you needn't try it. It still works that way.

Every cathedral, real or analogous, is built on settled science. Some of it involves architectural calculations, some of it involves missing or rotted food in the fridge, coffeepots with the burner left on all night, undisposed trash, messy counters. The results are predictable.

York Minster was built by Archbishop Walter de Gray, the prelate of York. He's buried in the minster in an elaborately carved tomb. If you go there, you can visit it. Look at the expression on his effigy's face. This is not the look of someone basking in the triumph of Gothic edification. It is that of someone who discovered baked-on grounds in the bottom of the coffeepot.

Science is ever with us.

The Molting

Sometime in the mid-seventies, I impulsively bought a bomber jacket. It was on sale at the time, because one end of the collar is semipermanently bent upwards, making it less fashionable than others that were available then. But it is heavy leather and well-made and has been a reliable companion from that time on. It usually hangs over the chair by the drafting table, a mediocre chair but a great hanger for frequently used clothing. Well, today I moved it to the closet. The shoes that typically sat beneath the chair also went into the same closet. So, too, will the long pants that accompanied them, just as soon as they are done sloshing around in the washing machine. Every last one of these items will stay where they are now deposited until sometime around Halloween. It is shorts, T-shirt, and sandals time ... for some time to come.

This morning, the dawn was overcast and warm, with a little bit of sticky thrown in. The dog didn't mind, but I took note. The afternoon walk will use a well-shaded route, by the mulberry trees or in the forest where the insects lurk; they keep us moving briskly. We will have showers this afternoon—not some front moving through but self-generated, where the moisture rises from the mainland and the marshes and rivulets, condenses into clouds, and then comes back down. Goodbye, spring. I hope you see me waving in your rearview mirror.

This spring was a pretty nice one, at least weather-wise. The weather was probably the least of our problems anyway. The problems are persisting, but spring is not.

Live oaks spread as much as any other kind, and ours grow non-Spanish mosses and ferns on the more horizontal branches as well as Spanish ones. The spring brought generous rainfall, perfect for them to molt and prosper. But now they are browning and withering. They will retreat and hibernate until autumn.

With the warmer weather comes the bounty of the sea, and we have participated. The garbage container outside the garage has attained a peculiar odor lately, that of well-aged shrimp shells. We bag them in sealable sacks, but the smell seeps through anyway. I believe that, in enough concentration, shrimp shell odor melts plastic. In the summer heat, the aroma may concentrate enough to kill the coronavirus. Somebody call the White House! My house will contribute a healthy supply if it does. Potential magic bullet solutions aside, shrimp in the evening compensates for many a hundred-degree day. In the rhythm of the year, we are past Girl Scout cookie season and into the time of shrimp, produce, and peanuts—boiled and raw. Soon will come the march of black cherries, summer produce at its height, and then the decorative gourds.

Among the early fruits and vegetables, the peaches are fibrous but sweet and the corn is small but still pleasing. Pies with local fruit have materialized at our house, and they also compensate for the heat and humidity. The secret to any local delicacy is to cook it as little as possible—let the taste of the actual food seep through.

The beach is a tantalizing option as well. Since I am allergic to crowds, I am usually off it by ten thirty in the morning or not on it until after six in the evening. When the beach is crowded, stadium seating rules and king of the hill tactics apply. That's not for me, and COVID concerns make the unacceptable even more so. Like an easy chair, the beach loses its restorative power when there are multiple occupants.

All of this assumes that we are to have a summer, but we have some autumn hanging around, too. The first tropical storm of the season, Arthur, swung by on its way to pound the Outer Banks. It is now called Post-Tropical Cyclone Arthur. After getting as far north as Virginia's Tidewater, it curved south again, though farther out to sea. If it completes the circle, the mosquitoes here better wear anoraks.

We haven't had a great influx of those vampire insects yet, no more than usual. However, the population of small lizards who dine on insects has boomed. They sun themselves on the hose reel, lurk in the pine straw, and keep watch for the mailman from inside the box. That may mean that we are due for a larger insect presence later. As long as they opt on outdoor living, they are bearable.

Early tropical storms to the contrary, I believe we will have summer. Summer is our defining season, just as winter defines the Upper Peninsula of Michigan. We dress for the occasion, a less complicated process than in the Upper Peninsula. We drink gallons of iced tea and other suitable beverages. We move the lawn chair to the garage and sit in a semi-stupor, watching the asphalt emit waves of heat. The cascade of fresh produce and sea bounty will nourish us. There are positives and negatives to summer, like any other season.

We will spend the summer as we normally do. We will abbreviate outdoor activities and sit at home in the air-conditioning.

We will cut back on social activities and await the big burst of galas and exhibitions slated for fall after the summer heat lessens. We will wander around town only when we really must, choosing the places we go carefully.

In other words, we will do the same things we've been doing in spring or should have been.

If we do so seriously, maybe we can go mask-less later this summer. The masks ruin glowing summer facial tans. Maybe the shops will open again, making the occasional outdoor expedition worthwhile. Maybe a dinner out will become possible, too.

Sometime in the 1200s, a Wessex composer wrote a song about the cuckoo singing loudly in summer. It's been around ever since. The mockingbird sings more sweetly than the cuckoo, and we have far more summer than Wessex could ever dream.

Maybe this will be the year that somebody puts that to music.

Pilferage

A few years back, I subscribed to an online music service. You tell it which songs or groups you like, and it plays those groups or songs, along with a lot of music it thinks is similar.

After some initial start-up problems, I was delighted. It works really well for me. I've created streams for jazz, classical, and the sort of things I play here at the station, among others. I hear pieces that I've never heard before, and I've added some to my permanent collection.

Good stuff.

The major start-up problem was that my initial choices led it to program Pachelbel's "Canon" for me.

I like the "Canon" well enough, but not three to six times an hour.

The problem is that many, many groups play the "Canon," and I was being treated to the same music from multiples of them. The "Canon" is always played more or less the same, so the differences are not outstanding. Pachelbel became neuralgia-causing: My left eye started to twitch every time I heard the cello intoning the introduction.

Well, we worked that problem out, and I can now listen to the "Canon" again with some enjoyment. There's still some blinking in that left eye, but that's a mild reaction. The "Canon" is fine—every once in a while.

Yesterday, on another program, my cohost and I played Maroon 5's "Memories." It's a catchy tune, with several unexpected chord progressions and a quirky set of lyrics. A nice piece of music, but my left eye started to blink again rapidly. I wondered at that and replayed the song several times at home, with occasional breaks for eye drops. I finally got it. "Memories" uses the same tune as the "Canon"—minus the moaning cello and drawn out violin notes.

Recycled music isn't exactly new, but I cannot bring myself to tut-tut at it. In this case, Pachelbel's work has been out of copyright for a few centuries now, so Maroon 5 is fully entitled to use it. Besides, it isn't the first. Examine the oeuvre of Vitamin C and Aerosmith, and you will find songs that may cause blinking. And I'm not the first to notice this—a very funny man by the name of Rob Paravonian did a five-minute riff on the problem—you can find it on the online video thingy under "Pachelbel Rant."

This sort of adaptation has been going on for decades. Elvis used opera, John Lennon used Chopin (but backward), and Broadway is filled with adapted tunes. If you want to hear the cavalry charge from Tchaikovsky's "1812 Overture" as you've never heard it, cue up Dan Fogelberg's "Same Old Lang Syne."

I have a great regard for classical music, and I grew up with it. But I also grew up with jazz. Jazz artists beg, borrow, and steal tunes and riffs from each other. Sometimes they steal from themselves. Thelonious Monk recorded several versions of his classic piece "Straight, No Chaser" while the rest of the jazz world was getting hold of it. Each version has a different feel, and often Monk played duets with people like Gerry Mulligan, who added their own bits to the piece.

So it's hard to say where borrowing stops and pilferage begins in the music world. In fact, the same is true of most creative endeavors. Have you heard the axiom "good writers borrow, great writers steal"? Do you know who said that? Nobody else does either. I have seen it attributed to T. S. Eliot, Oscar Wilde, Picasso, Aaron Sorkin, and a few others. The adage has been institutionalized, and there is no clear claim to ownership. And that's just the axiom—plotlines and character traits travel around the literary world faster than speeding jets. The art world works the same way, too. In entertainment like TV and movies, it's habitual, bordering on an addiction.

You still don't hear me tutting. I like covers in music, and there are some in literature that I find appealing. Sometimes people take ideas from other people and make it their own. Joaquín Rodrigo wrote a piece for guitar and classical orchestra that's become almost a national anthem, and if you are a guitarist and mess it up while in Spain, you'd best leave the country. But Gil Evans rearranged it, and Miles Davis and his band played it. Same tune, another classic. Many years later, Jim Hall adapted it again for a small group. Another classic.

Of course, there such a thing as overborrowing. A few years back, a novelist won a prize with several pages she had lifted from somebody else's work. The prize committee revisited the judgment. From time to time, the music world gets taken to court when somebody has blatantly copied. That's different.

One of the things that humans do is take an idea from somewhere else and apply it to the situations we face. The other part of that is to create situations where somebody *can* apply their previous knowledge. That makes computer processing, plumbing, and electrical work possible and most of the other things that we depend on, too.

The same is true for creative folks—they face standard situations as well. Stand on a stage and play music, entice people to venture to the movie theater, get them to buy a book. The key is to make them feel good about it after they've had the experience.

Nobody can do that with just the things that pop up in their own minds. All of them use the influences they've absorbed.

Some patrons become disappointed when they find out a work is based on another effort by somebody else. Not me. If you are going to entertain people, you put everything you've got into the moment of entertainment. If you use an idea you've absorbed as the basis, what of it? You can be memorable with what you do with it.

Just ask William Shakespeare.

Freedom

I qualify as an old person in just about any context you care to use, and old people are known to be temperish.

This week, I got impatient with the word "freedom."

It's one of those words, like "love" or "honor," that's particularly hard to pin down. Everyone seems to have their own definitions, and when you try to apply the word to any given situation, each person acts in a different way—some of them diametrically opposed to each other.

And because it's an elusive concept, you'd think that people would use it with caution. Like those other words, you'd be wrong. The word is used extravagantly by people who want to intrude into your mind, precisely because of the difficulty in defining it. It is good—everybody knows that—but beyond that, the definitions start to differ.

Freedom as a subject demands an object. You need to tell me precisely freedom *of* or *from* what before I can understand what you are talking about. Franklin Roosevelt took a stab at it and came up with four: freedom of speech, freedom of worship, freedom from want, and freedom from fear. That's a pretty good effort, but those are still abstract concepts. At more concrete levels, they get tangled up with each other. The four freedoms

came from a speech that Roosevelt gave in January 1941. They were an aspiration then, not an achievement, and they still are.

However you define it, I think freedom requires responsibility. You retain your freedom by acting responsibly in what you do and how you do it. At a very basic level, you get to walk around the streets if you don't shoot people or rob banks while you are doing it. There are more complex issues of freedom and responsibility that are every bit as important, of course, and those are the ones that cause controversy.

Edward Abbey, the environmentalist, was a convinced anarchist, and he found his freedom in wandering around harsh environments. He developed the skills to be responsible for not dying of thirst or hunger on some sunblasted rocky outcrop, so that worked for him. It kept him away from other people, who might impose responsibilities with which he was less comfortable. Being in a more populated place surely entails additional obligations. I don't have Abbey's sensibilities about many things, so I accept those responsibilities. I don't have his skills, and I don't particularly want to learn them.

Well, this week, I heard too many people splattering the term "freedom" around. None of them seem interested in the relationship of freedom to responsibility. I heard it from people face-to-face, and I heard it from public figures.

Some of them, mainly the public figures, demonstrated that their idea of freedom has more holes in it than a width of Belgian lace. The holes were there for people not exactly like them. They also seem oblivious to the responsibilities of their positions.

This whole discussion has special relevance in a public health emergency. The current lieutenant governor of Texas, whom I remember as a fitfully interesting reporter of high school sports many years ago, said that I should be proud to die for my country if I get COVID so he's free not to mask up. Nonsense. My death accomplishes nothing for the country. At a personal level, if I go out in public, I owe it to everyone else not to have COVID ... it's a responsibility. I can't guarantee it, so I wear a mask. I hope every other person will observe that duty. If somebody else's freedom to do otherwise infects me, it's misplaced. If it infects everyone around that person, it's worse than misplaced.

The other thoughts I had this week are mostly forbidden to broadcast by the FCC, due to the rather vivid language that goes on in my head. So I'll just talk about one of them. Between here and that thought, I'll report, just report, some of the things that went on this week.

This week, in a community west of Atlanta, a high schooler took a phone video of students crowding a hall between classes, mostly without masks, and then published it. The videographer was suspended, of course, because taking pictures in a hallway is forbidden, while crowding a hallway without protection during an epidemic is perfectly splendid. Testing revealed a number of COVID cases among the students, and the school

is being shut down for two days in the hope it can be cleaned and disinfected.

When asked about how school openings were going, the governor said (and this is a direct quote), "I think quite honestly this week went real well other than a couple of virtual photos." The crowded hallway wasn't the problem; depicting it was. Despite the obvious illegality of taking photographs that invade privacy or depict health risks, another student did the same thing later in Effingham County. It will be educational to see what the infection rates are after the incubation period, say, in two weeks.

In the number of new cases per one hundred thousand, averaged over the past week, Georgia had thirty-two on Monday and thirty-five on Tuesday and again on Wednesday. That was the highest total in the country on those days. We're number one—king of the hill, top of the heap. We beat out Florida, we beat out Mississippi, Tennessee, and Alabama. We even stomped Idaho, and it had a 17 percent increase on Tuesday. The national average on Tuesday was sixteen cases per one hundred thousand, by the way, so we're better than double. We were overtaken by Florida and the Virgin Islands later in the week.

It would probably be opinion to connect the infection rate with the school pictures and the governor's reaction, so I won't do that. Reach your own conclusions, please.

So here's the thought.

It's a corollary to the dictum provided by the poet and philosopher Ron White: You can't fix stupid, but you don't have to walk up and kiss it on the lips either.

It's probably infectious.

P. T. Bridgeport is a photographer, calligrapher, and uncompensated curmudgeon.

He is a member of the Savannah Art Association and occasionally exhibits his photographs.

At WRUU, he cohosts *Beyond the Liner Notes* and *Listening to Literature* on Fridays and has his own show, *When the Moon Sings*, on Saturday evenings.

A transplant from farther north, he resides in Savannah with the elegant and accomplished Ms. Hamden Bridgeport and their noble companion Stink.

He was a trombonist early in life but went through a program and now lives spit-valve free.

monte ceceri

In the early 1500s, it was from the heights of Monte Ceceri—otherwise known as "Swan Mountain"—in Fiesole, Italy, that inventor and artist Leonardo da Vinci let soar one of his experimental flying machines.

Envisioning a future where such fantastical creations would one day become reality, Leonardo desired to fill the world with awe-inspiring inventions and writing.

Like its namesake's Renaissance roots, Monte Ceceri Publishers, LLC, supports avante-garde writers whose works challenge current perspectives, inspire new paths, and speak to a modern-day humanism.

Based in Savannah, Georgia, Monte Ceceri is a proud member of the Independent Book Publishers Association and aims to publish books that raise issues of social, cultural, and philosophical interest, that cross disciplinary boundaries, and that facilitate cross-cultural dialogue through effective and engaging writing.

We welcome you to contact us.

Imprints

- **Monte Ceceri Publishers** (Nonfiction and Academic)
- **SwanHorse Press** (Fiction, Short Stories, and Poetry)
- **Pescaton Press** (Food and Science)
- **Bucket Goat Books** (Children and Young Adult)

www.ingramcontent.com/pod-product-compliance
Lightning Source LLC
Chambersburg PA
CBHW072110270326
41931CB00010B/1511